Alex Wall is an architect and Chair of Urban Design in the Institute for Local, City, and Regional Planning in the Faculty of Architecture at the University of Karlsruhe. He has published numerous articles on urban development, mobility, distribution, and leisure, including "Programming the Surface," in J. Corner (Ed.), *Recovering Landscape*; and the book *Cities of Childhood: The Colonie in Italy in the 1930s* (with Stefano de Martino). He is an urban design consultant for regional and international strategic development projects, such as "Masterplan Grünmetropole" Euregionale 2008. He is currently active in national and international research projects on contemporary urban development, among them Zwischenstadt (Daimler Benz Stiftung), and SHAKTI-Sustainable Urban Development Plan for Hyderabad.

Preface

Commerce is the engine of urbanity

Think of it as an Experimental Workshop

1903

| Garden Cities of Tomorrow, Ebenezer Howard | Victor Gruen (Grünbaum) born in Vienna on July 18, 1903 to Elizabeth Lea Levy, who was from a prominent Hamburg Jewish family, and Adolf Grünbaum, an urbane, middle-class Viennese lawyer. |

1909

| Goldmann & Salatsch Tailors and Mens Clothiers (Loos Haus), Vienna, Adolf Loos | Begins Volksschule. Family moves to a modern apartment (with transformable space for his father's office and reception) on Reimergasse 3, Vienna 1st District. |

1911

| Extension Plan for Vienna, Otto Wagner | Travels with family in the summers to visit relatives in many European capitals. |

1914

| World War I: Austria-Hungary joins Germany against Russia, France, and Great Britain. | First District's Realgymnasium, or grammar school. |

1918

| Armistice 11 November; End of World War I; Austro-Hungarian Empire broken up. | Cité Industrielle (project), Tony Garnier | Food supplies intermittant in Vienna, Gruen collects food distributed by American Quakers. Adolf Gruenbaum dies of the flu. Victor leaves the Realgymnasium, and continues his studies at the State Trade School for Architecture (Hoeherer Stadtgewerbeschule, Abteilung Hochbau), where he experiences anti-semitic discrimination. |

1919

| "Red Vienna": Social Democratic city council of Vienna institutes a vast program of social housing. | Welwyn Garden City, England, Louis de Soissons | Member of the Socialist Middle School organization (Bund Sozialist Mittelschuler) |

1922

| La Ville Contemporaine, Le Corbusier | Enters Vienna Kunstakademie (Vienna Academy of Arts in the Master School for Architecture), where he is a student of both Siegfried Sitte and Peter Behrens, and meets his future partner Rudi Baumfeld. After two semesters, has to resign his place to support his mother and sister. |

1923

| Country Club Plaza opens, Kansas City, MO, J.C. Nichols, Developer | Starts work at Melcher and Steiner, Architects and Masterbuilder (Stadtbaumeister). For the next 9 years carries out all aspects of building design, construction, and supervision, as well as management and negotiations with other architects. |

1925

| Bauhaus, Dessau, Walter Gropius | Travels to Paris. Sees the Ville Contemporaine and Plan Voisin project by Le Corbusier in Le Corbusier's Pavilion of the Esprit Nouveau at the Exposition des Arts Décoratifs. |

1926

| Schoken Department Store, Stuttgart, Erich Mendelsohn | Co-founder of the Political Cabaret (das Politische Kabarett). Gruenbaum, Baumfeld, and Langer: Competition for Vienna Municipal Housing Estate, 3rd Prize. |

1927

International Building Exhibition, Weissenhofsiedlung, Stuttgart, Mies van der Rohe (planner).

1928

Radburn, New Jersey, Clarence Stein and Henry Wright

1929

Starts working unofficially on his own projects. Strongly influenced by the work of Ernst Lichtbau, Oscar Strnad, and Adolf Loos.

New York Regional Plan, Regional Planning Association of America, New York. "The Neighborhood Unit," Clarence Parry.

„Black Friday," New York: Stock Market crash.

1930

Marries Elizabeth Kardos. Gruen writes the obituary "Adolf Loos Gestorben," in the *Arbeiter Zeitung*, Vienna.

Karl Marx Hof, Vienna, Karl Ehn Central Place Theory, the distribution of towns as central places, Walter Christaller

1932

Leaves Melcher and Steiner to start own practice. Converts family apartment into two flats and an office.

The International Style, Museum of Modern Art, Henry Russell Hitchcock and Phillip Johnson.

1933

Gruen reviews Le Corbusier's The City of Tomorrow, in "Die Stadt von Morgen," *Arbeiter Zeitung*, Vienna.

Charte d'Athènes. Le Corbusier states the four functions of the modern city–living, working, recreation, and circulation.

New Deal, Franklin Delano Roosevelt

1934

Gruen busy with many small remodelling and refurbishment jobs.

Boutique Immendorf, Vienna, Rudi Baumfeld and Norbert Schlesinger

With the support of Chancellor Englebert Dollfuss, the Austro-fascist *Heimwer* (militia) storm the housing blocks defended by social democratic tenants–the first armed resistance to fascism in Europe, defeated after three days of resistance. End of Social Democracy. U.S. Congress passes the first National Housing Act.

1935

Gruen's break into shop and store design, the Parfumerie Bristol, Vienna

Rockefeller Center, NY., Reinhard and Hofmeister; Corbett, Harrison and McMurray; Hood and Fouilhoux; Broadacre City (project), Frank Lloyd Wright.

1936

Stoff Singer, Vienna. Parfumerie Guerlain, Herrenmoden Deutsche, Herrenmoden Loewenfeld

Olympic Games, Berlin

1938

Gruen obtains the Affadavit necessary for emigration. Flies from Vienna to Zurich, then by train to Paris, London, and Southhampton where he and "Lizzie" board the Staatendam bound for America. In New York, works for an Exhibition Design and Installation firm, where he meets Elsie Krummeck. Then works as part of large model-making team for the „Futurama" city models designed by Norman Bel Geddes for the upcoming New York Worlds Fair.

The Culture of Cities, Lewis Mumford.

The Nazi annexation of Austria. Congress passes the first Federal Aid Highway Act.

1939

Lederer de Paris shop in association with Morris Ketchum; also the Steckler Store, Paris Decorators and others. As promised before leaving Vienna, Gruen produces "From Vienna," by the Viennese Theatre Group, composed of members of the Political Cabaret and members of the Viennese emigre community.

Masterplan for the Armour Institute (IIT), Chicago, Mies van der Rohe.

New York World's Fair; General Motors Pavillion, Albert Kahn (exterior), Norman Bel Geddes "Futurama" models. The future of the American City, seen by millions. Germany invades Poland, World War II begins.

1940

Gruenbaum and Krummeck, Designers, New York. Altman & Kuhne, Barton's Bonbonniere, and others. Begins work for the Grayson Co. First store opens in Sta. Monica. "Face to Face" in Apparel Arts, first publication in the U.S. Michael Auer joins G&K and runs New York office until jobs complete.

1941

Pearl Harbor attacked; U.S. enters World War II.	Baldwin Hills Village, Los Angeles, Johnson, Wilson, Merril, and Alexander, with C. Stein. After its bombing, Coventry, plans a new center based around a pedestrian shopping area.	Grayson's Seattle, Washington. Gruen and Krummeck rent a house and office on the Kings Road, Hollywood, Los Angeles. Gruenbaum registers as alien.

1942

Marries Elsie Krummeck.

1943

Linda Vista Shopping Center (San Diego), Gilbertson and Smith; Le Corbusier publishes Charte d'Athènes. Eliel Saarinen argues for the "organic decentralization" in *The City*.	Neighborhood Shopping Center, 194X, *Architectural Forum* (project). Rudi Baumfeld, who left Vienna after Gruen, arrives in Los Angeles via Prague, imprisonment in Campobasso, Italy, and New York. Joins Gruen and Krummeck.

1944

Congress passes the Serviceman's Readjustment Act ("G.I. Bill"); Veteran's Administration formed.	Greater London Plan, Patrick Abercrombie. *The New City*, Ludwig Hilbersheimer	Macy's, San Francisco. After receiving American citizenship, changes surname from Gruenbaum to Gruen. Karl Van Leuven leaves Disney to join Gruen and Krummeck.

1945

World War II ends in Europe and Japan.	John Entenza, Editor of *Arts and Architecture* magazine starts the Case Study House Program.	Gruen and Krummeck with Ernest Born: Interior refit with new flexible ceiling, Macy's Kansas City. Joseph Magnin's, Palo Alto, followed by Magnin's Sacramento and others.

1946

New Towns Act, England	New Farmers Market, Los Angeles, Deleena and Barbe: "where the farmer meets the movie star."	Gruen and Krummeck, main office at 8460 Sta. Monica Blvd., Hollywood. Open first branch office in San Francisco to deal with the Magnin's stores.

1947

Marshall Plan, Europe	Broadway-Crenshaw Shopping Center, Los Angeles, Albert Gardiner. Ketchum, Giná and Sharp plan multiple shopping centers around Boston (project).	Well received speech "How to live with your architect" at the Store Modernization Show in New York results in a pamphlet book of the same name (1949).

1948

Concerning Town Planning, Le Corbusier Drive-In Restaurant, Los Angeles, John Lautner	Harvey Park Shopping Center (project). Receives license to practice architecture in the State of California. Gruen and Krummeck break their 8 year relationship with Grayson-Robinson Co. for meddling with designs. Gruen makes first return trip to Vienna alone, and is devastated by the physical state of the city and the outlook of the people.

1949

Congress passes a revised Housing (Urban Renewal) Act. NATO founded.	GM Technical Center, Detroit, Eero Saarinen; The New Regional Pattern, Ludwig Hilbersheimer	Milliron's Department Store, Westchester (Los Angeles), CA.

1950

Korean War begins	Northgate Shopping Center, Seattle, Washington, John Graham	Mid-Wilshire Medical Building, Los Angeles, Victor Gruen, AIA, Edgardo Contini, Engineer; Feld Chevrolet Auto Showrooms, Maplewood, MO; Olympic Shopping Center, East Los Angeles (project); Eastland Shopping Center, Detroit (project).

1951

Victor Gruen Associates: Victor Gruen, Karl Van Leuven, Rudi Baumfeld, Edgardo Contini. Montclair Shopping Center, VGA with Irving Klein, Houston (project). Would have been the first air-conditioned enclosed center. Masterplan including factory, shopping center, and residential neighborhods for the Upjohn Co., Kalamazoo, MI (project). Gruen's first large-scale plan. Gruen remarries, sets up house, and reinstates his New York office in three floors of a Stanford White house on 31 West 12th Street. His third wife, Lazette van Houten, is the leading editor of the trade newspaper *Retailing Daily*.

CIAM 8 Hoddesdon, England; J.L. Sert calls for recentralization rather than decentralization. Alison and Peter Smithson propose the replacement of Le Corbusier's Four Functions (1933), with their *The Hierarchy of Associations*. Masterplan Chandigarh, Punjab, India, Le Corbusier with Max Fry and Jane Drew.

1952

50th Barton's Chocolates opens in Manhattan. VGA opens Detroit office to handle shopping centers. "Shopping Centers: The New Building Type" (article), Gruen and Larry Smith, *Progressive Architecture*.

Shoppers World, Framingham, Massachusetts, Ketchum, Giná, and Sharp. *The Heart of the City*, J. Tyhrwhitt, J.L. Sert, E. Rogers. United Nations Buildings, New York, Harrison and Abramovitz. Traffic Studies and Central Area Plan, Philadelphia, Louis Kahn.

1953

Downtown Appleton, Its Future?, Appleton, WI. Gruen's first proposal for a pedestrian downtown. Palos Verdes Peninsula: Masterplan and Research Center (project). *Shopping Centers of Tomorrow* (traveling exhibition)

Lijnbaan Shopping District, Rotterdam, van den Broek and Bakema. Tapiola Masterplan (Helsinki), Finland, O.I. Meurmann, A. Ervi

Dwight D. Eisenhower elected U.S. President Korean War ends

1954

Victor Gruen Associates move office from Sta. Monica to Doheny Drive. 100 employees. Northland Center, Detroit; Housing for Migrant Workers, Pacoima, Los Angeles, Victor Gruen and Arthur Gallion; "Dynamic Planning for Retail Areas" (article), *Harvard Business Review*.

Back Bay Center Development (project), Boston, P. Belluschi, C. Koch, TAC

1955

Gratiot Community Redevelopment, Detroit, MI (project), with Oscar Stonorov and Minoru Yamasaki; Unit System for California Schools (project); 3325 Wilshire Office Building ("Tischman Tower"); Penn Fruit Supermarket (prototype), Audubon, NJ; South Bay Marina and Residential Development, Redondo Beach, CA: VGA with A. Quincy Jones. $30 million contracts in Los Angeles and Detroit offices; "Cityscape – Landscape" (article), *Arts and Architecture*. "What the World Will Be Like in 1976" (project).

Congress passes the first Federal Air Pollution Act

The Chapel of Ronchamp, France, Le Corbusier. Disneyland, Anaheim, California, Walt Disney

1956

Southdale Center, Edina, MN; A Greater Fort Worth Tomorrow Plan. Plan for Green Bay, WI. "How to Handle this Chaos of Congestion, this Anarchy of Scatteration" (article), *Architectural Forum*.

Harvard Conference on Urban Design, J.L. Sert, Dean (Gruen presents Fort Worth); CIAM 10, Dubrovnik.

Congress passes the Federal Aid Highway Act (Interstate Highway Act).

1957

Eastland Center, Detroit, Michigan; Wilshire Terrace Apartment Building, Los Angeles; Valley Fair Shopping Center, San Jose, CA opens; Westchester Terminal Plaza, NY: mixed-use urban shopping center with offices and train station (project); Tomorrow's Airport, VGA-Edgardo Contini, (project); "The Planned Shopping Center in North America" (article), *Zodiac* 1.

Interbau, Hansaviertel, Berlin Hauptstadt Berlin (project), Alison and Peter Smithson, and Peter Sigmond. Brasilia, Lucio Costa and Oscar Niemeyer

1958

Seagram Building, New York, Mies van der Rohe and Phillip Johnson. Levittown, PA., Levitt Bros. *The Living City* (Broadacre City), Frank Lloyd Wright.

Masterplan Agua Caliente Indians, Palm Springs, CA (project); Masterplans for St. Paul, MN, and Green Bay, WI; Charles River Park, Boston, MA.

1959

Guggenheim Museum, NY., Frank Lloyd Wright. Roehampton (London), Masterplan for a new residential district, GLC, Hubert Bennett.

Kalamazoo 1980 (Burdick Street Pedestrian Mall), Kalamazoo, MI. World's Fair Plan, Washington D.C. (project). Wilshire Terrace Apartments, Beverly Hills, Los Angeles. City National Bank, Palm Springs, CA.

1960

Cumbernauld New Town (Glasgow), Hugh Wilson, Geoffrey Copcutt. Tokyo Bay Plan, Kenzo Tange.

Laguna Niguel Masterplan, Orange County; East Island (Roosevelt Island), NY, "new town in town" (project). Redevelopment Plan for Stamford, CN. Rose Marie Reid Swimwear Factory, Van Nuys, CA. Temple Leo Baeck, Los Angeles. *Shopping Towns U.S.A.*, Victor Gruen and Larry Smith.

1961

Berlin Wall erected.

The Death and Life of Great American Cities, Jane Jacobs. *Megalopolis* - Gottman. Nordweststadtzentrum, Frankfurt am Main. Apel, Beckert, and Becker. "Fun Palace," London (project), Cedric Price.

Gruen named Fellow of the American Institute of Architects (AIA). Whitney Estate Masterplan and Townhouses, Old Westbury, Long Island, NY (project). Cherry Hill Shopping Center, Cherry Hill, NJ. Masterplan for El Dorado Hills, near Sacramento.

1962

Cuban Missile crisis.

Reston New Town, VA., Village Center, Conklin and Whittlesey. Geodesic Dome over Midtown Manhattan, Buckminster Fuller (project). New Babylon, Constant Niewenhuis (project), *Silent Spring*, Rachael Carson. The White House Conference on Conservation set out to examine the deteriorating quality of the environment.

Midtown Plaza, Rochester, NY. "A Revitalization of the City Core," Cincinnati, OH. Randhurst Shopping Center, Chicago, IL. City Hall, Redondo Beach, CA. Gruen's third wife Lazette dies of a brain haemorrhage. Gruen's harangue against the misuse of the automobile led him to be labeled enemy number one (together with Lewis Mumford) of the National Highway Users lobby–a group whose goal was to protect highway funds from those who would use them in other forms of transportation.

1963

President Kennedy assasinated. Lyndon B. Johnson assumes U.S. presidency.

Guild House, Philadelphia, Venturi and Rauch. Free University of Berlin, Candilis, Josic, Woods. "Dynopolis," (project), Constantine Doxiades. Irvine New Town, Orange Co., CA, William Pereira, planner.

Gruen marries Kemija Salihefendic.

1964

Tonkin Gulf Resolution authorizing the bombing of North Vietnam.

Ghirardelli Square, San Fransisco, CA, Wurster, Bernardi and Emmons, and Halprin. *The View from the Road*, Kevin Lynch and Donald Appleyard. Columbia New Town, MD, James Rouse, developer, Morton Hoppenfeld, planner. "Plug-in City," Peter Cook (Archigram) (project). "Potteries Thinkbelt," Staffordshire (project), Cedric Price. Investigation into Collective Form, Fumihiko Maki

Fresno Central Area Renewal Plan and Fulton Street Mall. *The Heart of Our Cities*, Victor Gruen. Gruen converts a house in Bel Air, Los Angeles and an apartment on the Schwartzenbergplatz, Vienna as home-office Office. May Co, Department Store (prototype).

1965

Watts Riots, Los Angeles.

Litchfield Park Masterplan, Phoenix, AZ. "Sea World (Oceanarium)," Mission Bay, San Diego, CA.

1966

The Architecture of the City, Aldo Rossi. Sea Ranch, (clustered residential planning) Moore, Lyndon, Turnbull and Whitaker.

Masterplan "New City" Valencia, CA; Plymouth Meeting Shopping Center, PA for James Rouse. Phoenix Trotting Park, Phoenix, AZ (VGA and Impresa Grassetto, Padua, Italy; Merrywood housing Cluster, Fairfax, VA (project). New Cities U.S.A., Victor Gruen and Edgardo Contini.

1967

Central Area Plan, Boston, MA. South Coast Plaza Shopping Center, Costa Mesa, Orange Co., CA; Masterplan Teheran, Iran. Victor Gruen International opens in Vienna. search for design partner for VGA after Gruen retires.

Habitat, Expo '67, Montreal, Que. Megastructure project for Graphic Arts Center, NY., Paul Rudolph. *Society of the Spectacle*, Guy Debord.

Environmental Health Task Force charged with studying the effects of the pollution of air and water and urban congestion. The oil tanker Torrey Canyon sinks off the Scilly Isles.

1968

Gruen retires from VGA as per original partnership agreement and returns to Vienna. Victor Gruen Foundation for Environmental Planning, Los Angeles. Cesar Pelli appointed partner and head of design of Gruen Associates, and wins first prize in the international competition for a U.N. Center in Vienna. Gruen lobbies hard to support Pelli's project. Project is awarded to an Austrian architect and the U.N. withdraws from the process.

The Second New York Regional Plan

May '68: Widespread demonstrations in Western European cities; Civil disorder in America: race riots and a disrupted Democratic National Convention, Chicago. Martin Luther King assasinated. North Vietnamese and Vietcong mount the Tet offensive.

1969

Consultant for the new Towns program for Paris.

Design with Nature, Ian McHarg.

The Santa Barbara oil well blowout. Conflict between the energy industry and the natural environment. Richard M. Nixon elected U.S. President. The National Environmetal Policy Act (NEPA), creates the Environmental Protection Agency.

1970

Masterplan, Louvain-la-Neuve; La Défense Ouest, Paris (project).

"No Stop City," Archizoom (project).

1970 Earth Day: follows the succession of Clean Air Acts and the Clean Water Act.

1971

Galleria Houston, Houston, TX, Helmuth, Obata, and Kassenbaum (HOK).

1972

Central Area Plan, Vienna (project). Zentrum Glatt, Zurich (project executed by others). Zentrum für Umweltplanung, Vienna.

Defensible Space, Oscar Newman. *Learning from Las Vegas*, Robert Venturi. "Supersurface -The Journey from A to B," Superstudio (project).

1973

Centers for the Urban Environment - Survival of the Cities. The German edition: *Das Ueberleben der Staedte - Wege aus der Umweltkrise: Zentren als urbane Brennpunkte*, included The Charta of Vienna. *Meine Alte Schuhschachtel*, Victor Gruen: a collection of Gruen's writings from the 20s and early 30s.

1975

Gruen's last books: *Die lebenswerte Stadt*, (The Desirable City), and *Ist Fortschritt ein Verbrechen? - Umweltplanung statt Untergang* (Is Progress a Crime? - Environmental Planning or Downfall).

U.S. leaves Vietnam.

1976

Urban Growth Boundary, Portland, OR, the emergence of a new American planning. Quincey Market, Boston, MA, James Rouse and Benjamin Thompson Associates. Peachtree Plaza, Atlanta, GA, John Portman.

1978

Gruen receives the Gold Medal for his services to Austria (*Gross Goldene Ehrenzeichen fuer Verdienste um die Republik Oesterreich*).

Delirious New York, Rem Koolhaas.

1980

Gruen dies in hospital in Vienna.

The spreading out of cities, increasing traffic congestion, the uncertain role of the center, and problems of social and environmental sustainability have challenged design and planning over the past half-century. Architecture and planning are devoted to creating the built environment, yet in the past fifty years, architects have confined themselves to creating signature buildings, and planners have rebuilt downtowns or renewed historic city centers that fewer and fewer people have wanted to, or could afford to, live and work in. Where were architecture and planning when suburbia was first built out? And where was planning when interstate highways pushed through residential neighborhoods, and when the needs of new suburbs, aging downtowns, and regional landscapes conflicted with one another and required reconciliation?

In the 1950s and 1960s, debates about the impact of the regional shopping center, the re-building of downtowns, the role of urban highways, and the future of the American city filled the pages of professional and popular publications, yet few architects and planners met these issues on their own terms. Victor Gruen (1903-1980) is the commercial architect-planner who, perhaps more than any other, engaged and attempted to steer those trends. A shop designer in Vienna, Gruen fled after Hitler's annexation of Austria in 1938 and, by 1940, had become a prominent shop and store designer in New York. With his partner Elsie Krummeck he moved to Los Angeles, where, by the end of the decade, he was fully integrating his shops and stores into the new automobile landscape. More significantly, he began to preach to a national audience the virtues of a new building type, the regional shopping center, which was to change the suburban landscape and alter the course of urban development in North America. With his new firm Victor Gruen Associates (VGA), he continued to expand his work, moving from shopping centers to downtown redevelopment projects, and finally to creating masterplans for new towns and new cities. By the time Gruen returned to Vienna in 1968, his office had grown to 300 people, with design divisions in architecture, planning, engineering,

1 Clay, "Metropolis Regained," 13; Guzzardi, "An Architect of Environments," 137.

2 Gruen's New York shops are well featured in: Stern, Gilmartin, and Mellins, New York 1930, 1987; and, Stern, Mellins, and Fishman, New York 1960, 1995. One of the best articles on Gruen's role in the development of the shopping center is: Gillette, "The Evolution of the Planned Shopping Center," 1985. The conflict between the car and the city was well summed up in: Von Eckardt, "Escape from the Automobile," The New Republic, 1965. Gruen's masterplan for Valencia and the new town's subsequent development history is featured in: Wirtz, "Valencia, California: From New Town to Regional Center," (Unpublished manuscript), 1999; and Kaufman, "Valencia – More Than Just Another New Town," Urban Land, 1992. Finally, Gruen's little known project for the Cellular Metropolis resurfaced in: Hill, "Sustainability, Victor Gruen and the Cellular Metropolis, " Journal of the American Planning Association (JAPA) 1992. Gruen appears repeatedly in

The Harvard Guide to Shopping (see below). The first book on Gruen, Mallmaker (see below) focuses on his shops and shopping centers.

3 Compare for example, "The Suburbanization of Downtown," in Hardwick, Mallmaker, 2004: 209; with Leong, "Gruen Urbanism," in Chung et al, 2001: 383-4. Hardwick deemed Gruen's urban renewal projects as further exacerbating class and racial division in the U.S. Despite all of his reform minded theorizing about the city, Hardwick concludes that it is the juggernaut of shopping and the endless proliferation of shopping centers that are Gruen's legacy. In "Gruen Urbanism," Sze Tsung Leong is more accepting of Gruen's thesis that shopping as an activity, and the shopping center as physical metaphor for a city, were a basic unit of urban planning and thus a basis for the redefinition of the contemporary city. The Harvard Guide to Shopping does not take up the issue of class, racial, or gender separation.

interior design, graphic design, traffic and transportation, and urban systems. His last innovation was to create in Los Angeles and Vienna environmental planning foundations that were among the first of their kind in the world of architecture and planning.

Throughout his career, Gruen was a sought-after speaker in professional, academic, business, and political forums; he appeared frequently on radio and television; and he was known to two White House administrations. He published innumerable articles across the spectrum of professional and lay publications, as well as three influential books, *Shopping Towns U.S.A.* (1960, with Larry Smith), *The Heart of Our Cities* (1964), and *Centers for the Urban Environment* (1973). A public critic, Gruen questioned the role and the responsibilty of the architect in a mass society. In his lifetime he was known variously as the "pioneer of the shopping center," the "savior of the downtowns," and the "architect of the environment." At the height of his career he was called a "new urbanist," and *Fortune* described him as having "shown the skill of a surfboarder when it comes to riding the waves of the future, moving nimbly from store design, to shopping centers, and to city planning."[1]

Rediscovery

By the late 1960s, however, Gruen had slipped out of view. Yet recently both the popular and professional presses have rediscovered him as one of the best known shop designers in pre-WWII New York, as the architect who set out to make the regional shopping center a vital center of the community, as one of the architects who created downtown-revitalization plans that actually acknowledged the car while giving precedence to the pedestrian, as one of few architects who planned and built a new town, and as a theoretician who synthesized a humanistic and sustainable city model.[2] Phil Patton, writing in *American Heritage*, named Gruen "one of the ten people who have changed the course of our daily lives," and *U.S. News & World Report's* millennium issue, noting Americans who have shaped the modern era, said that Gruen had "changed the landscape of the continent"(Cohen, "A Mecca for Suburbanites," 50).

The current interest in the history of shopping and consumption culture and in the future of city and suburb has led to further interest in Gruen, but few authors and critics deal with him as a "citybuilder," focusing instead on his shopping centers and on Gruen himself as the "architect of consumption." Yet to Gruen shopping was not the end but the means for approaching what he considered architecture's real task: the struggle for the space and form of the contemporary city.[3] To explore his work in this light is the object of this book.

Victor Gruen contributed to architecture and planning in four areas, all stemming from his first work as a shop designer but moving far beyond it; and running through all of these areas of influence are also four thematic leitmotifs. In the arcades of his Viennese and New York shops, pedestrians could step from the flow of sidewalk traffic to pause, consider, enter, and perhaps buy; that is, Gruen understood how to create space and *mise-en-scene*. His shopping spaces were an interface between private commerce and urban public life, and the design and orchestration of this essential interface—so elemental to urban experience and culture—yielded the urban vision that would inform his philosophy and practice.

Gruen's first area of influence was of course in the shopping center. Yet in this he was driven by an urban-planning problem—to separate different kinds of vehicular traffic; and by an architectural goal—to recreate urban public space in the new suburban building type. Gruen wanted his centers to offer not just commercial but community and cultural space in the emerging suburban landscape. For him the shopping center was primarily an experiment in urban design, and he ultimately defined it in terms of its potential to renew old city centers and inform a new regional planning.

Gruen's second area of influence lay in his theories and projects for revitalizing American downtowns. He believed that the city center still had significant economic potential and could, through planning, accommodate the new twentieth-century icons of the city: highways, shopping centers, and parking garages. Gruen wanted the downtown to be the heart and brain for both the city and its surrounding region, and in his downtown plans he synthesized the opposing images of an automobile-oriented metropolis offered by Le Corbusier in the 1920s and '30s with the traditional public spaces of the dense European city, into a new image for postwar America.[4]

His third and fourth contributions to architecture and planning were more theoretical and much less discussed by contemporaries. Between 1956 and 1975, Gruen developed an abstract model for a networked, multi-centered regional city, the "Cellular Metropolis," as an alternative not only to the stark masterplanned image of Le Corbusier's *City of Tomorrow* and the anti-city model of Frank Lloyd Wright's *Broadacre City,* but also to the idea of continuous, *laissez faire* development spread over whole regions. He argued that cities do have an optimum size and thus the demographic explosion in the U.S. required new towns and cities, not just the endless expansion of existing ones. Finally, related to this theoretical work is the last of his contributions I will treat in this book. Gruen believed that architects and planners must defend the

4 Gruen, "Approaches to Urban Revitalization in the United States," 179. Gruen wrote: "My own urban and european upbringing, the fact that I have lived the first 35 years of my life in an intensely urban city, Vienna in Austria . . . and maybe especially the fact that my long years of residence in the classic anti-city, Los Angeles, gave me a most contrasting experience, has moved me to battle for the reestablishment of urban values and urban forms out of the conviction that the city, that great human invention for the facilitation of human communication, for the exchange of goods and ideas, is irreplacable as a cradle for human progress of all types."

5 Gruen, "The Planned Shopping Centers of America," 160.

environmental quality of life in cities, and in 1968 and 1972, he created environmental planning foundations in Los Angeles and Vienna as forums for the emerging ideas of the sustainable city. His idea of environmental planning began as a focus on urban public space, but later led to a plea for sustainable planning based on humanist culture and the ecological sciences—the urgent goal of planning today.

Informing all of Gruen's theory and practice are leitmotifs that he articulated in his many publications and speeches—and that continue to be urgent today. First is the role of commercial retail architecture and planning in the building of the city; commerce, Gruen believed, was the motor of urban culture. Second is the battle between the car and the city, which Gruen saw as a question of values—should urban life be dominated by technological or humanistic values? The third leitmotif is what he believed to be the architect-planner's most essential task: to make environments for transformative urban experiences, to create public space as a forum for social, cultural, and commercial exchange. And fourth is what he believed to be the role of the architect in the age of mass consumption, suburbanization, and mobility: given the increasing size and complexity of projects, the architect must be a communicator, manager, and interdisciplinary team leader.[5]

"Grabbing Fortune by the Tail"

Both personal and historic factors let Victor Gruen innovate in four such wide-ranging aspects of architecture and planning. In the rush to build a new America after WWII, his experience as an architect of retail situated him in the fast-moving field of shop and store design, a field that, with an expanding population, not only required innovation but, thanks to both individual and institutional investors, could pay for it. Thanks to federal intervention—the Veterans and Housing Acts—in the immediate postwar years, a new suburban landscape was emerging and badly needed retail and public facilities; Gruen seized the chance to promote the regional shopping center not only as a shopping and communal space, but also as an emergency center for civil defence. Then, when the physical deterioration of the downtowns and the need to adapt business and shopping districts to increasing automobile use required attention, Gruen could adapt the spatial structure and program of the regional shopping center for the downtowns. Here too federal intervention to support urban renewal and the new urban highways helped Gruen establish himself as an urban planner—although the problems of planning and building downtown would prove to be difficult.

Further, as his partner Edgardo Contini said, Gruen not only had unorthodox and novel ideas but "was very effective in selling them."[6] In this a detail from Gruen's early personal history is important, as it resonated through all his work: in Vienna he had been the impresario of a social-ist cabaret troupe, the Political Cabaret (das politische Kabarett). He managed the action on stage; controlled every aspect of display, lighting, and mood; and manipulated the audience as emcee, and all of this made him an extremely persuasive speaker and effective leader of a large architectural and planning organization. This theater background is, further, the key to his focus on public spaces–the stages for popular culture–in his urban and suburban projects.

The combination of commercial retail architect and progressive environmental planner makes Gruen one of the singular personalities of postwar architectural culture. He was not, as he said himself, one of the great "form givers" of his era, nor even among its most original thinkers.[7] His brilliance lay, rather, in his ability to synthesize a commercial practice with a philosophy of urbanism; his willingness to engage compromise; his ability to identify what could get built; and, finally, the urgency with which he addressed the question, What kind of city do we want?

Despite the enormous influence his work has had upon the American landscape and daily life–or, perhaps, because this influence has been so pervasive as to be indiscernible–the role of this central figure in American architecture has become obscured. With this book I want not only to fill a gap in the record of the architectural culture of postwar America, but to inject Gruen's arguments about the city into the current debate about the development of the contemporary city. I will focus on Gruen's innovative theories and projects in his American practice between 1938 and 1968, espe-cially with respect to the terms he set for himself: the return–by means of a new planning–of the city center and urban culture as the focus of the social life of the region. The context for his urban vision, however, was the "triumph" of the suburbs, the collapse of American downtowns, and vast demographic change; thus this book is the story of conflict between the ambition of an architect and the transformation of American society and its cityscape and landscape. Despite the difficul-ties that Gruen faced, many of his intentions and strategies are still valid; the debate in which he vigorously engaged still dominates architecture, planning, and the city.

6 Interview between Anne Gray and Edgardo Contini. March 19, 1988. Part Four: 5.
Interview, unpublished biographical notes, and articles of Edgardo Contini, Collection of Ann Gray, Los Angeles. Contini's articles span from 1941 to 1987.
7 Guzzardi, 77 In a backhanded compliment, the English critic

Reyner Banham characterized Gruen in his book *Megastructure*, 1976: "within this aggressively successful commercial designer there lurked–as *The Heart of Our Cities* reveals in page after page–a Viennese aesthete who shared most of the design aspira-tions of his more visionary colleagues."(42) Banham included Gruen's Fort Worth Plan and his project for Roosevelt Island.

The migration of Gruen's practice from Vienna to New York, then to Los Angeles and back to Vienna, together with his evolution from a shop designer to an international planner, has yielded the structure of this book. The projects are described in four parts: 1. "Commerce is the Engine of Urbanity," discussing Gruen's shops and stores in Vienna, New York, and California; 2. "Think of It as an Experimental Workshop," about the regional shopping center; 3. "The Car and the City," which deals with urban-redevelopment projects; and 4. "Alternatives to Sprawl: Gruen's Theory of Citybuilding," discussing projects for new towns and new cities. The projects are described relative to their planning, program, execution, and reception. The 1950s and 1960s presented a dramatically changing context–material, territorial, social, and cultural–that demanded creative responses if possible from architecture but certainly from planning. Each of the four parts therefore contains a brief discussion of the context or preconditions for Gruen's involvement with the different building types; project "reports"; and then the aftermath, or consequences, for Gruen and the American cityscape and landscape.

The roughly chronological structure of the book reflects the expanding scale of Gruen's projects as his authority grew. We should bear in mind, though, that Victor Gruen Associates was a general practice producing a wide range of buildings such as office buildings, banks, apartment buildings, restaurants, and private houses, many not corresponding to my four categories and some of which were well known at the time. Further, due to the stop-and-go nature of the work, an architect will be involved in a number of projects simultaneously, and between the late '50s and early '60s, Gruen was involved in four categories. This may be seen in the Timeline. (p. 4)

Commerce and the City
Architectural Culture and Trade

The role of commercial retail architecture and planning is a leitmotiv in this book about the building of the contemporary city. Victor Gruen saw commerce as one of the basic elements in establishing or renewing urban culture–certainly not the only element–and believed that a diverse architecture and urban design of retail could restore the attractive power of downtown and create new public spaces and new images for the city. One of the apparent contradictions in Gruen's work is that it is precisely his development as a designer of "consumption spaces"–from small stores to suburban shopping centers to downtown shopping districts–that was the basis both for his commitment to making public space, and for his role as an urbanist and environmentalist. Gruen attempted to link these apparently incompatible areas.

In a career that stretched over four decades, Gruen–either alone or with partners or his firm–designed some 40 shops, 15 department stores, and 44 shopping malls, in all about 44 million square feet of shopping buildings.[1] Yet many architects considered retail design and planning to be outside the main stream of architectural practice. Gruen was one of many architects and designers who fled Europe for the U.S. in the 1930s, some who became became emissaries of the International Congresses of Modern Architecture (CIAM)–the Modern Movement in architecture; others who became prophets of high design, representing the ideals of the Bauhaus or the Arts and Crafts movement in Vienna; while others rose to prominent university positions.[2] Victor Gruen belonged to neither the CIAM nor the academic elite, and he experienced some discrimination from the elite European modern architects as well as from established American architects because he was "trade." When Gruen arrived in New York, he remarked that, in comparison with Vienna, shop layouts were often done by store-furniture supply firms, and department stores frequently had their own layout division.[3] Architects seemed loathe to gain a reputation as retail specialists. Morris Lapidus, the prolific shop designer and renowned hotel

1 The status of Victor Gruen Associates (VGA) and the scope of the firms work is described in: "100 Largest Architectural Firms in the U.S.," *Architectural Forum*, Apr. 1963: 111; and the office books: Victor Gruen Associates - Architecture/Engineering/ Planning, 1958; and 1968. The portfolio of projects gives equal prominence to all areas of work. See also: Herman, "Three-Ring Circus," 2001: 742.
2 The impact of the designers, architects, engineers and planners who emigrated Austria is covered in Boeckl, M., (Hrsg), *Visionaere und Vertriebene*, 1995. For the impact of Bauhaus architects, and the architect and planners who were part of the CIAM, see: Mumford, E., *The CIAM Discourse on Urbanism, 1928-1960*, 2000.
3 Gruen, *Ein realistischer Traeumer: Ruckblicke, Einblicke, Ausblicke*, 110. (hereafter: *Traeumer*). Morris Ketchum made similar remarks, see: Ketchum, *Shops and Stores*: 9. With regard to architects currently in practice, Dan Herman also claimed that they often have kept their commercial retail work hidden, see

also Herman's "High Architecture," 2001: 390-401. Yet a look at the trade books of the time, for example, Labo, *Architettura del Negozio*, 1937, reveals nearly every well known modern architect and modernity from nealy every well known modern architect.
4 Lapidus, *The Architecture of Joy*, 73. Qtd. Hardwick, *Mallmaker*, 20. Gruen and Lapidus were colleagues. Despite Lapidus' remark, he was a prolific shop and chain store designer in the late 1940s and early 1950s.
5 Zola's *The Ladies Paradise*. Qtd. Grunenberg, "Wonderland: Spectacles of Display," 18-21. The most recent translation is Emile Zola, *The Ladies' Paradise*, (1883), trans. Brian Nelson, Oxford: Oxford University Press, 1995.
6 For the colonization of the suburban market by department stores, see Clausen's "Northgate Regional Shopping Center," 146; and, Kenneth Jackson's *Crabgrass Frontier*, 257. This development in a single city is described in Dyer, "Markets in the Meadows", and Longstreth, *City Center to Regional Mall*, 1997.

architect, observed that as an architecture student at Columbia University, he had believed that store design was not architecture at all. "Stores were designed by draughtsmen, who did not need degrees in architecture." [4] Many architects who made handsome shops, department stores, and, later, regional shopping centers did not include these projects in monographs of their work, for example Roosevelt Field Shopping Center, N.Y. (1956), by I. M. Pei. Even Morris Ketchum, who innovated in shops, department stores, and shopping centers, did not emphasize these projects in his monograph. Gruen, however, understood that the marketplace was a place of exchange and communication, an interface between economy and society, and that, as he claimed in *The New Yorker*, "merchants, more than any other group, had created the city"(25).

Until recently, commerce, particularly retail shopping, has been a neglected theme in architecture and urban design. But we cannot discuss the 19th-century city without addressing the social, commercial, and programmatic impact of the department store, and the recent interest in the corresponding history of the suburban and urban shopping center in the development of the late 20th-century city is long overdue. Urbanists have criticized the homogeneity of the suburbs and the phantasmagoria of the shopping mall, but the rise of the department store in the mid-19th century was the most prominent and spectacular manifestation of the new culture of uninhibited consumption. The effect on shoppers, mostly women, of luxurious and exotic architecture and goods immediately found its place in literature such as Emile Zola's *The Ladies' Paradise* (1883); and already by 1872, the Bon Marché in Paris was promoted as an essential tourist stop.[5] Louis Sullivan's Carson Pirie Scott in Chicago and Daniel Burnham's Selfridges in London were internationally known department stores that informed the zeitgeist of their cities. In early 20th-century America, further, department stores played a "precursor" role in the initial settlement of the suburbs. Beginning in the 1920s, Sears, Roebuck and Co., having observed that automobile registrations had outstripped the parking spaces available downtown, developed an aggressive strategy of locating new stores at the edge of cities where there was ample free parking. In Chicago and in Los Angeles, department stores such as Marshall Field's, Bullock's, and the May Co. soon followed suit.[6]

Architectural culture's distance from the typological and programmatic developments of trade was perhaps exacerbated by the influence of European modern architects in America, particularly members of the early CIAM in the 1920s and 1930s, whose interest in the development of city planning focused first on the structure of the city, and then on the form of housing. Commerce was nowhere to be found in Le Corbusier's "four functions" of the modern functionalist city: dwelling, work, transportation, and recreation. In their rush to replace the old city, did modern architects, with their focus divided between luxury villas, "Existenzminimum" apartment blocks, and district and city plans, forget the everyday activity of shopping? The American critic Lewis Mumford claimed that the cultural and civic role of cities, as they would be represented in a civic core, was the missing "fifth function" of the modern city.[7] Yet if towns and cities are to have a civic and cultural center, there must be a marketplace nearby. The linkage between public social space, the community center, and shopping area, achieved in the Greenbelt Towns produced under President Franklin D. Roosevelt's New Deal Program, was, however, a blind spot for modernist urbanism. This was a significant omission. Church, town hall, and marketplace equal "city." The planned shopping center would take its place among a variety of spaces that have become synonymous with "city" and urban culture: agora, souk, trade fair, market square, galleria, and department store, and Gruen referred to this history in exhibitions, lectures, and articles. As much as on cathedrals, palaces, and museums, the history of architecture and the city is dependent on these spaces.

7 Mumford, *The CIAM Discourse on Urbanism*, 142. The author refers to Lewis Mumford's review of J.L. Sert's *Can Our Cities Survive* in the New Republic in early 1943. Mumford named the cultural and civic role of cities, as they would be represented in a civic core, the "fifth function." See also Deckker, *The Modern City Revisited*, 2.

8 Gruen's writings from the 1920s and 30s were gathered together in his *Meine Alte Schuhschachtel* 1973. See "Adolf Loos gestorben," 1933: 117-19.

9 Peter, "*The Oral History of Modern Architecture*," 20. Gruen remarked, ". . . . a person who impressed me very much was Adolf Loos. Loos not only built but he wrote . . . . I believe many young people were very excited by what he had to say. I always remember that he used to show us a beautiful British-made suitcase and say, "This is design." . . . . I was so excited about him that I was deeply moved when he died." Later he would often refer to the influence of Loos. For example, see Gruen, V., "The better to see, reach, and touch," where he wrote " . . . .the basic principles of good design were as discernable in 1931 as they are today.

The Shop and Architectural Culture in Vienna

Distinctive shops and stores have always contributed to the character of streets and public spaces. This was particularly so in early 20th-century Vienna, where Gruen grew up and first practiced. Here the opposing polemics on design could be traced not only in major buildings but also in the most recent shops and stores. In the political, social, and economic turbulence after World War I, when Gruen began work as an architect, the Viennese architectural scene was animated by often bitter debates not only on the nature of design but on the form of cities, and he could see directly the work of several of the founding figures of modern design and planning. The theoretical background for questions of design relevant to the small works that Gruen began to take on had been the opposing views on the relationship of art and industry to architecture expressed by the architect Josef Hoffman (1870-1956) and the architect, designer, and polemicist Adolf Loos (1870-1932). Hoffman sought to achieve an artistic totality by bringing the highest level of attention and creativity even to the most everyday objects, while Loos believed that the amalgamation of art and purely utilitarian objects compromised the integrity of both. The impetus for their debate was the ornate decoration and delight in the unreal favored by the Viennese bourgeoisie. As Janik and Toulmin wrote in *Wittgenstein's Vienna*, "Under no circumstance should an object reveal its purpose by its shape—ornament had become a way of distorting things, an end in itself, rather than an embellishment." This was the impulse for Loos' attack on ornament; he rejected the use of applied art as a cultural cosmetic to screen reality. The nature of reality in design and architecture, he believed, was functional utility. Both Hoffman's and Loos' arguments could be measured in their shops and stores. Hoffman's Altmann & Kuhne luxury chocolate shop was on the Graben, and the utility combined with elegance of Loos' Knize Men's Outfitters (1913), also on the Graben, became a benchmark of design throughout Gruen's life. Loos found no contradiction in creating rational functional spaces for his men's clothing stores, albeit with luxurious materials. Loos' activities as polemicist, practitioner, and aesthete impressed Gruen deeply (he wrote an obituary of Loos for the Arbeiter-Zeitung in 1933).[8] Years later, Gruen still believed the principles of design established by Loos: "Close to fifty years ago, the architect Adolph Loos designed a large men's store in Vienna, which would be no less workable and aesthetically pleasing today than the best of current design in the field."[9]

Other prominent European architects built handsome shops, often early in their careers. Erich Mendelssohn's department stores built in Germany in the 1930s for the Schocken family are well known, Willem Dudok's Bijenkorf department store in Rotterdam was a striking example of Dutch modernism, and Oscar Nitschke's *Maison de la Publicité*, a mixed-use building planned for the Champs Elysees in Paris in 1935, was a dramatic example of incorporating media into a façade. Because of the comparative lack of resistance to change and the pressure of commercial competition, shop owners were open to new ideas. As Gruen later explained, shops had their own language of detailing, required an understanding of merchandising, were small, and required fast execution: they were thus perfect testing grounds for new concepts. When Gruen fled to New York after the Nazi *Anschluß* in Austria, he was not the only immigrant to bring with him design ideas that found form in shops; as the authors of *New York 1960* put it, "Shops were the advance messengers of the new trends of European architecture" (Stern et al, 374). If American architects and some of the exiled European elite considered shop design "trade" or a minor practice, other well-known European architects along with Gruen, such as Friedrich Kiesler, displayed no such hesitancy. In *Contemporary Art Applied to the Store and its Display* (1930), Kiesler demonstrated how modernist principles of abstraction, simplicity, and asymmetry could be joined with advertising, entertainment, and spectacle. He made clear the correlation between the store window and the theater stage, a correlation that Gruen was to take further in his own work and imbue with ideas about urbanism: "Why doesn't the show window hold instead of a display—a play? A stage play. Where Mr Hat and Miss Glove are partners. The window a veritable peepshow stage. Let the street be your auditorium with its ever-changing audience. Has nobody tried to conceive plays for merchandise?"[10]

10 Kraus, E., "Thoughts on Friedrich Kiesler's Show Windows," in Hollein and Grunenberg, (Eds.), *Shopping*, 125. The quote is from "Some Notes on Show Windows" (undated typescript), Austrian Frederick and Lilian Kiesler Privat Foundation, Vienna, 3. See also Kiesler, F., *Contemporary Art Applied to the Store and its Display*, 1930.
11 Kwinter, S., "Virtual City: the wiring and waning of the world," *Arch+* 128, Sep. 1995. The "Gruen transfer." Kwinter wrote: "This term refers to a threshhold, the moment when a shopper's purposive behavior and directed, coherent bodily movements break down under the barrage of excessive narrow-spectrum stimulation and continual interruption of attention. The unconsciously bewildered shopper, rendered docile, cannot help but drift into the prepared pathways and patterns of externally induced consumer activity, unfocused but exquisitely suggestible to gentle but firm environmental cues. It is estimated that as much as 90 percent of shopping mall transactions concern goods that the shopper had not planned in advance to buy, yet did so after the Gruen transfer took hold."

The Shopper as Willing Victim?

Until recently, architects have mostly remembered Gruen as a villain who pioneered the shopping center, and critics have coined the expression "the Gruen Transfer" to describe a reputed phenomenon that occurs during a visit to a shopping center: in the presence of a dazzling array of goods, one loses one's purpose and begins to drift, transformed into a pliant and uncritical consumer purchasing random items.[11] But, first, Gruen simply perfected what every good shop designer practiced: the art of catching the eye of the passer-by and making of him (and especially her) a customer. In 1940, writing in *Apparel Arts*, his first U.S. publication, he described this process as lowering the potential customer's resistance with an alluring display of merchandise, which would entrance the now defenseless individual and spirit her through the entrance door. And, second, Gruen argued that this "manipulation" was more complex than sheer consumption-engineering; the shop window, and especially arcade spaces, were part of the theater of the street: window shopping was as intrinsic to urban culture as sitting on a stoop or chatting on a corner. One definition of urban design is the city seen from the perspective of the pedestrian, and the interest of marketing consultants has been described as terminating at 15 feet above street level; both are describing the fundamental urban space of the city—the street. In exploiting their skill and wit to create customers out of passers-by, store architects and merchants in fact created the atmosphere of the street; designers doing shops were "citybuilding" at the most intimate and everyday scale. For Gruen, this notion was supplemented by his experience as a cabarettist, which gave him a sense for the dramatic and didactic space of the theater stage. Although he would not write about this synthesis until much later, he would combine these early experiences of creating space and a *mise-en-scene* into his concept of new suburban and urban public spaces.

Part 1 documents Gruen's development as an architect in Vienna; his reincarnation as one of New York's prominent shop designers; and the establishment of his office in Los Angeles, where he graduated from popular chain stores to experimental projects for shopping centers. The last project in this section is Milliron's, a hybrid department store that balanced flows not only of people and goods but also of vehicles, and thus stands both as an automobile-age transformation of the small street-front shop and as a harbinger of the new suburban commercial landscape.

Store design is not the antithesis of city building and city planning; what appealed to Gruen about retail architecture was that it was space designed not just for commercial but for social exchange and thus was inherently urban. For Gruen, urban shops and stores formed the critical foundation of his later career as a space maker, urbanist, and humanist.

Although Gruen is most important for the projects and theories he developed during three decades in the U.S., he spent the first 35 years of his life, including his first 10 years of professional activity, in Vienna. Gruen (born Viktor Gruenbaum) grew up in a comfortable social and cosmopolitan milieu that deeply influenced his vision of urbanism. The work and social life of his father, a prominent lawyer with many clients in the theater, was particularly formative: all daily excursions—to offices, courtrooms, theaters, and cafés, undertaken on foot or by horse-drawn carriage in the First District, Vienna's historic center—became the basis for Gruen's philosophy of what it meant to live in a city, his model of urbanity. Everyday activities of urban life—including work, leisure, and family—should be no more than a short distance from each other, and the spaces between each destination—streets, sidewalks, parks, squares, and everything that filled them—were quintessentially urban.[12] These elementary experiences would be tempered by Gruen's exposure as a student to the opposing ideas of Camillo Sitte, who believed the city was a theater and championed a picturesque urbanism, and Otto Wagner, who believed the city should be an efficient and practical urban structure as the basis for commercial development.[13] In 1925, these different images of the city were thrown into the starkest relief when Gruen traveled to Paris and saw the dramatic drawings and models of Le Corbusier's "Contemporary City" and the "*Voisin Plan.*"

12 *Traeumer*, 41-2. "(Upto the outbreak of the first World War) . . . . the day began with my mother and father being served breakfast in bed, then at the large marble table in the bedroom, they would leisurely bathe and dress . . . . finally around 10:00 my father would set out to the office, where he (would start the day) by dictating letters . . . . regularly we could observe through the children's bedroom window, my father making his pleas in the business court across the street. After the traditional mid-day meal at home, my father would set off to the Café de l'Europe on the Stephensplatz, in order to take care of business contacts . . . . From the Café he returned to his office to take care of correspondence or meet with clients. With great pride I went with this elegant man—with his black hat, stiff collar, and walking stick—to appointments at the Carl Theater. While he met with the Director Eiberschutz, I sat in the darkened theater and followed attentively the rehearsals . . . ." (author translation) A different version ot this text exists in *Die Lebenswerte Stadt*, 156-7.

13 For a general discussion of Viennese urbanism at the turn of the century, see: "The Ringstrasse, Its Critics, and the Birth of Urban Modernism," in Schorske, "*Fin-De-Siecle-Vienna,*": 24-115. The current questions of theming and the city have renewed the relevance of Sittes's classic text, *City Planning According to Artistic Principles* (see Collins and Collins Eds.), originally published as Sitte, *der Staedtebau nach seinen kuenstlerischen Grundsaetzen*, 1889). Sitte, who believed that the artistic and modern were antithetical, championed a picturesque urbanism based on the irregular streets and squares of the medieval and renaissance city. The city was a theater, and the principal role of buildings was to frame the intimate corridor street and pedestrian plazas so that these spaces could act as the stage for urban public life. The architect-planner Otto Wagner, on the other hand, believed the role of the urban planner was to provide an efficient and practical urban structure as the basis for commercial development. Transportation was the key to growth, and his plan for the extension of Vienna of 1893 was structured by four circumferential road and rail belts, of which the nineteenth-century *Ringstrasse* would be the first. Gruen's own urban vision would be a synthesis of the public spaces of Sitte, the acceptance of the automobile by Le Corbusier, and the importance of commerce expressed by Wagner.

14 *Traeumer*, 79. Later, Friedrich Scheu, a journalist who fled Vienna for London, published *Humor als Waffe*, which describes the Political Cabaret. See the chapter "Der Weg zum Politischen Kabarett" (The Road to the Political Cabaret), 19-34. Gruen came to the Political Cabaret via his activities in various socialist youth organizations and his love of the theater. Scheu's book is dedicated to Victor Gruen. Gruen's account is in *Traeumer*, 69. "The political cabaret stood . . . at the focal point of my creative life."

By the time Gruen began practicing under his own name, the vast municipal housing program begun by the Social Democrats was being completed. The only opportunities were small works for progressive clients who sought the contemporary design of a single room or an apartment, often including the design of furniture, fittings, and lighting–a whole living environment. Among Gruen's first independent projects were such designs for single or groups of rooms, always with moving partitions and transformable furniture units. The Gruen-designed living environments were a synthesis of modern and moderne, simple and comfortable, making an easy context for both modern chromed-steel furniture and fittings and traditional pieces, be they Persian carpets or period furniture. As much as possible, the furniture was built-in, often with folding or sliding panels that enabled an area to change its function. Shelves were terminated by a lighting-standard, full-height cabinets transformed into martini bars, conveniently projecting into space, and domestic rooms were transformed into offices by day. The work required constant supervision on site, and numerous visits to the small workshops of the cabinetmakers, metalworkers, and upholsterers that were typical of small-scale Viennese industry.

An important job, despite its small scale, was the chance to carry out small alterations in the house Adolf Loos built in Hietzing in 1912 for Dr. Gustav Scheu, which gave Gruen not only an intimate understanding of the spaces and ambience of Loos but also a chance to enter the progressive intellectual and political circle of the Scheu family.[14] Beginning in the turbulent year of 1934, Gruen was able to move his design work in a new direction that would both engage his theatrical imagination and launch his career: the design of shops and stores–first façades, then interiors, and occasionally a complete store. He claimed he had never liked domestic work because of the conflicting desires of family members, whereas the agenda of a shop was certain. Important too is the fact that the shop, unlike the private residence and perhaps more like the theater, is a place of social interface, a semi-private place with a direct and active relationship to the public and the street.

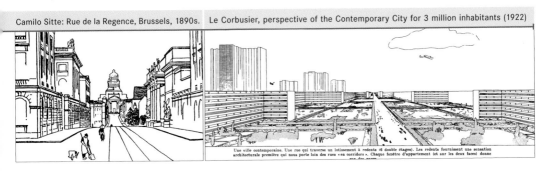

Camilo Sitte: Rue de la Regence, Brussels, 1890s.   Le Corbusier, perspective of the Contemporary City for 3 million inhabitants (1922)

Gruen's first shop to draw attention was the Bristol *Parfumerie* in the Bristol Hotel with an address on the Ringstrasse. Working with a façade only 8' 3" (2.5m) wide, Gruen glazed the entire front, framed in stainless steel on a base of black marble, so that the white lacquered interior space of the store became part of the street space; he further dissolved the store's narrow confines by using the well-known device, employed by Loos, of a mirrored rear wall with an additional mirrored band along the ceiling. Gruen had turned the shop's small size and intimate scale to advantage. The play of the initials BP, worked into the chair upholstery and, in blue and pink, set into the blacktop tables, resulted in a review in *Display* magazine, the first English-language publication of Gruen's work.[15]

Perfume Boutique in the Bristol Hotel (1935). The combination of a white-laquered interior, augmented by mirrors, both enlarged and dissolved the tiny store space.

15 "Initials in the Decorative Scheme," *Display*, 233; and Gruen, *Traeumer*, 81.

16 Shamp, "Victor Gruen, designer of Kalamazoo Mall, Dies." The project is not listed in Gruen's "List of Work Done in the Years 1924-1937," but neither are other larger scale buildings he is alleged to have done under pressure from the local Nazi Party such as the *"Kraft durch Freude"* Halls.

17 "Les Boutiques,"*l'Architecture d'Aujourd'hui*, 18-19*;* and, Augenfeld, "Modern Austria, Personalities and Style," 165, 171. The *l'Architecture d'Aujourd'hui* showed the Bristol Parfumerie,

Parfumerie Guerlain, and Herrenmoden Deutsch. See also *"Glas" (Österreichische Glaserzeitung*, no. 8/9, 1937, which showed four pages of Grünbaum shop facades, including the Parfumerie Bristol (1935), Singer Store (1936), Parfumerie Guerlain (1936), Herren Moden Deutsche 1936, Piccadilly Store (1937), and Park Confisserie.

18 Gruen's production in Vienna is documented in a job list, which is dated Vienna, May 15, 1937, 10 months before the Anschluss. It was translated in Los Angeles in 1951. See: List of Work Done In The Years 1924-1937. LoCVGP.

Two years later he further explored the spatial relationship between shop and street, this time at the Singer store on the Rotenturmstrasse. Here Gruen created a recessed "arcade" entrance flanked by display windows, making an intermediate zone between pavement and shop entrance so people could step out of the stream of moving pedestrian traffic and, as he would later express it, begin their subtle transformation–enacted by light and space–from mere passersby to customers.

Within this limited sphere of activity, Gruen became in a few years quite successful and began his first larger-scale work, the renovation of a department store on the Mariahilferstrasse.[16] All of his shop conversions specialized in the use of glass with different lighting effects. In these projects, the fundamental mechanism of the façade as "eyecatcher" and display window as an introduction to another world from the space of the street was worked out with the minimum detailing that was dictated by the project budgets.

In the mid-1930s, Gruen's work began appearing in architecture and trade publications. In 1937, the journal *"Glas" Österreicher Glaserzeitung* featured the façade treatments for seven

The Singer Fabric Store on the Rotenturmstrasse (1936) with its bold neon sign and walk-in arcade space.

shops and included the Bristol *Parfumerie*, the Singer Store, and *Herrenmoden* Deutsch. In April 1938, both the *Architectural Review* and *l'Architecture d'Aujourd'hui* gave Gruen his first European exposure. In the former, Felix Augenfeld, writing about the modern movement in Vienna, claimed that "one must not look for large modernist monuments but rather small private dwellings, a few country houses, and the middle-class living room." He described the simple elegance of Gruen's *Herrenmoden* Deutsch shop as particularly characteristic of Austrian modernism (Modern Austria... 171). The same year, *l'Architecture d'Aujourd'hui* published the Bristol Parfumerie, *Herrenmoden* Deutsch and *Parfumerie* Guerlain, and compared Gruen's work with the best current work in Paris.[17] But it was an inauspicious time for this promising beginning; in March, Nazi Germany annexed Austria, and Gruen, a Jew and well-known leader of socialist agit-prop theater, the Political Cabaret, abandoned his career and fled to the U.S.

When Gruen reached New York, he was hardly a well-known architect and had none of the stature of the Bauhaus masters, many a generation older, who were making their way to London, Boston, New York, or Chicago. He wrote in his autobiography that all he had acquired at the State Trade School for Architecture and as the supervising site architect at Melcher & Steiner was skill as a technician and construction manager. His architectural vision had been won through reading, attending public lectures, and traveling. As leader, emcee, and actor in the Political Cabaret, however, he had mastered fantasy, organizational skill, persuasiveness, and empathy—and these were what he brought to the U.S (Traeumer, 85-6). Despite this claim, in Vienna Gruen had carried out more than one hundred small projects, absorbed the ideas and techniques of Loos, and developed a conviction about urban space, public life, and the city.[18]

In the Deutsch's Men's Fashion shop (1936), Gruen contrasted an eye-level inset vitrine with a one-and-a-half story glazed shop window.

Facade for Richard Löwenfeld's women's fashion store, Vienna (1937)

Hermann Lederer, who, before fleeing Austria, had been proprietor of luxury leather goods shops in Paris and Vienna, was familiar with Gruen's work and, learning that he too had emigrated, asked Gruen to do his first American store.[19] The building owner, however, refused to turn part of his building over to an unknown refugee, who was, moreover, an unlicensed architect. Finally a compromise was reached whereby the owner proposed that Morris Ketchum, a young American architect designing the adjacent Ciro store, stamp and sign the drawings.

The prime location of Lederer's Store at 711 Fifth Avenue meant that the density of pedestrian traffic would make a normal flush show window easy to miss and impossible to stand before. Gruen therefore decided to treat the façade of the store as a frame with a cut-in "arcade" space, the device he had used in the Singer store. This would increase the street frontage and create a space for pedestrians to pause out of the flow and admire the leather goods.

Light and glass would characterize the arcade: the ceiling consisted of ribbed translucent green glass with concealed light sources so that the lobby was illuminated; along the two sides of the arcade, as well as on either side of the fully glazed entrance door, Gruen set six small glass vitrines that cantilevered into the arcade space and were surrounded by the same light-grey glass he had used in his European stores; in the middle of the arcade he placed a stainless-steel and glass vitrine similar to those found in museums, which gave a serene focal center to this tiny urban space, while the luxury leather goods in the side vitrines were dramatically spotlit.

Lederer's was featured not only in the architectural and trade presses but also in the daily newspapers and weeklies; it was named "Store of the Month" within the trade as well as being featured in *Women's Wear Daily*. Lewis Mumford, writing in the *New Yorker*, however, criticized both the Lederer's and the Ciro stores for disturbing Fifth Avenue's quality as "one long picture window" and likened Lederer's to a seductive peep show for eager consumers.[20] After this, Gruen and Ketchum received further commissions for shops and stores, notably Paris Decorator's on the Grand Concourse in the Bronx, and the Steckler Store on Broadway and 72nd Street, which featured an arcade front with an even deeper setback.

19 *Traeumer*, 106. Gruen's list of the jobs he had completed in Vienna shows a small conversion for a Leo Lederer 1934.
20 Mumford, "The Skyline: New Faces on the Avenue," *New Yorker* (Talk of the Town). See also "Lederer Front Is New Departure," *Women's Wear Daily*; and "Store of the Month," *Store of Greater New York*. All of these in LoCVGP, OV 11.

"Trade," *Architectural Forum*, October 1940, includes Steckler and Lederer Shops, Strasser Studio, and the Altman & Kuhne shop, 286-291. Gruen was thrilled when after a fire in 1963, he was asked to redo the store exactly as it had been originally created. In 1976, the store was demolished and gave way to a standardized chain store design.

Lederer de Paris (1939). Restrained elegance on 5th Avenue. Below, extending the public space of the street: Lederer's rectangular arcade and Morris Ketchum's concave façade for Ciro's.

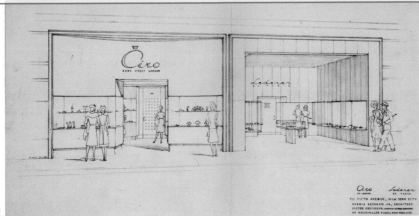

Having parted ways with Morris Ketchum, Gruen joined with designer Elsie Krummeck, founding Gruen and Krummeck, Designers, in November 1939. Krummeck had studied at the Parsons School of Art and Design, and by the time the World's Fair in New York opened, she had contributed to the design of over 25 exhibits. With her background in display, where one had to sketch and conceptualize quickly, she created the visual concepts for façades and interiors using Conti color sticks, oil pastels, and later air-brush, as well as designing the details, graphics, and packaging. Her skills would complement Gruen's gift for organizing people and finding new clients.[21]

Their first job together was a store in the Gotham Hotel at 700 Fifth Avenue, opposite Lederer's, for the Viennese confectioners Emil Altman & Ernst Kuhne, now also refugees. The merchandising practice in the elegant Altman & Kuhne store on the Graben in Vienna, designed by Joseph Hoffman, had been to display their entire candy assortment in cases and to have a smartly uniformed sales assistant arrange the customer's selection in special boxes. Instead of an "inset" arcade, Gruen gave the New York shop a plate-glass window on the street line with no display behind; thus the entire interior functioned, as the *Architectural Forum* expressed it, as show window. In December 1939, a "Broadway style" opening took place, and the *Architectural Forum* later wrote,

The uniformed assistant, the elaborate display cases, the selecting and wrapping process all taking place in an interior of satin, mirror glass, stainless steel in bright colors was nothing if not theatrical . . . certainly the intimacy and scale of the merchandise–the individual chocolates–gave the shop the air of luxury and intimacy . . . . [22]

21 Elsie Krummeck-Crawford, author interview, 1998; and, *Traeumer*, 113. In early 1936, Elsie was making miniature model figurines that set the theme of eight shop windows at Bonwit Teller. See Austin, "Elsie Krummeck has dramatised with her patented metal dolls . . .,"1936; also "Act Out Day's Program for Customers in Series of Store Windows." *Womens Wear Daily*, 1936; and *Dry Goods Economist*, Aug. 4, 1936: 18. Elsie said that at the time she met Victor, city planning was certainly not on his mind. He carried his Vienna architectural work in an old suitcase.

22 *Traeumer*, 120. See also: "Altman & Kuhne Shop,"*Architectural Forum*, 90. See also "Trade" *Architectural Forum*, 289, 291.

The interior combined sensuousity, whimsy, and–with the choreography of selection and display–drama.

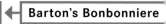

The success of Altman & Kuhne brought a new client, Stephan Klein, who had also come to New York from Vienna, where he had learned the chocolate production business and seen Gruen's shops. Klein, who had set up a chocolate factory with his brothers in Brooklyn, wanted to produce a chain of popularly priced candy stores that would fill a niche in the American market between mass-produced candy bars sold in drugstores and luxury chocolates sold in shops like Altman & Kuhne. Several shops already existed in Brooklyn, but this new Barton's was to be the chain's debut in Manhattan. The tiny store space was on 82nd Street and Broadway, in a middle-class area. The show window, which turned a corner and returned to the entrance door (thereby creating a half-arcade), dissolved the barrier between the street and the interior, giving the illusion of greater space—yet another instance in which Gruen modulated the distinction between street and interior, public and private, audience and spectacle. Gruen and Krummeck, who designed not only the façade and interior, but also the name of the business ("Barton's Bonbonniere"), the logo, the stationery, and the wrapping paper, set a serpentine wooden screen by Artek opposite a mirrored wall to separate sales and storage areas, and further reinforced the sense of space with semi-circular ceiling fittings. White and grey stripes in the open front created a perspective pull towards the magenta entrance door, which was inset with a grid of portholes; these candy-stripes became the store trademark. After its opening in 1941, Klein commissioned a further five stores. Barton's was Gruen and Krummeck's first chain of shops.[23]

Each of these early shops, in both Vienna and New York, demonstrated variations on a theme intensely worked out in the detail design: shopping as not just a raw exchange of money and goods but an activity that is social, interactive, theatrical, aesthetic, and involving motion and flow: an activity that is profoundly urban.

23 Stern et al, *New York 1960*, 582. Also *Traeumer*, 118. Before commissioning Gruenbaum and Krummeck, Klein had already opened several shops in Brooklyn. About twelve years later Gruen received a telephone call out of the blue. It was Stephan Klein, now having built 49 Barton's shops. For his 50th store, Klein wanted Gruen to create a new image and logo for the future. Klein had bought a rowhouse across from Macy's. Gruen called Alvin Lustig, the renowned designer who was doing the graphics for Northland, and the lighting designer Kevin McCandless to create something special. See "Playful chocolate shop," *Architectural Forum*, 100-09, and Stern et al, *New York 1960*: 582.

24 Elsie Krummeck Crawford, author interview, 1998. Also Traeumer, 125-27. Gruen and Elizabeth Kardos had divorced amicably.
25 "Getting Twenty-Four Hours of Service from Store Fronts," *Chain Store Age*. Base of the columns, there were scales, where customers could check their weight before entering a display with the theme "clothes reduce your apparent weight."

In 1940, Gruen parlayed a request to alter some drawings into the chance to produce new plans for a downtown department store on the West Coast. After a successful presentation, he and Krummeck were flown to Southern California by a flamboyant entrepreneur, Walter Kirschner, who intended to build a chain of stores selling low- and mid-price fashions to the thousands of women generating their own income by working in war-production factories. Gruen and Krummeck scouted store locations in a dozen cities across several states, in a trip that was a crash course in commercial real estate, store management, and financing, and that ended with the commission to design all subsequent stores for the Grayson company.[24]

Gruen and Krummeck's first Grayson's store opened in Seattle in 1941. Located downtown, it shared the same preoccupations with material, light, and color as Gruen's previous store designs, but its scale was enormous, and its tone—unlike the quiet luxuriousness of some of the New York shops—was in keeping with the flashiness and lower prices that would appeal to the popular market Grayson's sought. Krummeck's dominating façade approached a graphic quality at the scale of the whole street. Supported by two giant, copper-colored columns, the vast, four-story, yellow concave shell façade, which rose from the main entrance, was dramatically lit at night, and, with its giant neon letters and deep entrances animated with built-in and island vitrines, it set the pattern for many of the Grayson's stores that would follow. Access to the store itself was by a bridge crossing a sunken display area with a tableau of uplit live models and mannekins. Gruen and Krummeck seemed to have combined Radio City Music Hall with a department-store atrium; from the entrance, one could see into three levels of the store—another dissolution, on a grander and more lavish scale, of shopping space, theater, and street that was so vital to Gruen's urban vision.[25]

Designed to dominate the street! Grayson's Seattle store (1941), where one entered through a crowd of mannekins. Plans and sections show the extent to which the space of the street has been drawn into the selling strategy of the store.

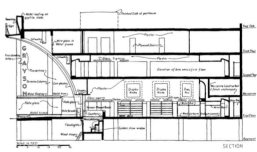

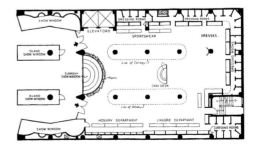

Their second Grayson's, on Crenshaw Boulevard in Los Angeles, marked the beginning of a crucial shift in Gruen and Krummeck's work, a shift to the new automotive context of Southern California, which would profoundly affect Gruen's evolution as space maker preoccupied with movement and flows. Postwar affluence, increasing car ownership, and expanding suburbs, anchored initially by the commercial strip, were producing a new automobile culture. In its heyday during the '50s and '60s, the strip would of course generate its own building types—supermarkets, bowling alleys, coffee shops, and motels—but already in the '40s, traditional urban types had to be rethought for the new automobile environment. Unlike stores in dense East Coast downtowns, where many customers arrived on foot or by public transport, the new suburban strip stores on the West Coast catered to both the pedestrian and the private driver, who most often entered the store from a parking lot at the rear. The Crenshaw Grayson's was thus markedly different from the downtown store in Seattle and followed a general change in store design: it had two "fronts" of equal importance. Gruenbaum and Krummeck devoted as much attention to the rear parking-lot entrance as to the "main" entrance on Crenshaw Boulevard. The parking-lot entrance had large-scale lettering and a sweeping, convex-curved glazed façade. At night the curtains, drawn by day, were opened to show a fully lit interior.

Not only were individual stores adapting themselves to the automobile, but, increasingly, many stores were located along shopping strips or in shopping centers of varied type. In 1942, writing in *Architect and Engineer*, Gruen enthused on the progress of store design in the more open West Coast urban environment, where automobile access was as important as pedestrian access:

Designing stores on the west coast has presented new problems and new possibilities . . . . The wide open arcade front and the sightly parking lot entrance, for example, could not be carried out anywhere so well as in California . . . . [26]

26 Gruenbaum, "Some Notes on Modern Store Design," *Architect and Engineer*. In *City Center to Regional Mall*, Longstreth believed Gruen and Krummeck's Santa Monica Grayson's Store (1940) was their first work in Southern California (433,n. 38).
27 A record number of women were entering the workplace—some 4 million between 1940 and 1944—taking jobs in wartime factories that formally would have gone to men. Their disposable income was a boon to the Grayson specialist stores, which were opened in just the cities that had war industry factories. See "How Main Street Stole Fifth Avenue's Glitter," in Hardwick's "Creating A Consumer Century," 100-102. This dissertation is particularly strong in its coverage of shops and the rise of chain stores during the war years.
28 For Grayson's "Victory Stores," see "New Stores Opened By Ingenious Use of Substitute Materials," *Chain Store Age*: 24; and "Chain Apparel Shop-Gruen and Krummeck plan a 'Victory' Store

with non-critical materials," *Architectural Forum*: 89-91.
29 Gruen was surprised to find that even these temporary store installations were published in the best magazines. *Traeumer*, 149
30 Forristal, "Grayson's Growth," Wall Street Journal. The Journal wrote, ". . . . the growth of Grayson-Robinson Stores, Inc. has been especially striking . . . . between 1938 and 1945, the company has assumed national stature. It now operates 28 stores but has recently acquired Robinson's Women's Apparel, Inc. with 17 units. With the Robinson chain absorbed, the way was paved for the invasion of the rich Manhattan retail market through the acquisition of S. Klein-on-the-Square, Inc." See also: Grayson-Robinson Stores, New York, Annual Report for the year ended September 30, 1946. LoCVGP, OV 14. Hardwick (2000) believed that in these years the fees for the Grayson's stores accounted for 89% of Gruenbaum and Krummeck's income, 132 (note 12).

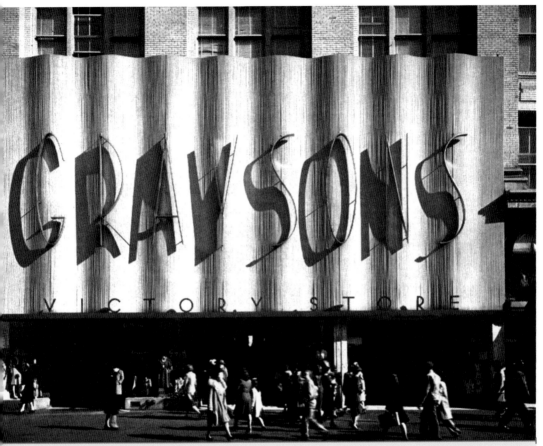

Building without glass, steel, and concrete; Grayson's "Victory Store" in San Francisco (1943?) comprised three stores "joined" by a common facade and supergraphics.

Victory Stores

When the U.S. entered World War II in 1941, the War Production Board placed restrictions on building materials, slowing or halting projects altogether. Grayson's, however, wanted to stick to their development schedule to take advantage of the anticipated consumer demand generated by the millions of working women who would have a new disposable income.[27] To keep to schedule but get around the restrictions, Gruen and Krummeck developed ingenious methods of construction. Using fireproof fabrics stretched over timber frames for walls or suspended to form mock ceilings, for instance, they literally built stage sets for selling until the war was over. In at least two examples, the 739 South Broadway store in Los Angeles and the San Francisco store, two or three older stores were combined without structural alterations to produce larger "new" Grayson's stores. To conceal the multiple entrances and different façade treatments, Gruen and Krummeck suspended large fiberboard and wooden screens over the entrances of both stores.

Eager to integrate the war effort into their merchandising strategy, the "Grayson's" logo on both store façades was flanked by the slogans "Buy War Bonds" and "Victory Store." As was normal in store refurbishment, all remodeling was carried out without interrupting business.[28]

Gruen and Krummeck's dexterity enabled Grayson's to continue expanding and make a fortune during the war, while consolidating the designers' reputation as merchandising and construction experts in the retail field. Grayson's strategy to dominate the street was well featured in the architectural and trade press, although later Gruen would claim that he was surprised that these stores received such publicity. Aside from the stage-set façades and dramatic uses of light, he admitted that there was little design—only strategies for how much could be built for how little cost in the shortest time.[29] But there was no need to demur; it was the "style for the job." Gruen's statement hides the fact that Grayson's aggressive marketing, Kirschner's desire for publicity, and Gruen and Krummeck's desire to establish themselves dovetailed perfectly; as Mark Jeffrey Hardwick points out, "their joint success during the war years was no coincidence."[30]

31 Gruen and Krummeck's adaptation to Southern California is ironically described in "How should we live?" *Traeumer*, 135, 138.
32 In his book *Shops and Stores*, Morris Ketchum, Jr. gave Gruen and Krummeck, together with Ernest Born, credit for devising and perfecting the flexible ceiling in their 1944 refurbishment of the Macy's San Francisco store, 137-9. See also Gruen, "The Case for the Flexible Ceiling." The Macy's Kansas City and San Francisco refurbishment jobs were well known in the building trades for their use of removable suspended ceiling panels, which also incorporated lighting, as well as custom designed movable partitions and knock down display fixtures. The Macy's work was not only a break from the regimen of the Grayson's stores, but also a platform for further work for major department stores and, ultimately, the regional shopping center.
33 "Retail Stores: A Critique," Progressive Architecture. See also Ross, "Elegance and Sophistication," *Display World*; and, *Interiors (Industrial Design)*. Aug. 1947: 98. Gruen and Krummeck opened their first branch office in San Francisco to deal with Joseph Magnin stores in Northern California, which by 1950, included Palo Alto, Sacramento, San Fransisco, San Mateo, Oakland, and Reno, Nevada. Magnin's were to become over the years the shining light of retail on the West Coast hiring, among others, Rudi Gernreich in the 1960s. Gruen's, and particularly Rudi Baumfeld's, long association with Joseph Magnin Stores was to last through the 1970s. Gere Kavanaugh, Designer. Author interview, Los Angeles 1998, 2000.
34 With their growing office, Gruen and Krummeck were emerging in an exciting architecture and design scene in Los Angeles. Krummeck was part of a small group of women designers that included Ray Eames, Florence Knoll, and the Viennese architect and interior designer Liane Zimbler. The architecture scene was dominated by a previous generation of Viennese, Rudolf Schindler and Richard Neutra, but a younger generation of local architects was emerging that included the designer Charles Eames and architects such as John Lautner, A. Quincy Jones, and later Craig Elwood and Pierre Koenig. In 1945, partly in reaction to the over-standardization and low quality of average subdivision tract houses, John Entenza, editor of *Arts & Architecture* magazine, started the Case Study House program, which encouraged young architects to work with new materials to create new prototype houses. Although Gruen and Krummeck were not part of the Case Study House program, they would soon be joined by the Italian engineer Edgardo Contini, who had worked as the consulting engineer on projects by the Eames's, Lautner, and A. Quincy Jones. For Gruen and Krummeck's early years in Los Angeles, see *Traeumer* 138-46.

As the Grayson's work was getting underway, Gruen and Krummeck, with some prodding from clients, settled permanently on the West Coast and married in 1942 (Gruen for the second time).[31] By this time, he had received American citizenship and changed his name formally from Gruenbaum. The expanding workload enabled them to move their office from their rented house on the Kings Road to Santa Monica and expand their staff, but they were frustrated with the repetitiveness of the work and sought to widen their professional activity. In April 1943, in a special issue devoted to architecture after the end of the war, the *Architecture Forum* published Gruen and Krummeck's first design for a neighborhood shopping center—an important project that I will return to in Part 2. In a few years they began to work for the nationally renowned Macy's department stores, carrying out successful and well publicized renovations of Macy's San Francisco and Kansas City stores. Working with architect Ernest Born, Gruen and Krummeck developed one of the first installations of the suspended flexible ceiling, with interchangable lighting grills and fireproof acoustic panels.[32] From this innovative work came the chance to create "high-style women's apparel" stores, beginning in 1946 for Joseph Magnin. Whereas the "extrovert" Grayson's stores set out to dominate the streetscape with their brash façades, the Joseph Magnin's stores let Gruen return to the elegance and intimacy of the Lederer's and Altman & Kuhne New York shops. The Joseph Magnin stores built in Sacramento and Palo Alto were discreetly furnished, with a refined use of materials and lighting to convey intimacy and elegance and "to beguile the customer, to attract her eye and her mind and hand to the acquisition of merchandise."[33] The Magnin stores represent a pause, then, from designing for the street and its complex social and vehicular currents, and instead a focus upon another theme that would preoccupy Gruen and find expression repeatedly in his work as it evolved from shop to city: control of mood, how a designed space can influence how one feels and behaves.

Meanwhile, the expansion of the office's retail work required additional personnel. First to join the office was Karl Van Leuven, who had worked on cartoons and animation at the Disney Studios. Then Rudi Baumfeld, Gruen's schoolmate, who, having fled Vienna for Prague, had then made his way via Italy, where he had been imprisoned, and New York before finally reaching Los Angeles. With his Viennese experience of free-standing buildings, interiors, furniture, lighting, and color, Baumfeld would ultimately take over the department-store work and the role of chief designer.[34]

Corner detail, Joseph Magnin's, Sacramento (1946). The Sacramento Union reported that 50,000 people jammed the downtown for the September 5th preview.

MARCH 1949

STORES

March 1949
*G79₃

STORE DESIGN

THE RETAIL PRICING
SITUATION

THE MONTH IN
RETAILING

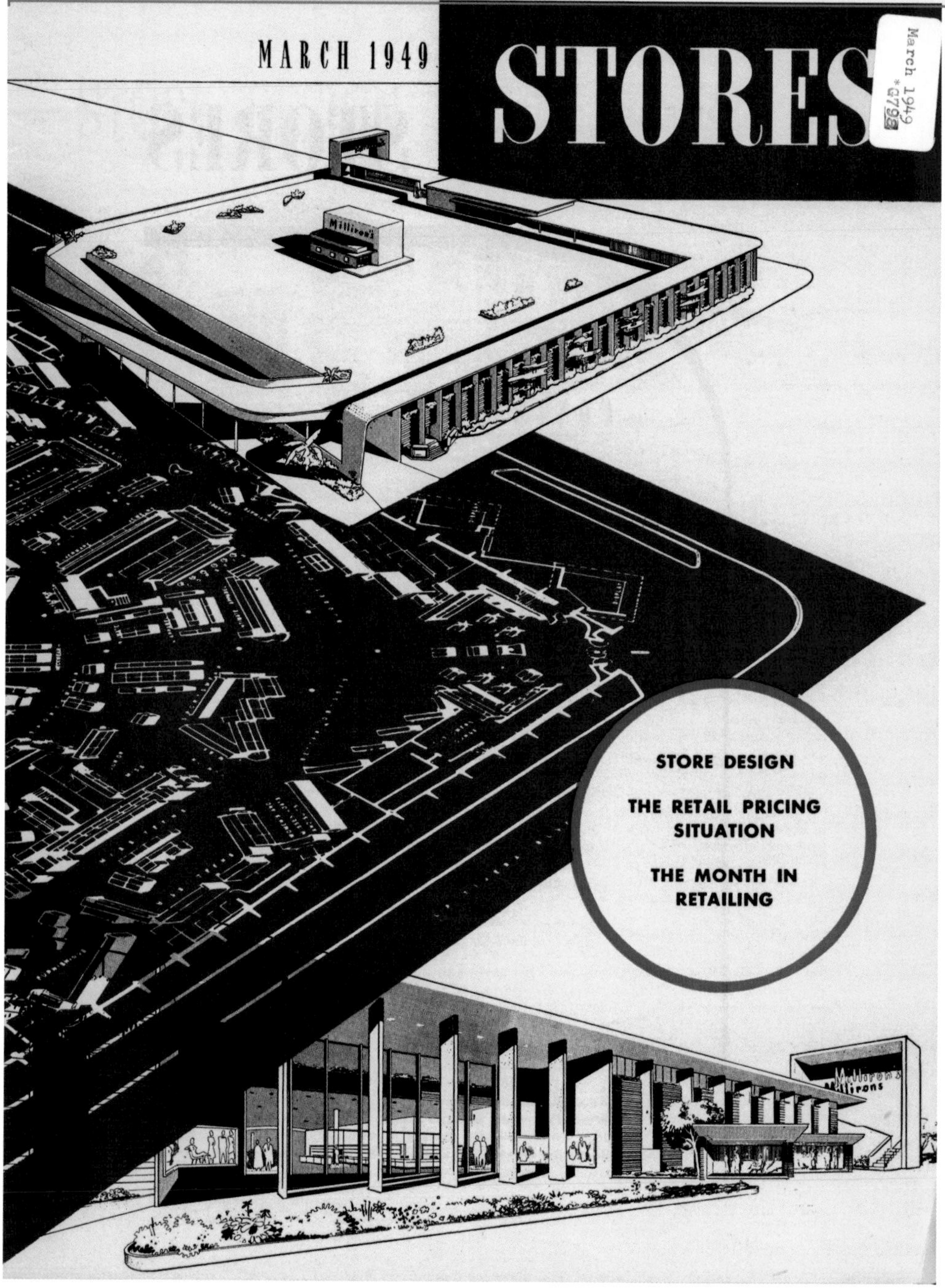

35 Milliron's in the larger Los Angeles context is described in "Something New in Stores," *Architectural Forum*; "Markets in the Meado-ws," in Richard Longstreth's *City Center to Regional Mall* (1997): 238-247; and Greg Hise, "The Airplane and the Garden City": 154-8.

In 1947, Gruen synthesized ideas about merchandising and designing for the automobile in the office's first commission for a free-standing building—a department store to be built as part of a commercial center for Westchester, a newly planned area that would be home for workers in the new defence plants. The military build-up during and following WWII stimulated suburban home building in Southern California, and Westchester, lying in the middle of Los Angeles' expanding "southland communities" of Culver City and Redondo, Hermosa, and Manhattan Beaches, was planned to support a population of 50,000. The community's commercial center, which would cover 72 acres (32 Ha.) of the project's total of 3000, had been started in 1942, and in 1946, Gruen was awarded the job for Milliron's first branch store.[35] The new department store, which sold low- and medium-priced merchandise, would be located in the center of the shopping district with 600 ft. (182m) frontage divided equally between 88th Street (La Tijera) and Sepulveda Boulevard.

Plan and aerial view of Milliron's location in the planned commercial area in the newly built district of Westchester.

At Milliron's, Gruen experimented with building type, store layout, and access. Given the retail program of a project that, downtown, would have been a three-story department store, Gruen instead convinced his client that it would be most economical to compress the program into one story, eliminating the need for elevators and fire stairs. The single-story store, however, occupied more space on its lot than a taller structure and reduced the area for parking; Gruen also set the building back from both streets, further reducing the parking area. These decisions, seemingly antithetical to car-based design, in fact allowed tactics that more boldly addressed the car: Gruen placed the parking on the roof, his most dramatic and startling dissolution of store and street so far. And, to maintain the store's presence on Sepulveda, he set a tower-like structure with the Milliron's logo at the north end of the main façade, forming a landmark that both separated the store from its neighbors and acted as a billboard for oncoming motorists. Tower and roof area were thus a newly evolved form of "arcade," catching the flow of potential customers, while an appendage of the building itself provided the sort of "display" that the shop-window itself once did.

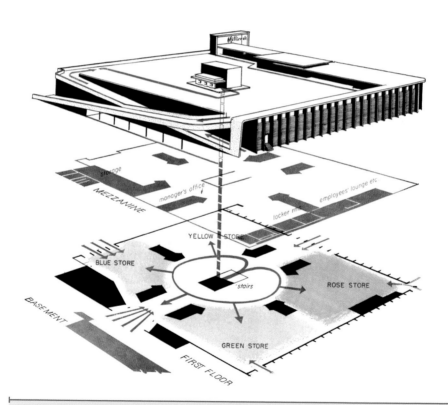

Exploded projection showing circulation and color-coded store areas.

Nite view of store side entrance with ramp to roof entrance behind.

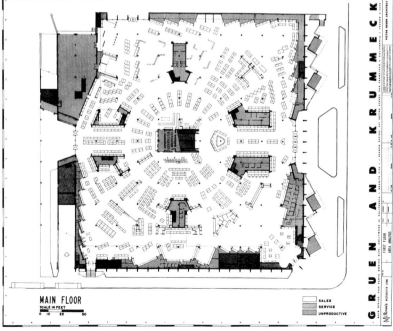

MAIN FLOOR
SCALE IN FEET
0 10 25   50

☐ SALES
▨ SERVICE
▧ UNPRODUCTIVE

GRUEN AND KRUMMECK

VICTOR GRUEN ARCHITECT

FIRST FLOOR
AREA ANALYSIS

Milliron's WESTCHESTER STORE

"In the hymnic transfiguration of the traffic, of the stream of passers-by, of the machines and the noise of the city street, futuristic motifs come to life. . . . here, the store is no uninvolved observer of the whirring cars and the traffic streaming here and there; rather, it has become an absorbing, participating element of motion."[36]

There were in fact three modes of access, each manifesting a different balance between automobile, pedestrian, and merchandise. The entrance on the main façade was flanked not by show windows but by four small display pavilions angled to face oncoming traffic on Sepulveda; the pavilions, constructed of wood and plate glass and clad in brick, were equipped like theatrical stages with footlights and a catwalk. From the rear parking area, one entered the store beneath the crossing roof-access ramps, passing small specialty shops that served both inside and outside. The most theatrical entrance was from the roof: dominating the rear elevation was a pair of dramatic highway-scaled scissor ramps leading cars to the roof parking area, from which escalators then brought customers down to the center of a large circular sales floor. The roof parking area had its own program with four departments: a creche, beauty parlor, the Penthouse Drive-Up restaurant with a view over the airport, and the 250-seat community hall that remained open outside store hours. With his early shops, Gruen had captured the interest of the passing pedestrian by use of public space, vitrines, and lighting. Facing onto busy Sepulveda Boulevard, Milliron's tower, scissors ramps, and stage-lit display pavilions were designed to catch the attention of the automobile public: the same design principles and impulses that had informed each of Gruen's shops were now completely refigured to meet a larger scale, a more variously mobile audience.

Having convinced his client that he could pack a three-story department store not only into a single level but also into a single space, Gruen experimented inside with a circular merchandising layout, arranging the different departments radially from the center of the store, where the escalators descended from the roof deck. A circular central area, divided by two broad aisles connecting the front and rear entrances, organized the merchandising groups into four quadrants. Spatial definition and orientation were given by six full-height enclosures called "pylons," which housed stockrooms, offices, fitting rooms, and services, which helped Gruen achieve an above-average net percentage between selling, circulation, and service areas. To further orient the shopper, Gruen used color: each of the four merchandising sectors had a basic color theme, while the circular central area was light grey. Built-in loudspeakers broadcast subdued music and store announcements. The flexible ceiling, lighting, and display furniture that Gruen had developed for Macy's enabled the retail layouts to be quickly changed.

---

36 Urban traffic: Erich Mendelsohn's "new partner" in the environment that determines the exterior form of architecture. Erich Mendelssohn. Qtd. in Pfeiffer, H-G., "The Origins and Development of the Department Store from the Middle of the 19th Century until the 1930s." in *Architecture for the Retail Trade*, 1996)
37 Gruen, "Triple Target for Economy," 17. See also: "Something New in Stores," *Architectural Forum*, and Gruen, "Architect's Complete Control of Design and Furnishings Effects Large Saving for Owner." $14 per sq. ft. was achieved with $9 invested by the landlord and $5 fixtures and fittings to be paid by Millirons. *Southwest Builder* and *Contractor* noted the advantageous figures for the sales area of 66.5%, service area 21%, and non-productive areas of 12.5%. The $105,000 invested in reinforcing the roof slab, constructing the ramps, and the escalators with the single flight main stair was compared with an estimated $300,000 which would have been spent on the vertical circulation for a three-story building.

Milliron's opened on Saint Patrick's Day, 1949, to even more than the usual fanfare. There were three days of opening events, with fashion shows, beauty pageants, and speeches by community and civic leaders. The store was open three nights a week to appeal to men, who preferred shopping in the evening; 24-hour telephone shopping was available; charge accounts were offered; and customers could pay their utility bills in the store. John Muchmore, a store executive, said, "We want to coordinate our store activities to the best advantage of the community." Gruen himself liked to call Milliron's "a store without lost motion" and "a new type of department store fitted to the needs of a suburban area."[37]

Local boosters had touted Westchester as "the model residential community of the decade," yet having opened to considerable national publicity, the district developed more slowly than anticipated until the early 1950s. The continuous expansion of Los Angeles airport limited growth to the south, and Sepulveda became ever more heavily used as a traffic artery for the city, making communication across the boulevard difficult for shoppers. The idea that a shopping district could be developed on both sides of a busy boulevard was shown to be false– similar problems would beset the popular Crenshaw Boulevard shopping district–and marked the end of this model for a suburban center. Department stores and their architects would have to find a more compact and shopper-friendly way to reach the expanding suburban market.

Already by 1940 in New York, Gruen and Krummeck had moved to the forefront of contemporary shop and store designers, and this gave them not only considerable coverage in the design and trade press but a venue for articulating design concepts to the American public.[38] In 1941, Gruen and Krummeck's shops and stores were featured in two survey articles in *Architectural Forum* and the *Architectural Record*. Morris Lapidus, in a critical survey of stores for his article, "Store Design, A Building Types Study," for the February 1941 *Architectural Record*, included Barton's, Manhattan, for its storefront and again to illustrate interiors; Grayson's, Santa Monica, for its "facade as poster"; and Paris Decorators on the Grand Concourse, Bronx, New York City, to illustrate how to make an entrance. In September *Architectural Forum* published the first survey of the office's work, "Recent Work noting that besides their retail work, their projects included apartment interiors and residences, as well as the design of packaging materials, china, glassware, and furniture. Emerich Nicholson, writing in 1945 in *Contemporary Shops*, described Gruenbaum and Krummeck's use of the "arcade" as a breakthrough in shop design and a progression in the concept of the shopfront from merely a two-dimensional 'poster' attracting people to an interior, to a three-dimensional space connected to the city's streets by the open front. He illustrated both solutions with the example of Lederer's and Altman & Kuhne:

Two of the finest shops in America face each other across New York's Fifth Avenue. The Lederer shop, which sells handbags, gloves and other women's accessories, is severely tailored, precise and formal in appearance. Altman & Kuhne's candy shop is soft in line, frivolous in color, and sug-gestive of nothing quite as much as a tray of Viennese pastry. Under no circumstances could the two designs be interchanged. Yet both are modern in the best sense, and both, incidentally, use the open front. (Nicholson, 45).

A Thousand Little Stages ← The Dynamics of a Store

One of Gruen and Krummeck's first chances to articulate their concepts uniting shop, theater, and street came in June 1940, in an *Apparel Arts* article called "Face to Face." Besides the theatrical extravaganzas of the theater district, they wrote, thousands of glamorous little shows were put on by the merchants of the city, and "the stages of these little shows [were] the storefronts," which performed the magic of transforming pedestrians, step by step, into customers. The agents of this manipulation were architectural–space, form, light, and material–and the technique animat-ing and synthesizing these elements was, in Gruen and Krummeck's case, stage design: always sprinkled through his arguments were references to stage, theaters, actors, and performance. "The psychological effect of this system," he wrote, "is to overcome the 'phobia' of entering a store."[39] Gruen wrote in the *Architectural Forum* that the exterior of the store was a synthesis of advertising poster and exhibit, while the interior should be a sales factory. This hardly meant that the interior should be industrial; indeed, he wrote, "the buyer must enjoy being in this room so much that he is ready to pay for this privilege by buying more than he originally intended" ("Recent Work," 191).

Romantic Functionalism

A crucial element in Gruen's interiors, one derived directly from his cabaret experience, was lighting; he frequently wrote not merely about its technical applications but also about its use as a tool to create the right psychological atmosphere. He was prone to using such phrases as "the feminine touch," which he defined as a certain atmosphere created more by emotion than objective factors. "This atmosphere must elevate a woman to higher levels than her home could," he wrote in 1947 in *West Coast Feminine Wear*; "it should elicit a holiday feeling, a sense of exhilaration."[40] To do this, he said, the store space must operate somewhat as a theater interior. Excepting the often bold façade and entrance treatments, the Grayson's stores—especially during the war years—were modest enough inside and devoted primarily to volume selling; and although Milliron's deployed various lighting strategies, it too was geared toward volume selling. At Magnin's, however, he was able to create a more subtle experience and emotional impact by manipulating light and shadow. Gruen believed that in store design, carefully controlled light could help induce the emotions normally inspired by sunsets, moonlit nights, and the starlit sky. "We use light for its psychological effects," he said in the January 1953 *Lighting and Lamps*. "Our functionalism is romantic . . . our romanticism is entirely functional."[41]

The Merchandising Concept is the Starting Point

Although based in L.A., Gruen by 1949 had developed a national overview of retail design based on his constant travel and work for the Grayson Company, the Barton's chain, the Joseph Magnin Stores, and Macy's, and he had been developing his theories in articles published in the trade press, such as *Apparel Arts*, *Display World*, *Women's Wear Daily*, and *Chain Store Age*, as well as in lectures to the National Retail and Dry Goods Association and National Store Modernization Shows. The success of Milliron's gave Gruen a chance to articulate further ideas. Like his earlier shops, Milliron's attracted local and national attention; some commentators saw it as a new model for the suburban "department store of tomorrow." Of course, suburban department stores were in themselves hardly new, and older examples of roof parking could be seen locally, but Olga Guelft, writing in *Interiors*, believed Milliron's embodied a number of trends: single-story stores would be built on inexpensive land in suburban areas as part of the regional merchandising strategy of department stores; the street entrance would be less imposing than the entrances from the parking areas; ramps would lead to additional parking on the roof; and new flexible fittings, fixtures, and ceilings meant that the department store of the future would operate like a giant stage set that could be transformed overnight.[42] Milliron's was, already, a department store designed with the attributes of a shopping center.

38 Gruen's first article was (Gruenbaum and Krummeck) "Face to Face," in *Apparel Arts*, June 1940, which featured Lederer's, Altman and Kuhne, and Elsie's sketches for the first Grayson's stores.
39 "Face to Face," 52; see also, Gruenbaum, Krummeck and

Auer, "The Case of Displayman versus Store Designer."
40 Gruen, "Store Design for the 'Feminine Touch'."
41 Gruen, "Lighting Today's Interior," 31. See also Gruen, "Lighting Fixtures Used for their Psychological and Decorative Value," 46.

With his experiments at Milliron's, the technical innovations at Macy's, and the interior design at the Joseph Magnin stores, together with his earlier New York work, Gruen had embedded himself in retail culture and was becoming established as a merchandising expert—a position that, as we'll see, would influence his beliefs about the role of the architect. In pitching himself to prospective retail clients, he argued that Milliron's was successful because the architect had exercised complete control—over the merchandising concept and layout, the building, the interior design, the furniture and fixtures, everything down to the plates and table linens for the restaurant—and this had achieved the most economic solutions in terms of cost, space, and operation. Setting Milliron's back from the street, for example, not only provided a better perspective for motorists but created an opportunity for landscaping, which meant that the building would not have to be clad in expensive protective finishes such as marble or ceramic tile. Likewise, the compression of the building into a single story represented an enormous savings, despite the costs to reinforce the roof and construct the ramps.

Soon after the opening of Milliron's, Gruen and Krummeck published a brochure entitled "Merchandising Controls Store Design," in which they presented a summary of the theories and methods by which their work had developed over the years. Pitched at potential commercial clients rather than the architectural community, the brochure presented store design as a synthesis of merchandising, cost control, and design flexibility. "The first step in planning a store," they wrote, "is by no means to draw up the construction plans, but must always be the merchandising survey, the crystallization of merchandising aims, needs and methods." Merchandising, Gruen claimed, controlled the structural grid, the layout of departments, lighting, fixtures, and even atmosphere. The tool for developing the merchandising concept was a form used to analyze an individual shop, a sub-department or department in a larger store, or an entire floor of a department store. Working from the survey sheets, they could project income from individual spaces, the quantity and method of display and storage, and the amount of service areas required. The survey thus exposed the performance demanded of the structure, after which design could begin. Milliron's had come to Gruen as a three-story department store, but after he had conducted the merchandising survey, he designed it as a single-story, 300x300 foot structure, with some departments located on the roof parking lot.

When merchandising needs have been analyzed and merchandising aims clearly stated, then and only then can the design of the structure . . . proceed. Never shall the structure or the building be permitted to make merchandising its slave, pressing it into spaces and shapes not suited for it" ("Merchandising Controls Store Design," 2, 4).

In his California stores, Gruen was able to work at a larger scale, for national chains, and in the case of Macy's, for a full-scale internationally known department store. Yet the work for Grayson's was quantitative, and the work for Macy's in San Francisco and Kansas City, despite the technical innovation of the flexible ceiling and demountable store furniture, was basically refurbishment of an existing building and creating new façades. It was with Milliron's that he was able to experiment with the site layout, building, access and circulation, and a new programmatic relationship between retail, services, and public space. The hybrid department store's greatest significance was its demonstration that the automobile was an instrument and force for typological change—Milliron's was designed to serve flows of vehicles, people, and merchandise.

Through a growing number of articles and frequent lectures, Gruen by 1950 was becoming a national commentator not only on retail, but on suburban development and the conditions in the downtown cores of American cities, which so affected the fortunes of his department-store clients. Most important of all, he was experimenting with designs for a much larger and integrated retail building complex—the regional shopping center—a new and exciting building type emerging simultaneously in different parts of the U.S.

In New York, as Richard Longstreth observed, Victor Gruen, Morris Ketchum, and Morris Lapidus had immersed themselves in the science and strategies of merchants to an extent matched by few other architects (*From City Center to Regional Mall*, 234-5). Bringing this experience to Southern California, Gruen joined local architects who had been specializing in department stores, such as Albert Gardiner, Welton Beckett, and Albert Martin. The accelerating growth of new communities, together with the expanding population and increasing automobile use, had already led to the proliferation of farmers markets, shopping strips, and shopping districts. For many architects, planners, and critics, this metastasizing landscape of consumption seemed an affront to city and land, and so they ignored it, thereby missing out on the birthing of this landscape. Commerce is the engine of urbanity; overlooking or denying it meant, in the late '40s and early '50s, stepping out from the most critical field of development that was to define the American landscape after WWII. Gradually, all traditional urban and architectural building types would be recast for the suburbs. It would be the architects who had gained experience in retail and accepted the reality of increasing use of the private car who would be able to conceive the regional shopping center, the pioneer building ensemble of the future city.

---

42 Guelft, "Department Store of the Future: Milliron's Could Be the Model." Roof parking had been used since the 1930s and could be seen locally in Sear's Pico Boulevard Store built in 1938-9, although none of the other roof parking stores approached the theatricality of Gruen's design. Roof parking remained an exception rather than the rule, perhaps as subsequent suburban development generally provided enough land for parking.

From his vantage point in the fast-developing, commercial, and car-oriented culture of Southern California, Gruen in 1952 was convinced that the shopping center needed to be more than a "collection of stores." The brash Grayson's stores, Milliron's, and even his best shops were merely single objects along street or strip—all façades and interiors, part of no larger settlement idea. Both commercial strip and subdivision lacked public spaces, what Gruen called "crystallization points," supported by social and cultural functions. Yet, as the Cold War got underway, there would be no return to the collective values embodied in the community centers of the Greenbelt Towns built during the New Deal. Gruen claimed that whatever the politics, the need for social and cultural activity—"that primary human instinct to mingle with other human beings" —had not disappeared. Already by the mid-1940s, he knew that the shopping center could fulfill these needs; the architect needed to realize a concept that, besides providing for its commercial program, would include other functions, all organized by a network of public spaces. With his eye on the city, Gruen wrote that the suburban shopping centers might "well be regarded as satellite downtown areas, offering much of what the metropolitan centers give," and indeed, that the retail capacity of large suburban shopping centers was the equivalent of a large town, or a small city.[1] In support of his argument, Gruen's lectures and articles included illustrations of historical European market squares and buildings. He was stretching the point, but it would be precisely the combination of retail, social, and cultural functions, and public spaces that he would bring back to the city in his later urban redevelopment projects.

1 Gruen and Larry Smith presented this argument in their article, "Shopping Centers - The New Building Type," published in *Progressive Architecture* in June 1952. See pages 67-8. They wrote: "The shopping center of tomorrow will more than its name implies . . . a center for shopping. The shopping center of tomorrow will, besides performing its commercial function, fill the vacuum created by the absence of social, cultural and civic crystallization points in our vast suburban areas." . . . What are the requisites to the fulfillment of this function of social and cultural center?" Gruen (and Smith) wrote, was "to go beyond the commercial needs"(a program of mixed uses), "take advantage of the existence of public areas" (create a network of public spaces), and "to realize an architectural concept."

2 Richard Longstreth, author interview, Washington, D.C., 1997.

The New Building Type

The regional shopping center was the new building type that came to define the American suburban landscape of the 1950s. For Victor Gruen, it was neither the destroyer of the old city, nor a machine for consumption. It played a pivotal role in the development of the contemporary regional city. However harsh the judgements against the shopping center, its developers, architects, or the consumption culture it fostered, this new type emerged out of the most diverse and ambitious precedents. Many factors, some from as far back as the 1920s, gradually coalesced to yield both the crucial context for the regional shopping center and several different prototypes between the late 1940s and mid-1950s. The new building type did not therefore just appear overnight, nor can it be attributed to any one individual, despite Gruen's reputation; as the historian Richard Longstreth aptly put it, "There is no paper trail leading to the origin of the shopping center."[2] Rather, in certain streetcar suburbs, in the few Depression-era Greenbelt Towns, in planned wartime defense-industry communities, and, above all, in the federally supported build-out of the postwar suburbs, the shopping center—in different form, scale, and name—became an integral part of the process of experiment and change in American settlement.

From the mid-1940s, the coming of the regional shopping center was a hotly debated topic; the demographics around U.S. cities were rapidly changing, and the need for retailers to respond to these changes meant that department store executives, developers, and architects all followed one another's projects with great interest. From his base in Los Angeles in the early 1940s, Gruen understood that the shopping center would be a key component within the "planned experiment" of American settlement; a successful center would not only function as a social and cultural center for its surrounding communities but also continue to evolve into a regional subcenter. Through a barrage of articles and speeches beginning in 1948, Gruen became an aggressive promoter of the new building type, theorizing a context for its development within a new urban and regional planning, all before his first center had opened. Well into the early 1950s, the regional shopping center was open to different interpretation, and there was ample opportunity for making serious mistakes, as Gruen himself wrote in *Progressive Architecture* in 1952, having learned, by then, from his own experience (Gruen and Smith, 70).

The potential that the new building type opened up for Gruen was fourfold. First, the regional marketing strategies of downtown department stores represented, together with the highway network and the build-out of suburbia, a vital stage in the evolution of the American regional city. Second, the possibility of adding social and civic functions led to the regional shopping centers being conceived of, at the turn of the 1950s, as agents of recentralization.[3] Third, the ensemble of buildings of the shopping center was immediately perceived as an experiment with direct relevance to the redevelopment of downtown.[4] Finally, the management and maintenance techniques of the regional shopping center were seen by some as a model practice for the "management" of urban shopping districts, and by extension, the entire downtown.[5]

The emerging suburban landscape and the deteriorating urban cityscape were the twin contexts Gruen set out to engage from the 1940s to the 1960s, so before turning to his work, it is worth briefly considering the political, economic, and social forces that precipitated America's urban and suburban revolution. Gruen was an urbanist and considered himself a defender of the social, cultural, and spatial qualities of the city, but he was as much involved in the production of the suburban landscape as he was involved in the struggle against it. Business interests and politicians institute social, cultural, and economic trends; architects and planners react to them. Victor Gruen sometimes succeeded in tailoring his projects to exploit the possibilities provided by the Acts of Congress, but at other times he was overwhelmed by the Acts' consequences. What then were the instruments and agents of this transformation—how and why did this landscape come into being?

3 Welch, "Some Projects in the Northeast," 7. The shopping center as an agent of recentralization was recognized in the early 1950s. Besides Welch and Gruen, Jose Luis Sert demanded that sprawling suburban development be oriented to urban sub-centers. See Sert, J.L., "Centers of Community Life," 6, and "Summary of Needs at the Core," 164-8, in Sert et al (Eds.) The Heart of the City.
4 "New Thinking on Shopping Centers," Architectural Forum, 122.
5 See: Roush, "Kalamazoo Mall Turns 30"; Steinhauer, "New York

and the nation"; and Jones, "Downtown of Tomorrow?"
6 Olsen, Better Places, Better Lives, 12. James Rouse will appear several times. His career intersects with Gruen's in a number of ways: directly as developer of some of Gruen's regional shopping centers, principally Cherry Hill, NJ and Plymouth Meeting, PA; and indirectly as one of the framers of the 1954 Housing Act, as a critic of urban renewal, and as developer of Columbia, MD, a new town contemporaneous with Gruen's Valencia, CA.
7 Albrecht, "Introduction," World War II and the American Dream, xxi.

Depression, War and Recovery

The Depression after the stock market crash of 1929 was a disaster for homeowners, the housing market, and related industries. In 1930 alone, some 100,000 home mortgages were foreclosed, and by 1933, 50 percent of mortgages were at default.[6] In reaction, President Roosevelt's "New Deal" legislation in planning and housing established, in 1934, the Federal Housing Administration (FHA), which brought drastic change to the housing market, resulting in the establishment of real-estate development as a fulltime profession. For the rest of the 1930s, America focused on recovering from the Depression, but the entry of the U.S. into World War II on two fronts–Europe and Asia–required the mobilization of society, the transformation of existing industry, and the creation of new industrial centers. The wartime economy produced remarkable prosperity that ended the great Depression and was the starting point for the postwar economic boom. The creation of countless defence industry plants, many of enormous scale, to produce planes, ships, and armaments required a vast number of workers, men and women, white and black. The scale of the defense-industry installations and the number of people involved forced the government to enter the housing market, and the creation of the large defense-housing projects during World War II forced homebuilders to employ industrial methods to increase their production. By 1944, as the prospect of victory came in sight, the country began to focus on peacetime conversion: soldiers to workers, women workers to wives, and armament factories to producers of cars, trucks, domestic appliances, and building materials.[7]

The traumatic experience of war sharpened the appetite of returning soldiers for a stable and prosperous lifestyle. In seeking the bases for the later culture of consumption, Robert Friedel writes, "The contradiction of sacrifice and prosperity left their permanent mark on American life . . . . The conflicting forces of the war years reshaped the material and domestic culture that both reflected and reformed the most basic aspirations of women and men–to be at home, to feel comfort, to experience a measure of well being." The government and private industry set out to meet these aspirations and expectation. The explosive population growth, coupled with a flourishing economy, resulted in a vast new market of consumers hungry for the goods that had been in short supply during the war, but, more immediately, for new houses and new cars. The cities, however, were not able to meet this demand for new and better housing, nor were they under the kind of planning pressure for rebuilding that was the case in the bombed cities of Europe–and they were never designed for the number of automobiles that Detroit was producing. The high cost of building within a city made development of land on the periphery attractive.

The history of suburbanization of America and the dispersal of the city has been well told by several authors, and my interest is not to repeat their work but to link it to Gruen's developing ideas about the city.[8] The suburban landscape has suffered under two myths: that it is an unplanned chaos, and that it is a mirror of private enterprise; both myths have for a long time hindered productive analysis. Architects often criticize suburbia and sprawl as spontaneous, chaotic developments that are rude manifestations of the real-estate market. Yet, as Paul Adamson argues, the build-out of the suburbs far better represents strategic planning that separated residence from nearly all other functions, industrial production methods developed during the war and applied to housing, and developments in the real-estate and banking businesses. The second myth, popular with politicians, developers, and investors, is based on the idea that private enterprise and not government intervention is the foundation of American commercial strength and success in the world; statutory planning controls and state-funded development belong to "socialist" Europe. To make sense of the American landscape today requires examining the immediate postwar years. In 1998, the Fannie Mae Foundation commissioned a survey that asked academic and professional urbanists to rank the top 10 influences of the last 50 years on the American metropolis, and then to rank the 10 most likely influences for the next 50 years. In his article "Past and Future Influences," summarizing the results of the survey, Robert Fishman cites the overwhelming impact of the federal government on the American metropolis, especially through policies that "intentionally or unintentionally promoted suburbanization or sprawl."

8 Besides Jackson's *Crabgrass Frontier*, see for example: Peter Mueller, *Contemporary Suburban America*, 1981; Peter Fishman, *Bourgeois Utopias: The Rise and Fall of Suburbia*, 1987; Peter Rowe, *Making a Middle Landscape*, 1991; and Dolores Hayden, *Building Suburbia - Green Fields and Urban Growth*, 2003. As referred to above, the decisive role of World War II was set out in an exhibition and catalogue: *World War II and the American Dream*, curated and edited by Donald Albrecht, 1995. The great migration of African American's is told by Nicholas Lemann in *The Promised Land*, 1991.
9 Garvin, *The American City* (1996), 5, 155; see also: *Congress and the Nation*. Vol. I, 1954-64 (1965). The FHA not only provided the fiscal structure for suburbanization but was also active as an advisory body for developers. The Land Planning Division of the FHA, directed by Seward Mott, published and updated various aspects of subdivision planning practice such as incorporation of common open spaces as well as lot sizes, alignment of streets and intersections.
10 Hanchett, "U.S. Tax Policy and the Shopping Center Boom of the 1950s and 1960s," 1082-1110. Hanchett claimed that a section of the 1954 Internal Revenue Tax Code, which enabled investors to depreciate real-estate investments on an accelerated basis–profit-making investments could be shown as paper losses, thus reducing tax liability–was as much a reason for the explosion of shopping centers as rapid suburban growth or racial strife. This was rebutted by Kenneth Jackson, who accepted accelerated depreciation as merely one of a number of factors contributing to sprawl, especially the cheapness of land on the periphery, the weakness of land-use controls, and subsidized automobile travel. See Jackson, "All the World's a Mall," 1114-1115.

Opportunity, Mobility, and Segregation

The far-reaching legislation passed by Congress popularly known as the Housing, Veterans, and Highway Acts specified not only where and how development could take place, but also which social groups would benefit from it; they established new patterns of mobility; and they provided the financial security that was the basis for private development and industry for decades to come.

The availability of federally insured mortgages for first-time homebuyers was made possible by the National Housing Act of 1934, which created the Federal Housing Administration (FHA). The Act, which regulated rates of interest and the terms of every mortgage that it insured, encouraged banks to invest a major portion of their capital in housing. Alexander Garvin observes that the Act enabled consumer desire to become consumer demand, and indeed it was a financial instrument that raised American home ownership from 44 percent in 1940 to nearly 66 percent in the 1990s.[9] Yet two aspects of the Act have generated enormous social inequity and tension: the FHA refused to insure mortgages on older houses in typical urban neighborhoods, and until the mid-1960s, FHA-insured mortgages were limited to race-restricted housing in the new suburbs—African Americans would be excluded from new homes, schools, and an accelerating suburban economy. The 1949 revision to the act was also the basis for the downtown redevelopment and public housing projects, popularly known as urban renewal. Second, the Serviceman's Readjustment Act of 1944, popularly known as the Veteran's Act or "the G.I. bill of Rights," established the Veteran's Administration (VA), which guaranteed mortgage loans and college education fees for the millions of servicemen returning from World War II. Third, the legal and financial measures to establish a national system of highways, which had been brought to Congress several times, finally passed as the Federal-Aid Highway Act of 1956, and provided further encouragement for developers and merchant home builders to seek sites farther from the city center. The act supplied the funding of 41,000 miles of Interstate and Defense highways, of which 6000 miles would be built in and around cities, planned for completion by 1972. Finally, the Congressional amendment to tax legislation in 1954 allowing "accelerated depreciation" on commercial development on suburban greenfield sites made it far more profitable to invest in strip centers, shopping malls, and suburban industrial parks than to put money into new or existing structures downtown.[10] These measures, largely the results of collaboration between private industry and the federal government, were the mechanisms that started an "urban and suburban revolution" and spawned the consumption landscape that continues to evolve today.

The acts created opportunity and mobility. For the white middle classes, America was undergoing fundamental change not only spatially and demographically but culturally—a nascent consumption culture would emerge from the coming together of rising prosperity, television, and the need to equip all those new homes. The dispersal of development from the old pattern of cities and streetcar suburbs into the surrounding region rendered traditional methods of planning and urban design obsolete. New planning and new building types were needed for living, working, education, and shopping, all based on convenient automobile access.

The dispersal of American industry, had begun when World War II broke out. By the time of the Korean War, the ability of the Soviet Union to produce an atomic bomb gave discussions on the merits of dispersing industry, and even cities, a special urgency. Gruen, who had described the potential role of a regional shopping center in civil defense in 1943, returned again in 1951, to argue for the significance of the regional shopping center as a new kind of subcenter in the city-region. Two years later, in a memorandum entitled "Regional Shopping Centers and Civilian Defence," Gruen again touted the "planned, coordinated" center and not the "strip center" as an important component of a dispersal program for civil defence. Among the potential advantages for defense were the planned service tunnel and truck-loading area, together forming a 50,000-square-foot sheltered area constructed in reinforced concrete; parking lots, which presented large paved and drained surfaces; dispersed sanitary facilities; and a central power plant capable of furnishing heat and emergency power for a large concentration of people. All of these features could enable a shopping center to become an emergency evacuation and relief area quickly and efficiently.[11]

Precedents from Private Development and Public Planning

The numerous precedents for the regional shopping center have been well described by others, and Gruen himself referred to these in his books and articles.[12] The examples which were most influential for his development were those in which the formal, operational, and programmatic aspects contributed to the center's character as a central "place" that was essentially urban.

The earliest project relevant especially for its management was Country Club Plaza, described as a "shopping district," begun in 1923 by the developer J. C. Nichols and still in business today. In a prefiguration of retail marketing strategies that would become institutionalized 25 years later, Nichols advertised all the shops and stores under the name Country Club Plaza. He planned his shopping-district comprehensively, with all phases of the development controlled by a single entity, the development company.[13] Nichols was particularly concerned about traffic:

11 Gruen's speech, "Controlling Factors in the Establishment of Regional Shopping Centers," revealed that already in 1943 he understood the basic factors that would make a shopping center project viable, such as demographics, market area, driving times, spatial organization, and the need for a developer to control the area surrounding the center. In 1951, the theme of the National Conference of the A.I.A. in Chicago was "Defense on the Periphery." See both Gruen, "Defence on the Periphery," 1951, and "Regional Shopping Centers and Civilian Defense, 1953. The extent to which Gruen positioned himself—and his shopping centers—relative to cold war fears is explored in Mennel, "Victor Gruen and the Construction of Cold War Utopias,.

12 Precedents for the regional shopping centers are described in: Gruen and Smith, *Shopping Towns U.S.A.*,12-13, 17-19; Gillette, Jr., "The Evolution of the Planned Shopping Center," 449-51; Crawford, "The World in a Shopping Mall," in Michael Sorkin (Ed.), *Variations on a Theme Park,* 19-21; Garvin, *The American City,* 101-8; Longstreth, *City Center to Regional Mall,* 268-338; and Rowe, *Making a Middle Landscape,* 109-24.

13 See Longstreth, "J.C. Nichols, the Country Club Plaza, and Notions of Modernity," 121-35; and in the wider context of out-of-town shopping districts, "A Guaranteed Neighborhood," in Longstreth, *City Center to Regional Mall,* 171-4. Gruen considered Country Club Plaza, the pioneering shopping center (*Heart of Our Cities,* 189).

14 Greenbelt Shopping Center, Crescent Road, Greenbelt, MD, 1936-37, (D.J. Ellington, R.J.Wadsworth, architects, H. Walker, planner, Clarence Stein, advisor) see Stein, Towards New Towns for America (150); and, Baker and Funaro "Shopping Centers: Design and Operation,"(232-5).

15 "The Town of Willow Run," *Architectural Forum*; and Longstreth, *City Center to Regional Mall,* 171-4.

through-traffic could move around the center, while access roads led shoppers to the parking lots and garages, which were among the first purpose-built in the U.S. As Country Club Plaza was deliberately planned beyond the reach of the streetcar network, planning for the movement of people, goods, and cars was a starting point.

Under Franklin Roosevelt's New Deal Resettlement Administration Program, the planned community of Greenbelt, Maryland included a shopping and community center where pedestrian and automobile movement were segregated from each other. Pedestrians from the neighboring residential developments could walk directly to the center, which offered not only shops but a school, public baths, and community rooms.[14] The Greenbelt Town's "social" model of a mixed use center was directly taken over in the military-industrial build-up during World War II. Two well known examples were Saarinen, Swanson, and Saarinen's Willow Run shopping and community center project, which the *Architectural Forum* described as a spacious image of a suburban "town" center that "accepted in the most realistic and economic manner the existence of the automobile," and offered the best guide to postwar planning yet produced.[15] Willow Run's combination of cruciform and pinwheel plan, paved and planted public areas, and mix of social, civic, and commercial functions would reappear in Gruen's best shopping center projects.

Country Club Plaza, Kansas City, MO. Preliminary concept drawing for a City Beautiful shopping district, 1922, E. B. Delk; George Kessler, planning consultant.

Greenbelt

Willow Run

Willow Run, Michigan, a new town for war workers. The project is a proto-type for shopping center and suburban community planning.

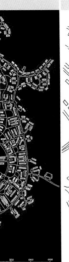

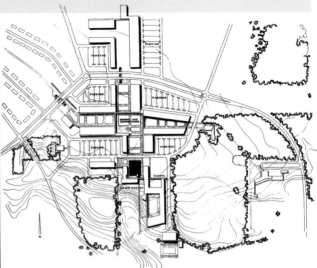

Linda Vista

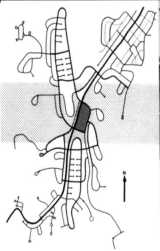

"GRASS ON MAIN STREET" BECOMES A REALITY

Plan of the war workers community of Linda Vista, near San Diego, CA, 1944(E.F. Gilbertson and W.R. Smith, associated architects); and view of the "village green" from the September 1944 Architectural Forum.

SHOPPING CENTER, LINDA VISTA, CALIFORNIA

16 "Grass on Main Street" (Linda Vista), *Architectural Forum*, 83. Linda Vista Community Plan. Public Buildings Administration, Washington and Gilbert S. Underwood. Linda Vista was the first project authorized under the Lanham Defence Housing Act, 1940. Linda Vista Shopping Center, 1943-4, Earl F. Gilbertson, Architect; Whitney B Smith, Associate Architects; for the National Housing Agency. See also: "Neighborhood and regional shopping centers," in Ketchum, *Shops and Stores*, (266-285); and Longstreth (1997): 295-8.
17 Rouse, "Why aren't there more good shopping centers?,"

166, 170. See also: *Women's Wear Daily*, 5 November and 10 December, both in 1959. Meredith Clausen noted that after the bankruptcy of Shoppers World, the center was taken over by Allied Stores, owner of the Bon Marche' and Northgate Center, which in turn hired John Graham to revise the plans. The center flourished under new management (160). For Shoppers World, see Ketchum, *Shops and Stores*, 281; also Rowe, *Making a Middle Landscape*, 14-15, 126-27; and Longstreth, *City Center to Regional Mall*, 332-5.

Willow Run was never built, but a smaller project, Linda Vista neighborhood shopping center, built near San Diego in 1944 by the Public Building Administration, offered a concrete image of suburban collective space. Retail stores were grouped around a central green space, landscaped with grass and trees, and bordered by sheltered walkways in front of the stores. Linda Vista was enthusiastically described as a demonstration of "Grass on Main Street."[16]

Two significant conditions precipitated the quantum leap to the regional shopping center: first, the entrepreneurial action of major downtown department stores seeking competitive advantage as they sought to capture the suburban market; second, the vast numbers of cars needing access roads and parking places. The formal organization and the operational efficiency of these elements at an unprecedented scale would be the challenge for Gruen and other shopping center architects.

Breakthrough: Northgate and Shopper's World

Despite restrictions on building materials during the Korean War, by the beginning of the 1950s, the first shopping centers began to appear. From a planning point of view, the conceptual breakthrough was the location of these centers where no concentrated residential development yet existed. The regional shopping center would, therefore, serve not a local population but a much larger and carefully measured regional clientele, some of whom would be willing to drive for up to 30 minutes. Access would be provided by the planned highways, which would create the structure of the outer metropolitan area, while convenience—in sharp contrast to the shopping conditions of both commercial strips and downtowns—would be provided by free parking and the separation of pedestrians from vehicles.

The first regional shopping center was Northgate, opened in April 1950 outside Seattle, Washington. Planned since 1947 by John Graham for Allied Stores, owners of the Seattle department store Bon Marché, Northgate literally transposed the layout of the city's main shopping street to a new location in the suburbs—Bon Marché was centered on the east side of a pedestrian "street," or mall, with rows of tenant stores along either side.

In June 1947, before construction had started in Seattle, the *Architectural Forum* reported that National Suburban Centers, Inc., would produce a number of large modular regional shopping centers surrounding Boston. The architects, Ketchum, Giná and Sharp, were designing not merely a single project but a regional retailing strategy. Their first built center Shoppers World, would be built near Framingham, 19 miles west of Boston, on a 70-acre site near the junction of regional highways. Unlike Graham's compact recreation of a city shopping street, at Shoppers World, two split-level store blocks, placed 80 feet apart, faced onto the central green "lawn." Two department stores were to close the ends of the 665-foot-long rectangular ensemble. Shoppers World opened in October 1951, but the second department store was not built, so the retail layout of the complex remained imbalanced. A further problem resulted from the design of the traffic flows: drivers turned directly from the state road into the parking lot, which during peak periods created annoying and dangerous congestion. Nine months after opening, Shoppers World defaulted on its loans, sending a chill wind through shopping-center development circles. A mortgagor took over the operation of the center, and gradually Shoppers World became successful.[17]

The two precedent setting models for the structuring of public spaces in the regional shopping center: above, the "street," exemplified by John Graham's Northgate, Seattle, WA (1950); and right, "the village green," exemplified by Ketchum, Giná and Sharp's Shoppers World, Framingham, MA (1952) and Sharp's projects for the Boston area.

18 Clausen, "Northgate Regional Shopping Center," 158. Clausen wrote that the goal at Northgate was financial success and not fine design (158). Much as Gruen and Krummeck had stated that same year in "Merchandising Controls Store Design," Graham repeated the generic retailing principle that merchandising should be the organizing principle of the project, and architecture merely a means of merchandising. Graham built Northgate as plainly as possible and eschewed diversions to shopping such as art or landscaping. "Parking and not art" was intended to be "Northgate's main appeal." The example of Northgate's narrow paved pedestrian mall was followed shortly thereafter by Albert C. Martin, Jr. at the Lakewood Center, Los Angeles, and Welton Beckett at Stonestown, San Francisco.

19 Gruen, "Dynamic Planning for Retail Areas," 55; Gruen and Smith, *Shopping Towns U.S.A.*, 76.

Northgate and Shoppers World each demonstrated a different spatial concept for the public areas built for their customers, who were mostly women and children. The "pedestrian street" at Northgate enabled the shopper to see displays on both sides. In this narrow space, any obstacle or novelty distracted from the ensembles' commercial purpose; there was no room for "frills."[18] At Shoppers World, on the other hand, Ketchum, Giná and Sharp created a large green space as the setting for the two-story arcade of shops. Whether as a reference to a village green, a formal park, or perhaps the suburbs themselves, the generous space was hardly urban; it didn't function as social space. Despite the connecting ramps, the two linear store blocks were remote from each other. Gruen praised the design intent at Shoppers World and the daring use of two shopping levels–Ketchum, Gina's and Sharp called this a "doubled-decked main-street"–that was accessed by bridges from the parking level, but he criticized the restricted access and the non-urban "green."[19] Gruen was at this time attempting to find an alternative model that would, by its public spaces as well as the shopping attractions, attract people and keep them. What follows are descriptions of three unbuilt projects in which Gruen wrestled with the scale and layout of the new building type.

Ketchum, Giná and Sharp's Middlesex Center (project), planned for Beverly, MA, 1949. Shoppers World, which opened near Framingham, MA in 1952 had a similar layout. Note how the nearby houses abut the shopping center.

In 1943 Gruen–still in partnership as Gruenbaum and Krummeck–had first been able to create a model of a local shopping center, not as part of a planned settlement but as a new element in an existing community. The chance arose when, anticipating an early end to the war, *Architectural Forum* editors George Nelson and Henry Wright, Jr., devoted their May issue, entitled "194X", to the future of a wide range of building types with sketch proposals by selected architects; Gruenbaum and Krummeck were chosen to project their vision for the neighborhood shopping center of the near future. The *Forum* invitation, Gruen later wrote in his autobiography, gave him the first chance to really consider how a shopping center could be designed to respond to "the deplorable state of affairs" in cities such as Los Angeles, where, he said,

rows of businesses and enterprises were strung together on both sides of the main streets, producing for shoppers endless long routine trips that could often only be undertaken with an auto. Shopping in this way was not only time consuming but also increased the through-traffic. Moreover, the space in front of the businesses was further reduced by parked vehicles, which led to additional conflicts between all types of traffic: private automobiles, buses, trailer-trucks, and pedestrians (Traeumer, 149).

DRUG STORE AND DINING TERRACE

---

20 Letter from Gruenbaum and Krummeck to the *Architectural Forum*, 26 Feb., 1943. AHCVGC, Box 54.

Showing how far he had developed his retail ideas beyond his ongoing work for Grayson's, Gruen wanted to exploit the "194X" submission to design one or more large shopping centers that would serve the entire metropolitan area. He and Krummeck first proposed three large retail centers, each capable of serving 25-30,000 people, and each combined with an office and cultural activities. Each center was conceived as a circular building 140 feet in diameter, forming an island in a traffic intersection. External and internal partitions were to be of glass, creating, under the great circular space, a kind of transparent bazaar or continuous arcade. Gruen argued that mixed-use developments with ample parking were already to be seen in Southern California:

The developments in Southern California seem so interesting to us because the cities and towns here have mostly been developed since the automobile became the most important means of transportation. We feel that shopping habits and sales organizations as they have developed here therefore indicate in many ways the possible developments in an automobile-rich postwar America.[20]

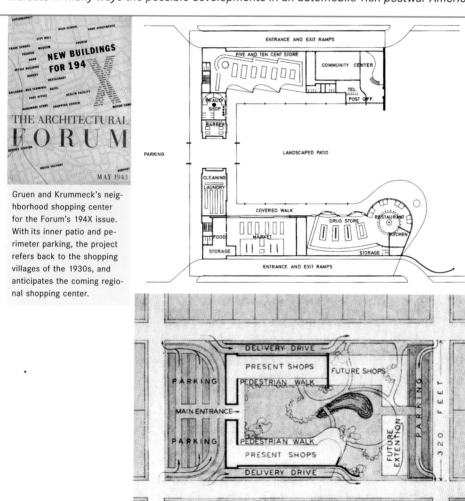

Gruen and Krummeck's neighborhood shopping center for the Forum's 194X issue. With its inner patio and perimeter parking, the project refers back to the shopping villages of the 1930s, and anticipates the coming regional shopping center.

After considerable correspondence, however, George Nelson insisted that Gruen and Krummeck submit the smaller and more modest neighborhood center for which they had been asked. They complied and submitted plans and perspectives describing a simple U-shaped building that enclosed a paved and planted garden court with parking at the front and rear. The "landscape patio" with a small pond would be the main attraction. The façades of the building were to be designed in an unassuming manner without advertising in order not to disturb the character of the surrounding neighborhood. A wide entrance led shoppers to the garden court, surrounded by an arcade, which sheltered the entrances of the shops. They could promenade along the storefronts, relax in the park-like atmosphere of the court, or, safely removed from automobile traffic, go directly to stores and businesses. The center would offer, Gruen wrote,

all the necessities of day-to-day living . . . . post office, circulating library, doctor's and dentist's office, and rooms for club activities, in addition to the usual shopping facilities. Shopping thus becomes pleasure, recreation instead of a chore. Larger centers could be built on the same principle, covering several blocks. Automobile traffic could be diverted around such centers or if necessary, under them.[21]

Create a Central Place and Establish the Idea of Community ← Harvey Park

With his eye on the evolving planning for Northgate and Shoppers World, Gruen had the chance to experiment and test his ideas in two projects near Los Angeles. The first of these was Harvey Park, published in "What to Look for in Shopping Centers," co-written with Morris Ketchum in the July 1948 *Chain Store Age*, in which both architects argued that regional shopping centers, aside from fulfilling their obvious commercial intent, were ideally suited to serve as social and cultural centers—the basis for community building in the new landscape of suburban subdivisions. The illustrations included a project by Ketchum, Giná and Sharp near Boston, and two perspectives of Gruen's Harvey Park, which was a project developed to a much larger scale than the modest proposals he had put forward five years earlier in "194X." Gruen's center consisted of a cruciform figure of pedestrian shopping streets flanked by tenant store buildings, which led to the edges of the site. Covered colonnades along the storefronts would provide protection from the sun and rain. At the center would be a large cylindrical department store, which reflected the circular merchandising ideas that Gruen was developing at the time for Milliron's. The 250,000-square-foot anchor, with its monumental seven-story storage and utility tower, was the form that would advertise the center and, when illuminated at night, would be a beacon or landmark, visible from the surrounding boulevards.

21 "Shopping Center," Gruenbaum and Krummeck. *Architectural Forum*, May 1943, 101.
22 Gruen. Qtd. Balcolm, Lois, "The Best Hope for Our Big Cities." "The surface between buildings, as well as an occasional link from one structure to another, will have gardens, walkways, covered malls, little shops and kiosks—the salt and pepper of a city." **23** Gruen and Ketchum, "What to look for in Shopping Centers,"

(63-6). See also Gruen, "Whats Wrong with Store Design?," 62. The drawing for an otherwise unidentified shopping center, named 'Harvey Park', is most probably a reference to developer Leo Harvey, who sought to develop a 70 acre shopping center, with a 300,000 square foot department store on Whittier Boulevard that would serve the East Los Angeles market. See also Longstreth (1997), 324-5.

In addition to the central department store and the tenant store blocks, there were to be numerous small enterprises–kiosks, refreshment stands, and vending booths–which Gruen would later refer to as "the salt and pepper" that enriches the urban environment.[22] At Milliron's, he had included social and cultural functions, and, in this much larger project, he included a movie theater and an auditorium where plays, concerts, fashion shows, and other performances could be staged. Harvey Park was certainly less retail-focused than Northgate or Shoppers World; municipal authorities had branch offices, meeting rooms were provided for civic groups, parents could leave their children at a nursery, and the social and cultural facilities were to be further complemented by medical and dental offices and a gas station. "People could shop for furniture, listen to a concert, admire the flowers," Gruen said. As he had written in *Chain Store Age*, rather than merely create a commercial establishment for repeated visits, Gruen's goal was thus to create a central place and thereby establish the idea of community:

It is the aim of our scheme to impress the center's facilities deeply into the minds of the people living in a wide surrounding area. The center shall become to them more than just a place where one may shop–it shall be related in their minds with all the activities of cultural enrichment and relaxation: theatre, outdoor music shell, exhibition hall.[23]

Gruen's "urban-suburban" shopping center hybrid–the storeblocks reach the edge of the site. Harvey Park, Los Angeles, project (1948).

In 1950 Gruen designed a second project: the Olympic Circle Shopping Center for East Los Angeles, to be located between Whittier and Olympic Boulevards, six miles east of downtown. For Olympic Circle, he rearranged the cruciform model of Harvey Park into a ring of store blocks, broken by the cylindrical department store. Four access roads, which ramped under the stores, met in a central roundabout with a drive-in restaurant. The new circular layout–with both internal and external parking areas–enabled the maximum number of vehicles to park as close as possible to the stores. The pedestrian shopping streets reappeared as broad arcades on both sides of the arc-shaped tenant store blocks facing the parking areas. Again Gruen anchored the project with a circular 240,000-square-foot department store, designed on a single floor with parking space for 300 cars on the roof, reached by circular ramps.[24] Besides the department store and drive-in restaurant, the center offered a 1,500-seat theater, a gas station, and a museum.

Despite experimenting with different modes of access, servicing, and store layout, Gruen wasn't able to reach a simple and convincing solution, and neither Harvey Park nor Olympic Circle was further developed. Customers at Harvey Park could enter the stores from the pedestrian shopping street, while deliveries would be made from sunken roads that ran along the parking lot side of the store blocks; yet while the design met his aim of separating pedestrian, private car, and service traffic, the sunken service roads were awkward. Similar to Eero Saarinen's Willow Run Community and Shopping Center project, the cruciform figure of Harvey Park organized a large irregular site into a comprehensible spatial form. The hybrid ensemble was partly urban, in that the shopping streets were terminated by pavilions that fronted onto the surrounding streets, and partly suburban, in that four parking fields filled in the quadrants. But Gruen never repeated this "urban-suburban" solution in later projects. The regional shopping centers built by Gruen and others were to be surrounded by their enormous parking fields, an urban design flaw that made it impossible to connect the center with surrounding areas. Although the Olympic Center would have admirably served the needs of automobiles and provided spacious arcades for pedestrians, as Gruen and Larry Smith later wrote in *Shopping Towns U.S.A.* (ii, 23), the front and rear access to stores at Olympic Circle would have created ambiguity from a merchandising point of view and posed security problems. The scheme was, further, hardly compact–one would have to walk the entire ring to see what was offered–and, worse, the flow of vehicles was limited by the capacity of the four access roads. Although this diagrammatic project was developed no further, Gruen would again try the "ring form" type in Detroit.

24 Olympic Shopping Circle, Victor Gruen, Architect. See also, *Los Angeles Times*, 22 Sep., 1950: Section I-p. 8. Longstreth shows the site to be the same for which Clarence Stein had produced a project two years before, Longstreth (1997), 328-30.

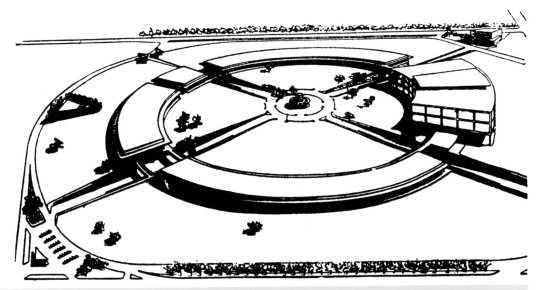

Olympic Circle, East Los Angeles, project (1950). While the Gruen and Krummeck project brochure showed a circular department store, *The Los Angeles Times* had shown a different design with the anchor store as an arc.

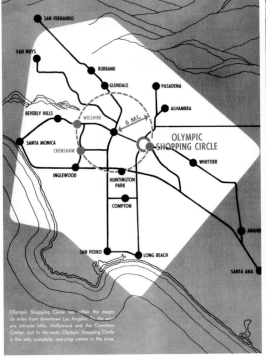

In 1949, Gruen traveled to Detroit, with the intent of meeting the Webber family, owners of the legendary J. L. Hudson Department Store, which dominated the downtown shopping district. As suburban development began to spread, it was clear that Hudson's would no longer be able to serve the entire region. To survive, the Webbers would have to follow the lead of stores around the country and plan for new suburban branch stores. After returning to New York, Gruen sent a proposal to Hudson's management analyzing the region's retailing future and proposing three possible courses of action: first, to build several free-standing branch stores in the suburbs; second, to build branch stores in existing shopping areas; or third, to develop a coordinated shopping center with the branch store as hub. Invited to Detroit to substantiate his proposal, Gruen argued that Hudson's should develop its own large, high-quality shopping center with a branch store as anchor. The size of the branch and the nature of its social and cultural services should, as with the downtown store, serve a catchment area of 500,000 people. Similar to developer Huston Rawls' retailing concept for the region around Boston, Oscar Webber, the family's patriarchal head, concluded that to serve the Detroit region he would have to build four such centers rather than a single branch. Webber then commissioned Gruen to analyze the Detroit marketplace and propose four suitable areas that could be developed over the next 15 years.[25]

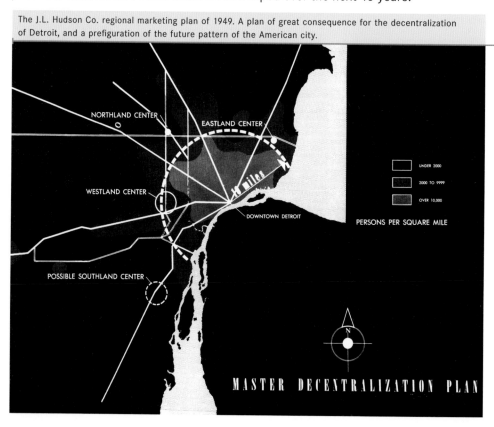

The J.L. Hudson Co. regional marketing plan of 1949. A plan of great consequence for the decentralization of Detroit, and a prefiguration of the future pattern of the American city.

NORTHLAND CENTER

EASTLAND CENTER

WESTLAND CENTER

DOWNTOWN DETROIT

POSSIBLE SOUTHLAND CENTER

UNDER 2000

2000 TO 9999

OVER 10,000

PERSONS PER SQUARE MILE

10 miles

N

MASTER DECENTRALIZATION PLAN

To prepare for the project, Gruen put together a team by inviting Karl Van Leuven, Rudi Baumfeld, and Edgardo Contini, the Italian engineer who was involved in an increasing number of Gruen jobs, to join him in an equal partnership, with himself as founder having the veto-right in case of hung decisions. In the new organization, Victor Gruen Associates (VGA), Karl Van Leuven would deal with client contact and relations, Rudi Baumfeld would lead design, and Edgardo Contini would be in charge of engineering. The survey and analysis carried out by Gruen and Karl Van Leuven yielded the following principles: each branch store center would need about 100 acres (43 hectares), far more than Northgate or Shoppers World; each should be approximately 10 miles from downtown; each should be located near two major traffic routes; and the immediate surroundings should be partly undeveloped. Further, additional land should be purchased to preempt "pirates" who would otherwise develop adjacent sites to capitalize on the number of visitors drawn to the area and the shopping center's own parking spaces.

Eastland Plaza ➔ Our Circular Period

In August 1950, *Architectural Forum*, focusing on the theme "Suburban Retail Districts," published as its cover story the Eastland Plaza project, the first of the shopping centers in Hudson's decentralization program. Eastland was to be built in the township of Gratiot, bounded by Kelly and Eight Mile Roads, a busy new home building area near prosperous Grosse Pointe. During the planning negotiations, Gruen had proposed a new zoning type—R.S.C. 1 (Regional Shopping Center Zone)—which set guidelines for parking, the separation of traffic and pedestrians, and the distance between the center and surrounding homes. To establish the retail sales potential of the center, Oscar Webber commissioned three independent surveys differing in method and approach. Gruen made a preliminary survey based on driving time-tests of between five and 30 minutes from the center to establish the market area and income; from this he established a gross and net retail potential indicating possible sales areas and parking requirements. Larry Smith, who had been the economic consultant for Northgate in Seattle, developed a feasibility study that was similar to Gruen's but used different time and income parameters. And Homer Hoyt Associates, who had been economic consultants for Ketchum, Giná and Sharp, conducted a market survey by giving out over a thousand questionnaires to housewives to analyze their shopping habits, their future shopping intentions, and their expectations should a large new shopping center be built. The consultants had established the market area, who their customers would be, and what their retailing needs were. All three surveys confirmed the viability of the location; each showed a retail sales potential greater than the projected sales capacity of the center.

Because of the narrow site, Gruen grouped the Eastland Plaza buildings in a long oval form with the circular Hudson's department store providing the anchor at one end and a theater or other public building providing the anchor at the other. The interior parking "plaza," reached by two

25 Gruen, *Centers of the Urban Environment*, The Northland Story, 22. For the "Emergency landing in Detroit," see *Traeumer*, 163; also Interview Ann Gray-Edgardo Contini, 1988, 5. Contini's version differs, claiming that Gruen was invited to Detroit on the basis of his recently published articles on shopping centers. In any event, Gruen had already met Foster Winter of the J.L. Hudson Co. in 1943; see above: Gruen, "Controlling Factors."

Shopping strip in a loop? The plan of a store block module shows the concept of two-sided access to stores, yielding a total arcade space of 3,300 x 15 ft. Eastland I (1949-50).

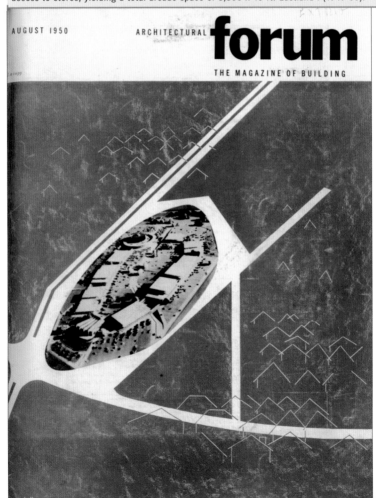

AUGUST 1950

ARCHITECTURAL **forum**

THE MAGAZINE OF BUILDING

access ramps, was to be sunk two feet below the sidewalks so that shoppers walking along the arcades could see across the center over the car tops. The interior-exterior parking arrangement enabled walking distance from car to store to be held down to 350 feet yet still accommodate the 6,000 parking spaces, each of which might turn over four to five times on a busy shopping day.

The project prospectus drew a large number of requests for space within the center, and the design proceeded quickly, but as Eastland was reaching construction drawing stage, the Korean War broke out and a freeze on strategic building materials was declared. While he waited out the freeze, Gruen completely revised his ideas about the spaces and flows of vehicular and pedestrian traffic. Despite the comparative studies undertaken by Gruen and his traffic engineer Lloyd B. Reid at both the Broadway-Crenshaw Center in Los Angeles and the Northgate Center in Seattle, Eastland's two access points would never have been sufficient for the traffic flows that would, for example, take place on a weekend or holiday. And the ambiguity of double-sided access to the tenant store blocks, repeated from the Olympic project, would clearly limit retailers' options for layout and security.

Like the Olympic Center project, Gruen's original plan for Eastland was never built. Years later, in *Centers for the Urban Environment*, he referred to these projects as "our circular period," and wrote that it was lucky they weren't built (193). Harvey Park had offered an intriguing balance between the pedestrian shopping streets and the parking fields. With the Olympic and (first) Eastland projects, Gruen focused too narrowly on the proximity of the automobile to the shops. There were arcades but no public spaces. With the partial exception of Harvey Park, in these early projects, Gruen had not yet given form and space in his design to his stated goal of creating a "place of (social and) cultural enrichment and relaxation" ("What to Look For . . . .," 63).

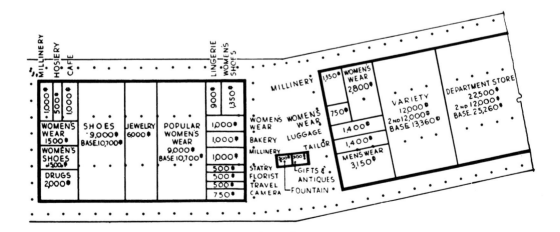

In the late 1940s and early 1950s, both retail trade and professional journals were busy with articles about not only the formal and operational characteristics of the regional shopping center but also, of enormous interest to Gruen as he developed his thinking, about the role of the architect in the undertaking. Gruen saw the challenge of building a regional shopping center as the chance for architects not just to undertake a large design and planning commission, but also to increase their status and influence. In its August 1950 article, "The Architect's Place in the suburban retail district," the *Architectural Forum* editors wrote that in designing a regional shopping center, the architect was

in a position of leadership almost unparalleled in his practice . . . . the architect is no longer the last man to climb aboard—at the mercy of the zoning ordinance, of the chain store's architectural department, of the real estate broker. Out on the meadows, he has a chance—as he has never had before—to control the traffic pattern, to help write a new zoning ordinance, to set the shape and depth of buildings, to control outside as well as inside space . . . . Ideally he will be called in while land buying notions are still a gleam in the developer's eye.

Perhaps with Victor Gruen or Morris Ketchum in mind, the *Forum* wrote,
The modern architect who opened up the front of the downtown store in the Thirties has come a long way. For his new job . . . . he needs to combine skills ranging from those of the traffic engineer and city planner to those of the chain store leasing specialist—not because he will dream of undertaking these jobs in his own firm but because . . . he will need to coordinate the work of experts in a dozen fields ("The Architect's Place...," 112).

The *Forum* projected these architects of "trade," once deemed to be at the edge of their discipline, as pioneers heading out into the city region to make order. At the time Gruen was working on the first Eastland project. He described his work with the Webber family, Larry Smith, and the consultants he had assembled as "a policy-making team which decides about leasing conditions, choice of tenants, location of tenants, traffic requirements, financial arrangements etc." (110). The *Forum* published a diagram of this corporate structure showing the constellation of client,

26 Larry Smith (1901-1967) was born in Canada and moved to Seattle forming Larry Smith and Co. in 1948. Working as a real estate broker with an expertise in bringing chain stores to small towns, Smith developed a format for precise market analysis. His break into shopping centers came with his work for the Equitable Life Assurance Society, one of the investors in the Northgate shopping center in Seattle. Foster Winter of the J.L. Hudson Co. then hired Smith to work with Gruen on the Eastland and Northland jobs. Working for most of the great department stores, Smith was to consult on nearly a thousand shopping center projects. Thanks to Michael Tubridy, International Council of Shopping Centers (ICSC), Albert Sussman Library.

27 Gruen assembled his arguments for the regional shopping center from the mid-1940s until his first built projects in the mid-1950s, and these may be followed in his published articles and speeches. For example, "mixed functions and public spaces" in "Shopping Center" (1943: 101), "completeness from a merchandising point of view" in "What to Look for" (1948: 22), "teamwork and cooperation" in The Architects Place in the Retail District" (1950: 110), "a new type of planning" in "Yardsticks for Shopping Centers" (1950: 23), "scientific analysis of traffic and potential market" in Shopping Center - The New Building Type" (with Larry Smith) (1952: 67-9). The center as a place for cultural, social, and leisure activities, and the necessity of separating different types of traffic is present in all of the above.

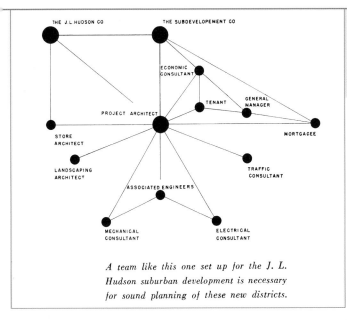

THE J.L HUDSON CO

THE SUBDEVELOPEMENT CO

ECONOMIC CONSULTANT

TENANT

GENERAL MANAGER

PROJECT ARCHITECT

STORE ARCHITECT

MORTGAGEE

LANDSCAPING ARCHITECT

TRAFFIC CONSULTANT

ASSOCIATED ENGINEERS

MECHANICAL CONSULTANT

ELECTRICAL CONSULTANT

A team like this one set up for the J. L. Hudson suburban development is necessary for sound planning of these new districts.

consultants, development company, and bankers. In the middle was the project architect. A full four years before he would open Northland, Gruen reveled in the chance to claim the leading role for the architect in the birth of the new building type. He indeed dreamt of undertaking all of these jobs, and he had just started to create the organization that could handle this scope of work. How else to build the new large projects for a mass society?

While Gruen was struggling with the formal layout of the regional shopping center, he was stating his ideas more clearly in publications, especially after he began to collaborate with the economist Larry Smith (1901-1967). Trained as an accountant and real-estate economist, Smith gained a national reputation as the management and economic guru for shopping centers, consulting on more than a thousand projects. His contribution to the commercial underpinning of Gruen's suburban and urban projects cannot be underestimated; he was later jokingly referred to as the "fifth Beatle" of VGA.[26]

Addressing his commercial clients, Gruen would describe the regional shopping center as a demonstration of a new type of planning, requiring intensive analysis, organization, and teamwork that precipitated changes in merchandising, building, financing, planning, and design, a complex organism that needed the synthetic vision and management skill of the architect.[27] To architects, however, he would emphasize the potential of the regional shopping center at both the macro and micro scales: first, its role in regional planning, and second, its social and cultural value to its surrounding communities. In "Yardsticks for Shopping Centers," published in *Chain Store Age* in February 1950, he made clear that the scale of the new projects, their level of investment, the extent of their supporting infrastructure, and their presence as new social and cultural centers meant that what was emerging went far beyond architecture's subculture of retail design and pointed toward a new kind of planning. "When they consider shopping centers . . . chain store real estate executives should begin to think in terms usually associated with city planning," he wrote (Yardsticks... 23). What distinguished the shopping center from other retail arrangements was that it was under the control of a single owner, and Gruen argued that the shopping-center developer should control as much of the surrounding land as possible for planned future development. Several professional and commercial uses fit well in the immediate neighborhood of a regional shopping center, such as offices, buildings for group medical practices or hospitals, schools, and apartment buildings. These would create, with the shopping center as the focal point, a new kind of multifunctional regional center.

In 1952, with only a few major centers open, *Progressive Architecture* devoted a major part of its June issue to the regional shopping center, and this issue established Gruen as one of the principal spokespersons for the new building type. In "Shopping Centers –The New Building Type," Gruen and Smith wrote of the urban capacity of the regional shopping center:

Regional shopping centers may well be regarded as satellite downtown areas, offering much of what the metropolitan centers give . . . . They will welcome the hordes of automobiles, which approach them, providing easy access and ample free parking space. They will offer restfulness, safety, and esthetic values. They can become places where suburbanites will visit for a short shopping trip, and also centers where they will want to congregate for many hours–both days and evenings.

Gruen, with Smith, then introduced the strategic elements for the regional shopping center that he would emphasize throughout his career: first and foremost, the organization and separation of traffic; second, a programmatic mix that would include civic and social functions; and third, the use of public art, landscaping, and other amenities to create a diverse pedestrian environment. The ability of the public spaces to support social and cultural activities would ensure the commercial success of the center. It was the public space–as much as the department store–that would be the attractor. "The shopping center of tomorrow will be more than its name implies. . . . [It] will, besides its commercial function, fill the vacuum created by the absence of social, cultural and civic crystallization points in our vast suburban areas."[28]

28 Gruen and Smith, "Shopping Centers . . .," 68.
29 Gruen and Smith, "Shopping Centers . . .," 70, 87, 104. See also Nichols, J.C., "Mistakes We Have Made in Developing Shopping Centers," 2-13; and "Suburban Retail Districts," *Architectural Forum*, 114.

In *Progressive Architecture*, Gruen wrote that he had learned both through his own experience and the experience of others: "Modern shopping centers are relatively new, the concepts are changing, new solutions are constantly sought, new problems arise. There is no tradition for the auto-age regional shopping center, no set of rules . . . . The experience has had a sobering effect on us; we have learned enough to realize how little we know."[29] Gruen had identified the core issue of shopping center design as a formal equation between access, parking, the mix of social, cultural, and commercial functions, and the public spaces in which the shopper could promenade, window shop, consider, and then buy.

Minutes From Town

People attending conventions and other visitors to Detroit can easily and quickly reach Northland Center via the John Lodge Expressway. Northland is actually only a matter of minutes from Detroit's Civic Center and the city's business section.

NORTHLAND
N🐻C
CENTER

OPEN

9:30 a.m.—5:30 p.m.
Monday through Wednesday
9:30 a.m.—9:00 p.m.
Thursday through Saturday

EXCITING
NORTHLAND

NORTHWESTERN HIGHWAY AND EIGHT MILE ROAD
IN THE
CITY OF SOUTHFIELD
MICHIGAN
ADJACENT TO NORTHWEST DETROIT

LITHOGRAPHED IN U.S.A. BY
EVANS-WINTER-HEBB INC., DETROIT

What follows are accounts of how he finally put his ideas in place in the spectacular breakthroughs at Northland and Southdale, and then a description of Cherry Hill, where the arcane formula of the regional shopping center came into conflict with social, cultural, and civic trends of the 1960s.

In 1951, Hudson's announced that its regional expansion plans had been revised and that the Northland Center was to be built first.[30] As with the Eastland project, while the new design was being developed, the economic consultants submitted their market research reports. Homer Hoyt, acting for Hudson's and basing his opinion on intuition, believed that the uniqueness of the project would carry it through. Larry Smith, however, based his analysis on existing shopping centers and concluded that Northland would not achieve the financial goals set by Webber: Gruen's proposal was too big and too expensive, and the formal arrangement of buildings and spaces had not been tried before. Smith's report scared off the institutional investors, and Webber, irritated by the disagreement between his economic advisors, decided that he was convinced enough to underwrite the project himself. When, well before the opening, all the retail spaces had been leased–300 applicants were screened for 80 tenant spaces–the insurance companies scrambled with each other to back the project.

In March 1954, after five days of special openings, Northland, the largest regional shopping center in America, opened. Built on a triangular site, bounded by Greenfield, Northwestern, and Eight Mile Roads, 12 miles from downtown Detroit, Northland would enable the J. L. Hudson Co. to serve a market as large as Dallas or Louisville yet independent of the market area of its

Northland's "pinwheel" plan. Building cluster with public spaces; site plan showing access flows and parking capacities; and model with reverse graded parking fields.

30 "Expansion plan revised, Northland center to be built first," *Hudsonian* 12,1951. Southfield Township approved the rezoning in 1951 and while approval was awaited from the Federal Government and the National Production Authority, construction drawings could begin. For the carefully planned sequence of openings, see Hardwick, *Mallmaker*, 125.
31 "Northland: A new yardstick for shopping center planning," *Architectural Forum*, 111.

downtown store. The principal formal characteristic of the center was the pinwheel plan of five tenant store buildings arrayed around the four-story J. L. Hudson department store, the single and centrally positioned magnet. The brick-clad square volume of Hudson's, articulated by the white reinforced-concrete frame, formed the monumental center to the ensemble and gave shape to the surrounding public spaces. The formal arrangement mirrored the merchandising concept. Customers would walk from their cars, past competing stores and through the public spaces before reaching Hudson's, embedded within the shopping center ensemble. This Hudson's was one of the largest department stores of any kind since the 1920s–470,000 square feet, 370,000 of them sales area–and exemplified the trend whereby branch stores were now being built larger than the downtown parent store.[31]

The five tenant-store blocks housed some 85 stores (with competing stores in the same price range placed close together), a small supermarket, and a garden center. The colonnades, which would protect shoppers from sun, rain, and snow, gave a visual unity to the store blocks themselves, allowing merchants to express their individuality in their treatment of storefronts and signs. Merchants were in fact encouraged to design their own façades, and Northland's owners paid the full cost of tenant fronts, which was considered unusual. VGA did, however, draft laws for the tenant stores: they may not, for example, place sale posters on shop windows, post signs in public areas, or use neon signs; display windows had to be visible and, even on Sundays, lit until 10 p.m. to attract visitors to the public areas, even though the shops were closed.

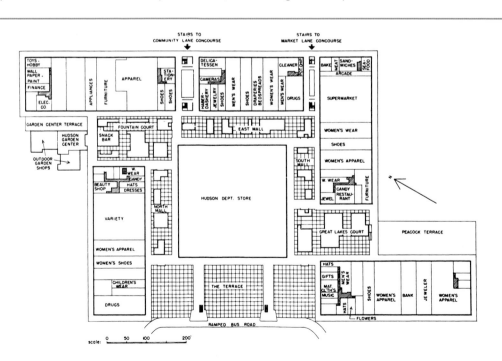

32 Gruen, "Is there a gap between architect and merchant?," 66, 70. Among the critics who questioned the costs of VGA's "frills," was S.O. Kaylin. Kaylin, in reviewing a speech by Gruen at the Institute of Distribution, reported on "what hard-headed businessmen might consider frills included by dreamy architects in the design of shopping centers." In a letter to the editor, Gruen clarified the economic benefit that would accrue to the shopping center that included social and cultural activities and spaces.

This kind of center "would develop magnetic powers to attract more people and to hold them for a longer time than if it were a commercial center. More people–for more hours–mean cash registers ringing more often and for longer periods." The art at Northland was described in "20th Century Bazaar," Life; and, "Architecture and Sculpture;" Arts & Architecture. The same year 13 preparatory sketch models of the sculpture were exhibited in the Seligman Gallery in New York.

Suburban Space

Northland was a cluster of buildings surrounded by 10 parking fields and set in the middle of the vast 300-acre (136 Ha.) site, well clear of the major access roads. Beyond the parking fields, a 300- to 600-foot-wide zone formed a buffer between the center and the surrounding residential communities. The legibility of the center's approaches and the ease and convenience of access and parking were of paramount importance and could not have been in greater contrast to a shopping trip to the downtown, or to stores along one of the ubiquitous "strips." Hudson's built its own circumferential divided parkway and secondary access roads to create a smooth flow of traffic from the state roads to the parking areas. To achieve convenience of vehicular movement, the different traffic streams—private cars, public buses, and service and delivery vehicles—were separated. Besides the parking fields for shoppers and staff, local and regional bus services would pull up to a bus station at one end of the ensemble, and a truck tunnel would enable deliveries to be made and the buildings to be serviced from below; Gruen had abandoned his sunken perimeter service road for the truck-tunnel solution used at Broadway-Crenshaw, Northgate, and at Walt Disney's new theme park in Anaheim, which was under construction.

Meet Me at the Totem Pole

All Gruen's ideas about compact, multi-functional space serving the new suburban communities came together at Northland. Between department store and tenant-store blocks were courts, malls, terraces, and lanes, all with colonnaded walks. The absence of vehicular traffic enabled crowds of people to enjoy these public spaces, whose fountains and sculptures were to capture the attention of mothers and their children, projected to be the most frequent users of the center. The design of the public areas themselves, rather than the elevation or the form of the buildings, would establish Northland's quality in the minds of shoppers. Gruen wrote that he shaped the open spaces between buildings as in European cities, "to create a successful strolling atmosphere," which to him meant a continuity of interesting experiences (*Centers for the Urban Environment,* 33). This he achieved by investing substantially in landscaping, artworks, and graphics. Edward Eichstadt, the landscape architect, gave each open area its own character—rhododendrons and azaleas in the Fountain Court, for instance, and magnolias in the South Mall—and had the great variety of plants labeled for garden lovers. To further enrich the public spaces, Gruen commissioned 13 artists to create sculptures, and this expense of some $200,000 on what most developers and merchants would consider "frills" sparked considerable debate.[32] While hardly part of a formal avant-garde, the sculptures, coordinated by Lili Saarinen and including works by Arthur Kraft and Malcolm Moran, operated at a human scale and became rendezvous points. Many reacted with wind and water, producing entertaining and playful movement; some dominated their spaces; others were partly hidden in the planting and had to be discovered. The number of people expected to move through a regional shopping center was equivalent to that at an airport or an international exposition, so clarity in the center's graphic communications was crucial. At Northland, the lettering and graphic design by Alvin Lustig extended into the architecture itself: Northland's watertower, with its giant "N," became a landmark in the flat landscape. [33]

All the physical comforts and visual pleasures at Northland expressed the Webber family's philosophy of community involvement and identity that had so characterized their downtown store. To substantiate Gruen's own claims that the regional shopping center must also support social, cultural, and civic functions, Northland included two auditoria for lectures and concerts, a series of clubrooms with a kitchen, several restaurants, a small infirmary, and a creche. The public rooms and the principal outdoor spaces were booked months in advance with fashion shows, exhibitions, musical performances, and "town meetings," confirming that the spaces filled a real need. Northland became a Detroit tourist attraction, and trade groups from foreign countries visited frequently. Only two stores were open on Sundays, but, surrounded by agricultural land and subdivisions, the center served then as a park, and people came to fly kites, race model planes and cars, conduct driving lessons, and photograph the sculptures and flowers in the courts. In "What Makes a Good Square Good?," Grady Clay wrote,

For a really screwball fountain, the place to go is Northland Shopping Center, north of Detroit. Here is a collection of jets and sculpture that would delight Rube Goldberg, and does delight constant streams of visitors . . . . People flock and stand, fascinated by the interplay of small wheels, levers, jets, spurts, and streams, a fantasy of motion and invention. Here, it seems to me, lies the promise of the future: the application of humor, inventiveness, and ingenuity to enliven display and entertainment.

33 Hornbeck, "Signs & Symbols in Commercial Architecture," 242-275. See also in same feature, "Architect Gruen States the Challenge that Graphic Design Presents," 244-6. Besides the graphic work of Victor Gruen Associates, the article went on to illustrate the graphic design by I.M. Pei, Eero Saarinen, Marcel Breuer, and Ketchum Giná Sharp.

34 Gruen, "Cityscape and Landscape," 19. "Cityscape-Landscape"–a seminal speech by Gruen, which includes most of his core concepts about the shopping center, the urban landscape, and the role of the architect–was presented at the International Design Conference, June 13-17, 1955 at Aspen, CO. The conference was divided into topics such as Communication, Light and Structure, Cityscape and Landscape, and Leisure. Besides Victor Gruen, other speakers in Cityscape and Landscape were Arthur Drexler, Henry Russell Hitchcock, Koicho Ito and Albert E. Parr. AHCVGC box 33. A slightly different version appeared in Ockman, J. (Ed.) *Architectural Culture*: 193-199.

35 Gruen, *Centers of the Urban Environment*, 26.

Clay concluded his remarks by asking, "Is there any reason [why] we can't have it in downtown too?" Yet no matter how much Gruen might argue for the importance of good design or the benefits of cultural events and civic spaces, only the commercial success of his project could render these arguments credible. "The 50 million people who came to Northland did one other thing also," said Gruen. "They shopped–they did it with so much joy, intensity and gusto that the sales figures per square foot of store area reached unprecedented amounts."[34] In terms of commerce and popularity, Northland was such a hit that the first year's sales at Hudson's were 30 percent higher than the estimate for the fifth year, and the number of daily visitors averaged not the 30,000 estimated, but 45,000. The only mistake at Northland, in fact, was in the amount of business predicted. Larry Smith had estimated that the center would do about $35 million in its first year and $50 million by the fifth–but Northland made $50 million in its first year and had passed $100 million by its third. When Oscar Webber asked Smith how it was possible after all of his analysis to get the figures so wrong, Smith replied that he had assumed Webber had intended to build a conventional shopping center. Hudson's had become one of the most profitable stores in the country.[35]

Northland's power plant and water tower. Partner in charge, Edgardo Contini. Before joining Gruen, he had worked with Albert Kahn.

Modern Architecture in the American Suburbs

The design research that went into Northland produced a new kind of architecture that could hardly be compared to "signature" contemporary public or institutional buildings, such as Frank Lloyd Wright's Guggenheim Museum in New York (1946-59), or Mies van der Rohe's Crown Hall at IIT in Chicago (1956). As an ensemble of buildings and spaces, Northland may be compared with Eero Saarinen's General Motors Technical Center outside of Detroit or the Connecticut General Insurance Company headquarters in Bloomfield, Connecticut, by Gordon Bunshaft for Skidmore Owings and Merrill, with its courtyards and landscaping by Isamu Noguchi. Although the Hartford Symphony Orchestra would play their summer program at Connecticut General, these two examples were principally private ensembles of splendid objects in landscape, where one arrived at work at nine and left at five. If Northland's public spaces were empty, as they were for *Architectural Forum*'s cover photograph, the buildings demonstrated no perfect proportions, no conceptual leaps in their structure, and no sublimely abstract curtain walls. Northland was commercial architecture and needed to provide generously for automobiles, merchandise, and, above all, people: the design of the graphics, landscaping, and placement of art was as important as the architecture. Its best contemporary counterpart–although in an entirely different context, the rebuilding of a city center rather than suburban development–was the Lijnbaan shopping area in Rotterdam, designed by van den Broek and Bakema and opened in 1953. The Lijnbaan was one of the first European renewal projects with retail as the major component and spatial determinant. With its 3,600-foot long pedestrian mall, enlivened by trees, flowers, sitting areas, play spaces, and sculpture, the Lijnbaan's ambience was very like Northland's. Both projects were commercial, but they were also examples of urban and civic design: they looked better with people, signs, and goods in them than empty. "They had to remain spatially coherent while organizing a clamorous diversity."[36] Arcades gave both projects a strong, clear expression, achieving a balance between weather protection, architectural expression, and transparency. The Lijnbaan, however, represented a deeper significance in providing evidence in the most concrete terms for the argument on which Gruen would soon focus: the regional shopping center as a new spatial model for retail that could be adapted for downtown.

Northland seemed a literal representation of modernist planning, the result of scientific analysis and rationally planned development, engineered to serve yet control the automobile, all on a cleared site. Aerial photographs of the newly finished shopping center show it as an urban fragment landed in a landscape of new subdivisions and remaining scraps of agricultural land. Despite its 'mid-century modern' style and the high quality of its construction, Northland was not really about architecture; it was above all an ensemble of urban spaces and shaper of public experience. The press seemed to understand this, describing Northland as a "satellite city" and an "intricate unit of traffic control, customer attractions and community services . . .

---

36 The Lijnbaan, Rotterdam: Planning, Department of Town Planning and Reconstruction, City of Rotterdam; Architects, van den Broek and Bakema; developer, The Visserdyk Group; Phase I, completed 1953. During the planning of the Lijnbaan, the width of the pedestrian mall was a point of contention, and this was an argument that would repeat itself throughout the evolution of the regional shopping center. The Lijnbaan shopkeepers wanted the mall as narrow as possible but the building regulations required adequate width for light, air and emergency vehicle access. The final width varied between 55 and 70 feet. See Kiek, "Europe's Fifth Avenue."

far from the conventional shopping center." In an extended review of the project in the June 1954 *Architectural Forum,* Jane Jacobs wrote,

This is a classic in shopping center planning, in the sense that the Rockefeller Center is a classic in urban skyscraper group planning, or Radburn, New Jersey, in suburban residential planning. Northland is a planning classic because it is the first modern pedestrian commercial center to use an urban "market town" plan, a compact form physically and psychologically suited to pedestrian shopping . . . the high standards in public signs; its uninhibited, generous and lighthearted use of art . . . its use of open spaces looks like a natural for coping with the rehabilitation of blight-spotted decaying shopping districts . . . this shopping center adds up to a new thing in town planning. But the Northland scheme has old roots. It is a rediscovery rather than an invention. ("Northland, A new Yardstick...," 103)

Jacobs compared Northland to the outdoor market space in Ludlow, an English provincial market town in Shropshire, but of course Northland was located in a suburban environment. Yet before the advent of the enclosed shopping centers, early regional shopping centers created an analog to traditional town and city marketplaces. Without the playful and nostalgic reproductions of Disney, Gruen, Ketchum, and others set out to create an eventful if rational ambience. Shopping centers have become so familiar to us that it is no longer possible to imagine the novelty of the variety of shops all anchored by a big city department store, but contemporary critics saw the importance of Northland; further, it was one of 10 buildings to represent U.S. architecture and planning in a State Department exhibition that traveled the world. It was also chosen as one of the most significant projects by the AIA at its centennial celebrations of 1957 and exhibited at the National Gallery in Washington, D.C.

The exceptionally positive reaction to Northland was enormously important to VGA. It vindicated Gruen's concept of architecture as the design of an environment, and of the architect-planner as coordinator of consultants in order to build the new large projects for a mass society.

For all of Northland's success, though, it was a model that, in the fast-developing field of shopping-center design, was short lived. Gruen repeated the Northland figure—a centrally positioned department store anchoring a cluster of tenant-store buildings and outdoor public spaces—at Bayfair, Oakland (1955); Glendale, Indianapolis (1956); the redesigned Eastland (1957); as well as at Valley Fair, San Jose (1957); and Maryvale, Phoenix (1961). But in September 1956, the design and concept of the regional shopping center would make a quantum leap with the opening in Edina, Minnesota, of Gruen's Southdale, America's first enclosed regional shopping center, a project that established a fatal contrast between the new conditions of suburban shopping and those in deteriorating downtowns. But in terms of Gruen's later work, the example of Northland's "cluster planning"—an ensemble of public spaces that represented a new concept of "center"—would become both a building block of downtown redevelopment projects and of local centers in projects for new towns and new cities.

| Montclair | ➡ | How Was a Customer to Shop in Comfort? |

While he was developing the original Eastland project, Gruen had his first chance to design an enclosed shopping center project when he was invited to join Irving R. Klein Associates of Houston, who were working together with Larry Smith, on the $10-million Montclair Shopping Center. In 1951, Women's Wear Daily announced the project—a 600,000-square-foot center on a 27-acre site—which had three unusual features that were nevertheless rational responses to site and climatic conditions.[37] First, because the developer, Russel Nix, had acquired two tracts

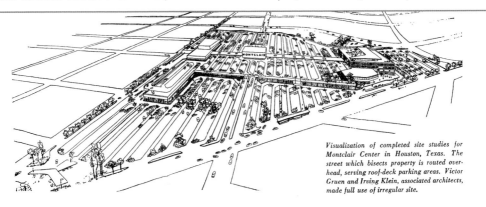

Visualization of completed site studies for Montclair Center in Houston, Texas. The street which bisects property is routed overhead, serving roof-deck parking areas. Victor Gruen and Irving Klein, associated architects, made full use of irregular site.

of land on either side of Weslayan Avenue at its junction with Bissonet, the architects proposed that Weslayan be run beneath the shopping center as an underpass, a solution that would cost $250,000. Second, in addition to ground parking for 2,000, there was to be parking for 1,800 cars on the roof in what would have been one of the largest roof parking areas "ever contemplated" in the U.S. Third, Houston's heat and humidity were appalling–how was a customer to shop in comfort?–so the architects planned to enclose and air-condition the pedestrian mall, a 900- by 70-foot space, which would have made it the first shopping center of this type. Running a street under the shopping center pointed up the awkwardness of Nix's "double site," but, as with roof parking, it was achievable with current construction methods. And although air-conditioning had been used in department stores since 1919 and was not unusual in Houston at the time, no one had ever conditioned such a large and multiple-tenanted public space. Korean War restrictions on building materials put the project on hold, however, and later, two smaller shopping centers were built. Gruen and his public would have to wait another five years to experience a climatized shopping-center space.

The Community's Living Room ← Southdale Shopping Center

Sometime in late 1952, Oscar Webber recommended Gruen to the Dayton family, who owned the Dayton's store in Minneapolis, one of the three largest department stores west of Chicago, with an annual business turnover of $60 million in 1953. The third generation of the store-owning family consisted of five brothers, who since 1950 had been considering alternative branch-store locations. Earlier that year, after market analysis and a site recommendation made by Larry Smith and Co., they had decided to go ahead with the development of a regional shopping center in Edina, seven miles south of downtown Minneapolis.

After visiting existing department stores and shopping centers around the country, Bruce Dayton, who would lead the project, set three goals for the new center: 1) it must be well built, with square-foot construction costs higher than normal; 2) it must have a potential for expansion from 560,000 square feet to 850,000 square feet; and 3) it must have a character so outstanding that it would become the premier shopping center in the area and provide a complete shopping service

Model of first project: Bruce Dayton and Gruen. Hermann Gutman, Gruen, and Rudi Baumfeld in central court.

38 Bruce Dayton, author interview, Minneapolis, 2001. See also Gruen, *Centers of the Urban Environment*, 33-39.

for the 206,000 potential customers who lived within a 15-minute drive. Despite Southdale's size—its 700,000 square feet of retail was the equivalent offered by a downtown store serving a population of 150,000—the Daytons believed that it would not threaten their downtown store but would serve an entirely new market, a view that in most other cities would be proved wrong.[38]

Gruen, whose first job for the Daytons was the renovation of their Rochester, Minnesota, store, was well aware of the Minneapolis climate—ferocious winters, hot summers, rainy springs and falls—that yielded an average of 126 good outdoor shopping days a year. So, from his early discussions with the Daytons, he had proposed that the central mall be covered and air-conditioned. The idea, he said, was inspired by the Italian gallerias, "where people pause to rest and sip aperitifs between visits to shops," but he had already developed the concept in the unbuilt Montclair project. To questions of feasibility and cost, Gruen argued that the central court could accept excess heat from the shops; that a controlled climate would allow internal façades of less expensive "Southern California" materials—plaster and wood—instead of stone or brick; and that the glazing for shopfronts could be crystal instead of plate glass, and this saving alone would pay for air conditioning. Most importantly, this air-conditioned court would not only neutralize the weather but create a forum for continuous events, thus folding culture, entertainment, and community activities into retail shopping. Southdale's Court was not merely public space; it would be a stage.

Site plan of first project (with a single department store), showing layout of planned community.
Southdale Shopping Center, Edina, MN (1953-6).

Although the impact of Southdale's interior court would later dominate popular reception of the project, in the architectural and trade press, the court was merely the first of three major "innovations" that Gruen and the Daytons were planning. From the beginning the Dayton brothers had similar ideas to the J. L. Hudson Company's marketing strategy for the Detroit metropolitan area; they too wanted to build a number of centers, but the immediate goal for Southdale, their first project, was not only that it be a market leader in the Minneapolis-St. Paul area, but that it be a magnet for an entirely new planned community. In order to block other commercial entities from building competing businesses adjacent to the shopping center, the Daytons, in consultation with Gruen and Smith, decided to develop the project as a complete "suburban settlement" of 462 acres (185 hectares), with the 84-acre shopping center at its core. Developing outward from the center's road system, the surrounding community would include commercial, service, and residential projects with generous landscaped buffer zones between them; the residential areas would include not only single-family homes and two-story garden apartments and townhouses, but schools, parks, playgrounds, and medical and dentistry buildings. After the drama of the interior court, Southdale's second innovative feature was that the department store–Dayton's–intended to be the center of a planned new community, rather than being an isolated building complex in a landscape of single-family houses.[39] Meanwhile, in "The Big Ideas in the New Shopping Centers," published in the March 1953 *Architectural Forum*, a model of Southdale was illustrated on the cover with a wry commentary within:

So the best shopping center planners have turned the tables to become community planners in self-defense. Southdale . . . . will control the development of what amounts to a complete village . . . . Here is the idealism of town planning actually become reality . . . . Frightened downtown merchants, please take note.

Throughout the early 1950s, architects were experimenting with different sizes and arrangements of the public open space in regional shopping centers; however, after the difficulties at the two-level Shoppers World, developers and retailers were wary of multistory centers. In "A Breakthrough for Two-Level Shopping Centers," the *Architectural Forum* triumphantly announced the end of the taboo and looked forward to more compact and urban centers. This was to be Southdale's third innovation: in comparison with Northland's 300 acres, Southdale would occupy just 84, with two main shopping floors, a fully programmed basement, and a services penthouse. Both the basement, which contained all loading, shipping, and maintenance

39 The idea was not new; the most progressive regional shopping centers of the 1950s were, in a limited fashion, continuing the idea from the Greenbelt Towns of the 1930s and the defense towns of the 1940s by joining community facilities and shopping to anchor a planned community. Perhaps the best example was Park Forest Plaza, built by Loebl, Schlossman and Bennett, 30 miles south of Chicago, and planned from 1946 as part of a "G.I. Town." Bennett brought the eastern edge of the shopping center right to one of the planned community's greenways, which was bordered by apartment blocks, thus giving direct pedestrian

access to nearby residents. Although much smaller than Gruen's regional shopping centers, this logical and "urban" design motif was rarely followed. See also, Randall, Gregory. *America's Original G:I: Town: Park Forest, Illinois*. Baltimore: Johns Hopkins University Press: 2000; and, Hayden, *Building Suburbia*, 141-6.
40 "A Controlled Climate for Shopping," *Architectural Record*, 193-4. See also, "600 Ton Heat Pump System Creates Eternal Spring," *Heating, Piping and Air Conditioning (HPAC)*; and, "World's Largest Heat Pump Revisited," *Heating, Piping and Air Conditioning (HPAC)*, 115-119.

functions, and the penthouse helped the center use space efficiently, maximizing selling areas on the two main floors. Besides housing services, the basement included a security control office, a children's petting zoo, and a post office, as well as low-productivity areas, such as the furniture store, which had a large basement area and a smaller "boutique" showroom on the main floor. The technological innovations necessary for the air-conditioning of the interior court attracted attention in the trade and technical press. In convincing the Daytons to air-condition the central court, Gruen had argued that heat produced by shoppers and lights would be drawn from the shops into the court and exhausted by fans in the roof. Later, however, Gruen, with his design engineer, David Berks, and consultant, Howard Wolfburg of the Carrier Corporation, inverted the original concept and used the court as a giant plenum. Instead of exhausting air from shops to the court, air was taken from outside, conditioned in the penthouse level, and supplied under modest pressure at the top of the court. The cooled air then flowed into the individual shops through long slots in their "external" walls to the court. Air, heated by shoppers and lighting, was then exhausted from the shops through shafts to the truck tunnel in the basement, and finally drawn up air shafts to the roof exhausts. The excess heat produced in the shopping areas warmed the external walls, which prevented heat loss during the winter months. The heat pump, at that time one of the largest in operation, contributed further to the efficiency of the system.[40]

Plan view of model of final project with axis swung 45 degrees for better vehicle and service flows.

Working model of central court with preliminary arrangement of escalator-bridge, sculpture, landscaping, and "street furniture."

As the planning and technical development was coming together, a threat emerged from one of Dayton's regional competitors. In 1953, the press announced that Donaldson's, another Minneapolis retailer, was planning to open a branch store in a regional shopping center only a few miles away. To avoid splitting the market, which could not sustain two large regional shopping centers, Dayton's convinced Donaldson's to become a second anchor at Southdale and agreed that Donaldson's could bring in its own architect, John Graham, who had earlier designed Northgate in Seattle. Southdale had already been planned, like Northland, as a "pinwheel square," but with the major exception that the Dayton's department store would not stand in the center but at the north façade, the vacated central area becoming the climate-controlled public space. The internal court, bounded by two floors of retail, was reached from the parking areas by six lanes, each lined with smaller shops and services. Six service cores, located within the store blocks, enabled the shops and stores to be serviced from the basement.

With a second anchor, the planning and merchandising concepts would need revision, and the fact that two architects of comparable prominence would have to work together introduced predictable tensions. The revised Southdale became an irregular rectangular building ensemble, comprising two department stores and four store blocks, set diagonally in the middle of its site.

"Breakthrough for two-level shopping centers," Architectural Forum's endorsement of the move towards more compact multi-level shopping center planning. Three early examples:
1 Southdale, organized around its internal court

2 Mondawmin, Baltimore, MD, James Rouse, Developer, organized around an open court and lane;
3 Shoppers World, Framingham, MA, Ketchum, Giná and Sharp, organized around its great "village green."

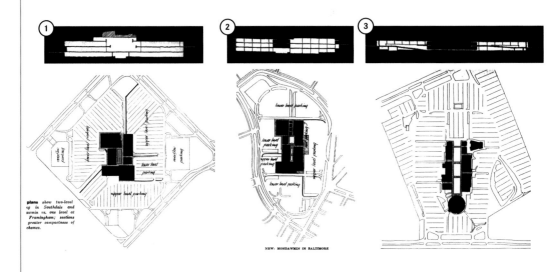

41 See: "Donaldson's Had Planned Another Suburban Center," *Minneapolis Sunday Tribune*: 5; "Donaldson's and Dayton's Merge Shopping Center in $15,000,000 Southdale Project," *Minneapolis Sunday Tribune*; and, "L.S. Donaldson Joins Dayton's In New Center," *Womens Wear Daily*; all in LoCVGP, OV 04, 57.
42 Gruen, "The planned shopping centers in America," 167.

Gruen and Graham agreed to place the two department stores diagonally opposite each other across the central court, with tenant-store blocks in-between, but they disagreed over the court's dimensions. Graham thought the central court was a luxury and would prevent shoppers from seeing stores on both sides of the mall space; he argued that the court should be narrowed to the width of a street, as at his Northgate.[41] The Daytons, however, supported Gruen's more generous dimensions: 240 feet long, 109 feet wide, and 50 feet high, split by a bridge and crossed escalators. "The idea that malls must be elongated mousetraps for customers," Gruen later said, "is held by people who haven't realized that the open spaces between buildings in a shopping center have functions all their own. In them can be located minor structures, like restaurant pavilions, exhibits, refreshment stands; and beyond that, their space should be so organized that they become places where the body and eye can rest."[42]

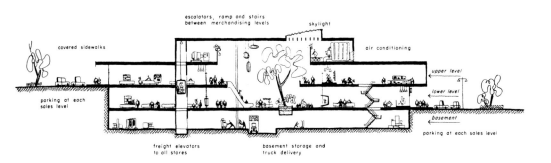

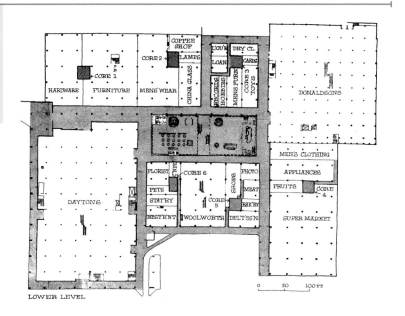

Ground floor plan. Besides stairs, elevators, and washrooms, the six cores in the tenant store areas contained ducts for exhausting the heat produced by shoppers and lighting. The department stores had their own air-conditioning and service cores.

Urban space for the suburban middle classses: "The court of eternal spring," with its cafe, exhibition area, and stage.

Opera Ball with the Minneapolis Symphony Orchestra

Fashion Show

43 Bruce Dayton, author interview, Minneapolis, 2001.

A Copy of Downtown?

Southdale opened in October 1956: America's first enclosed, air-conditioned mall. In "Pleasure Domes with Parking," *Time* magazine characterized Southdale as "piped music, splashing waterfalls, and clanging cash registers," but in "A Breakthrough for Two-level Shopping Centers" in December, the *Architectural Forum* focused on what it saw as the project's urban qualities:

Here we see architecture fulfilling one of its most creative roles: building a new kind of environment. The Southdale environment is quite unlike that of any other shopping center. There is nothing suburban about it except its location. For Southdale uncannily conveys the feeling of a metropolitan downtown; . . . Southdale (is not) a copy of downtown. Rather, it is an imaginative distillation of what makes downtowns magnetic: the variety, the individuality, the lights, the color, even the crowds . . . ("A Breakthrough...," 82)

What was "downtown" about Southdale was the experience of the internal court, which was both attractor and stage-set for visitors. Lighting and sculpture dramatized the court's volume—all this was indispensable to the illusion of being somewhere that was more than a building and more than a mere shopping center. Gruen intended that the lighting in the court reflect the time of day and even the seasons: there were no lights in the court ceiling, and, in the evening, the space was allowed to become slightly dim, lit only with hanging Japanese lanterns. "People in the court will know whether it is day or night, clear or cloudy," he wrote. "Even though they are protected they must feel that they are outdoors, because one of the court's chief functions is to provide psychological and visual contrast and relief from indoor shops" ("Winter or Summer," 127). Indeed, the Daytons planned to make the most of the festive public-square character of the court. It functioned as the community's living room, and Gruen was happy to cite the many public events soon crowding the Southdale calender. A stage could be equipped for fashion shows, concerts, and lectures, and there was sufficient space to house exhibits from paintings to new cars. Besides the continuous small exhibitions and performances, 5,000 people came to see the popular television quiz show "Truth or Consequences," which was broadcast nationally; the most popular event, though, was the annual Southdale Charity Ball, usually attended by 2,000 people. On Sundays, even when the stores were closed, people would drive to Southdale just to stroll around the court and window-shop on the upper terraces. Donald C. Dayton, president of the Dayton Co., believed such civic functions were good for business and helped the shopping center become an integral part of the community.[43]

As at Northland, Gruen commissioned works of art for the public spaces. Although the $50,000 budget was considerably less than at Northland, the effect in an enclosed space was strong. The sculpture varied from the abstract and spatial with the helicoidal birdcage and Harry Bertoia's "Golden Trees," steel tree-like frames with hundreds of bronze "leaves," to the more popular and figurative with Louise Kruger's two sculpted children on stilts, Dorothy Berge's "Three Acrobats on a Uni-cycle," and the cigar-store American Indian.

44 "New Thinking on Shopping Centers," 128.
45 "A Controlled Climate for Shopping," 193.
46 Larkin, "Closed Mall Pays Off in Leases – Cherry Hill," 55.
There was at the time a basic cost consideration. Stores at Northland had entrances both to the parking area and on the courts.

At Southdale, because of the air-conditioned court, external
entrances to the parking areas would have required double doors
with heated lobby in between. See also: *Centers for the Urban
Environment*, 36.
47 Smiley, (Ed.). *Sprawl and Public Space – Redressing the Mall*, 2002.

Introverted Architecture?

In the initial design—before Graham's project was incorporated—Gruen believed that the reserved exterior of his "introverted architecture" would be mediated by "big blocks of color and inviting entrance arcades, which would hint at the uninhibited interior nature."[44] The external elevation of the Dayton's store, consisting of a giant-order entrance porch, gave the exterior of the shopping center, set amidst acres of asphalt, the character of a single building. With the enlarged horizontal scale of the revised design, the center did not read as an urban structure; it consisted of low, interlocking, shed-type volumes. There were neither the see-through arcades, which were features at both Shoppers World and Mondawmin, James Rouse's new regional shopping center outside of Baltimore, nor the dramatic massing of the brick-faced Hudson's department store with the boiler chimney tower, which Gruen himself was using at Eastland (1957). Ironically, Gruen's open-air shopping centers, with their courts and malls, had a greater spatial variety. At Northland, Gruen had retained the double access to stores from his earlier unbuilt projects, but Southdale would be different, with store entrances opening to the inner court and lanes only.

In describing his inspiration for Southdale, Gruen often referred to the ambience of the Milan Galleria, but this reference falls flat, as that quintessentially urban structure stands several stories tall and has a mixed program of shops on the ground floor and offices and apartments above. At Southdale, as the *Architectural Record* gingerly put it, "something was missing that might have formally expressed the importance and exuberance of the center."[45] Against this charge of blandness, Gruen first argued that in earlier centers—perhaps referring to Milliron's—stores had to advertise themselves to attract drivers and create maximum visual effect on the highway. In contrast, Gruen said his enclosed shopping centers were examples of "introverted architecture." In deference to nearby residential areas, shopping-center exteriors should be simple and reserved—introversion and enclosure were essential for suburban commercial spaces to overcome the "vulgarity" of sprawling highway strips.[46] At the time, this kind of "introverted architecture" made any visual connection with the surrounding sites or communities difficult, if not impossible. Over the long term, Gruen's argument betrayed its inherent contradiction. Even the Randhurst shopping center outside Chicago, which had a three-story "pavilion" —a vertical food court—under a domed atrium, was, because of the enormous scale, merely a "pancake" building. To a certain extent, the indoor shopping centers reduced Gruen's role to that of a traffic engineer and interior designer. From a traditional urban point of view, the bland elevations were practicably mute; in starkest contrast to his urban shops, they offered nothing to the sidewalks and parking areas. In the most extreme sense his indoor shopping centers perfected the collapse between private shop and public street that had engaged Gruen from the start: at Milliron's he brought the car within the building, so to speak, by placing parking on the roof; now, with his enclosed shopping center he brought the entire street into the building—at the expense of the true public "streetscape" outside the structure. Today, in an effort to present a more lively character, the external elevations of many regional shopping centers are being opened up showing store-fronts and signage to the parking fields.[47]

Indeed, traffic-flow requirements further worked against any visual connection with the surrounding site. As at Northland, the Daytons constructed their own one-way peripheral belt road with 22 entrance and exit points to the nearby main roads, an investment in infrastructure of $1 million that, 20 years later, was described as one of the best access and exit systems in the country.[48] After clarity of access, the next most important goal was to separate the three types of traffic and confine each to its own area: service traffic to the basement or service courts; buses and taxis to their own stations; and private autos to the parking areas. To avoid inequality between the two main shopping levels, Gruen ramped adjoining parking quadrants alternatively to give access to the upper and lower shopping floors. The break with their surroundings, due to the vast parking fields and ring roads, was the price Gruen's shopping centers would pay for the creation of contained, focused pedestrian enclaves. As for the coordinated design of the surrounding community, because of cash flow problems, the Daytons began selling off surrounding land to other developers for single-family homes.

Shortly after Southdale's opening, Bruce Dayton brought Frank Lloyd Wright to Southdale. Wright called the place "a barracks." "What is this?" he said. "A railroad station or a bus station? . . . . The very appearance of the place repels me."[49] Unfortunately, his opinion of Minneapolis was no better; he recommended that the city itself be abandoned and started over. Despite his criticism, Wright seems at any rate to have understood that he was looking at a public building, where people and their activities were the central focus—and this of course had been Gruen's intention. It was hardly "designer architecture" and could not be seen in such a context. Although Southdale would never be integrated into a planned community, it would function as the shopping magnet in a commercial district that would serve its surrounding neighborhoods, and in this it was hugely successful. The addition of Donaldson's established the archetypal "dumbbell plan" shopping center—two department-store anchors with tenant-store blocks between, flanking the semi-public space of the mall. Southdale became the model for many subsequent Gruen shopping centers. Although he had demonstrated that the new model of an enclosed shopping center could succeed, it was a few years before Gruen would follow with Cherry Hill, NJ (1961), Randhurst, Mt. Prospect, IL (1962), Topanga Canyon, Los Angeles (1964), Plymouth Meeting, PA (1966), and South Coast Plaza, Orange County, CA (1967).

48 Crear, "Southdale 1951-71, 1971. LoCVGP.
49 "Minneapolis Crucified by Architect," *Rapid City Journal*. LoCVGP, OV 04.
50 Olsen, Better Places, Better Lives: 53. In addition, see: James W. Rouse: A Man of Vision, (obituaries and commemorative articles) The Enterprise Foundation; and, Ditch, S. and Rouse, P. (Eds.), "A Larger Vision," James Rouse and the American City . For further reference to Rouse's role at Cherry Hill, see Larkin, "Closed Mall Pay Off in Lease," 51.

The success of Southdale sparked an explosion of shopping centers across the suburban landscape, which in turn helped kill the inner cities. A second casualty was Gruen's original vision of the role the architect-planner should play in shopping center development. The final cut was that cynical developers, in pursuit of maximum profit, would reduce social and cultural functions and "frills" such as landscaping and sculpture to produce a purely commercial space. Gruen's Cherry Hill regional shopping center mirrored the beginning of this conflict, which would eventually prompt him to denounce the shopping mall altogether.

Constructed for the Philadelphia department store Strawbridge and Clothier in an underdeveloped farming community in Delaware Township, New Jersey, about seven miles east of Philadelphia, the Cherry Hill shopping center was conceived not only to respond to a market, but to react to the fact that the area was, as *Greater Philadelphia* magazine put it, "suburbia in search of a downtown," ("Cherry Hill," 29). Unlike in previous projects, though, here Gruen did not work from the outset with a merchant-owner but was brought in later by the developer: James W. Rouse. Gruen's vision of the architect-planner as the key figure in shopping center development, coordinating the many disciplines and responsible to both investors and the local communities, would be hard to realize. Although, in "Suburban Retail Districts," the *Architectural Forum* wrote that the architect, in synthesizing the skills of experts in a dozen fields, was the natural leader of the shopping center team (106), shopping-center development practice was changing quickly, and a new generation of developers would seize the chance that it presented.

In 1954, James Rouse, who had been active in mortgage banking and shopping-center financing, claimed that the regional shopping center required at least four different professions: the architect, the mortgage banker (lender), the builder, and the real-estate broker. Of all the players, the mortgage lender stayed with the project the longest and thus understood the work of the others the best. It was natural for Rouse to move from mortgage banking to developer.[50] In 1956 he formed a development company CRD (Community Research and Development). Having his own research, planning, merchandising, financing, construction, and management facilities, Rouse did not have to go outside his own shop at crucial moments in the center's development and construction cycle. Rouse, who was to become one of the most visionary and controversial developers in the country, always worked with architects, yet they were consultants serving his vision. Still, the coming together of Gruen and Rouse was fortuitous: both men believed passionately in the importance of the social and cultural role of the shopping center as the basis for its financial success. And their collaboration at Cherry Hill was enormously successful.

An L-configured center, designed for expansion along both linear axes, Cherry Hill was one of the first enclosed centers on the East Coast and also featured a principal internal space, the soaring "Cherry Court." It opened in 1961 to a crowd of nearly 100,000 people, who were delighted by tropical plants, a fountain, a Japanese garden complete with arching bridge and running water, and a fanciful wood gazebo where one could sit and relax. That same year, Delaware Township, after a long process of public debate, officially changed its name to Cherry Hill. The mall thus formed not only the symbol but the identity of its community.

Although Rouse was an ideal partner, and his (and Gruen's) standards had led to a regional shopping center of high quality, their collaboration was nevertheless the first sign of a debilitating trend. As Gruen himself had admitted, the chance to create something new at Northland and Southdale had much to do with the vision of his clients, third-generation department-store families who wished to maintain their reputation in their own city and metropolitan area. When, because of the innovative nature of their plans, they failed to win outside investors, they stood behind their projects—and architect—themselves. But after Southdale established the importance and success of the regional shopping center, two things happened: first, the development community, particularly the Urban Land Institute, began to codify the complex processes and web of relationships necessary to create a successful project; and then developers themselves, with their institutional investors, took over the primary role in shopping-center development.[51] As the formulas became standardized, developers began to dictate to their architects; an individual project would only be as good as the developer and the developer's support for his architect. With some exceptions, developers reduced the investment in public spaces, community services, landscape, and art and made the regional shopping center more and more what Alfred Taubman, the renowned shopping-center developer from Detroit, had called it: "a machine for selling, not an architectural problem."[52]

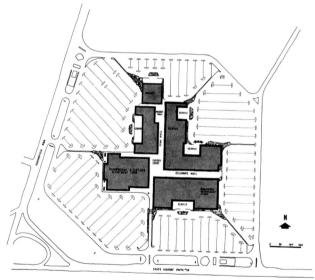

N

51 Gruen described this development in, "The Sad Story of Shopping Centers," 350-3. Gruen's idea that architects "lost-or lost control over-the shopping center," is only partly true; the early 1970s saw many innovative projects, some of which are described in Logan, Shopping Centers, 96-103. From the beginning there were articles followed by books on what the shopping center was and how to make one. Within this literature Gruen and Larry Smith were well featured. One of the first survey articles devoted to the new building type was Baker and Funaro's "Shopping Centers" published in *Architectural Record* in 1949; enlarged into the first full-length book of the same name in 1951. The following year, Gruen and Smith produced their 42 page article "Shopping Centers - The New Building Type," in *Progressive Architecture*. By the time of Gruen and Smith's landmark book Shopping Towns U.S.A. (1960), the Urban Land Institute had begun to put out regular bulletins defining good shopping center development practice. See, for example, McKeever, J. Ross, *Shopping Centers: Principles and Policies*, 1953.

52 Alfred Taubman. Qtd. Breckenfield, "Downtown Has Fled To The Suburbs," 85.

Cherry Hill shopping center, Delaware Township (later Cherry Hill), NJ (1959-61). Cherry Court. James Rouse replaced Gruen's landscape and furnishings with "Asian" themed gazebos and bridges and "tropical" planting arrangement.
Site plan. Gone are the expensive truck tunnel and basement service that enabled separation of service and shoppers traffic. Delivery and service courts are at ground level behind planted screens.

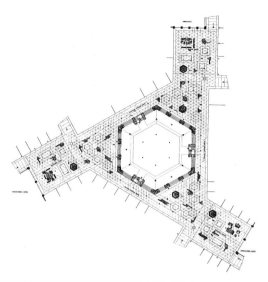

"Big pinwheel on the prairie." Mt. Prospect, IL, (1962). The first three-department store shopping center enabled Gruen to use a triangular planning geometry for great retailing efficiency. Under the 160 ft. diameter dome, the "pavilion," a raised structure with restaurants, cafes, and space for public events dominated the interior landscape. Despite the spacious and dramatic interior, Randhurst's exterior is a bland, shapeless structure.

53 "The Future Of The American Out-Of-Town Shopping Center," *Ekistics*: 96-105. The four regional shopping centers were: Shoppers World, Framingham (1952); Old Orchard, Chicago (1956); Lennox Square, Atlanta (1959); and, Cherry Hill (1961). See also in the same issue: Rouse, "The Regional Shopping Center: Its Role in the Community It Serves," 96; Montgomery, R., Summary, 100; and Comments, 103. Participants in the Panel were: James W. Rouse, President, Community Research and Development, Inc.; Roger Montgomery (Chief Urban Designer, Urban Renewal Administration); Richard Stein, New York; William Doebele and Martin Meyerson, both of Harvard University.

The Future of the Out-of-Town Shopping Center

At a 1963 conference on "The Future of the Out-of-Town Shopping Center" at the Harvard Graduate School of Design, development teams of four large regional shopping centers engaged in panel discussions with politicians, economists, and members of the design professions. One point on which both sides agreed was that local governments should take more control of the location of regional shopping centers. Representing Cherry Hill, Rouse partly echoed Gruen's ideas when he claimed that Cherry Hill was a "shopping town" and would function as a regional urban core, a claim that panelists criticized as being fraught with contradictions and simply not true. In summary, Roger Montgomery, Chief Urban Designer for the Urban Renewal Administration, argued that merchants were interested in their businesses, not in town planning; that shopping centers stimulated commercial sprawl, which was creating havoc with local zoning control; that inter-city settlement patterns should be the subject of regional planning and not marketplace roulette; and, finally, that "Cherry Hill supporters should not mistake cub scout dens, fashion shows and barber shop quartets for urban culture." [53] The discussion reflected the growing perception in development, planning, and government circles that the proliferation of shopping centers was creating abnormal pressure upon the city regions. Victor Gruen's idea of the architect-planner as the creator of new social, cultural, and commercial crystallization points in the suburbs was superceded by developers, who later, in extreme cases, would build shopping centers for an immature market just to preempt the competition.

Maintaining a regional shopping center's position in its marketplace was difficult enough, without having to contend with social, cultural, and demographic change. In comparison with Southdale, the subsequent history of the Cherry Hill Mall reflects more faithfully the regional shopping center's vulnerability to the vicissitudes of such changes, the demands of its investors, and the lack of regional planning. Its "odyssey," as Stefanie Dyer wrote, "from celebrated new downtown (sic) to aging suburban monolith in a span of ten years illustrated just how difficult the process of anchoring social value in the landscape of consumption became by the 1970s."[54] The claim, by boosters such as Gruen and Rouse, that regional shopping centers were both commercial and communal centers clearly had its limitations. Cherry Hill was prominent in the 1970s because it had become not only a place where teenagers were dealing drugs, but also an informal forum for political dissent. These different and competing uses of Cherry Hill's public space brought to national attention what has since become a well-known paradox of the regional shopping center: its "public" spaces were under single (private) ownership. As virtually the only public space in the suburban community, malls were the obvious place for political representation, and attempts by the shopping center's management to restrict political and social events, particularly demonstrations and leafleting, were overturned in 1994, when the New Jersey Supreme Court ruled in favor of a coalition of Gulf War protesters, setting a precedent for guaranteeing citizens greater free speech protections within malls. The conflict between who owned and those who could use the "public space" in shopping malls had indeed been in and out of the courts at all levels, including the U.S. Supreme Court, since the 1960s. In successive judgements, the space of the shopping center was described as the "functional equivalent of a sidewalk in a public business district," and the shopping center itself was likened to a "company town" and a "town center." Lizabeth Cohen cited Chief Justice Robert N. Wilentz of the New Jersey Supreme Court, in his decision in favor of the Gulf War protestors:

The economic lifeblood once found downtown has moved to suburban shopping centers, which have substantially displaced the downtown business districts as the centers of commercial and social activity . . . . Found at these malls are most of the uses and activities citizens engage in outside their homes . . . . This is the new, the improved, the more attractive downtown business district–the new community–and no use is more closely associated with the old downtown than leafleting. Defendants have taken that old downtown away from its former home and moved all of it, except free speech, to the suburbs. ("From Town Center to Shopping Center,"1070)

54 Dyer, "Markets in the Meadows." See especially, Chapter 5, "Creating a New 'Downtown' at Cherry Hill Mall," 329.
55 One of the first articles was Robert Goodman's "Dead Malls," in *Metropolis*, Nov. 1993. In 2000, the National Endowment for the Arts, together with the Woodrow Wilson School of Government at Princeton University, organized a conference where different strategies for the makeover of troubled or dead malls were presented; see Smiley, *Sprawl and Public Space*. Also: Herman, "Mall - Requiem for a Type (Obituary)," in Chung et al (Eds.): 464-475.
56 The making of Hamilton's collage, "Just what is it that makes today's homes so different, so appealing?," is described in Kirkpatrick, "The Artists of the Independent Group: Backgrounds and Continuities," 210.

The claims of Gruen, Rouse, Larry Smith, and other early mall boosters were, at least by this court, affirmed. In the 1970s, the commercial viability of Cherry Hill Mall faced a new threat, this time from a clash between community and real-estate interests. The shopping center was threatened by a newer mall just a few miles away, and Rouse had great trouble persuading Strawbridge's to accept another store at Cherry Hill in order to remain competitive. Yet the surrounding neighborhoods wanted no new development and tried to block the shopping center from adding new office, further retail, and other functions. While Cherry Hill remains in business today, this duplication of shopping centers in the same market area was a sign of the predatory nature of retail development and in many other places would lead to "dead Malls," which by the 1990s littered the American landscape.[55]

A Laboratory of Consumption Culture

The regional shopping center easily became the instrument that both nurtured and accelerated the postwar "culture of consumption." The lanes and plazas, but especially the internal courts, joined public or semi-public space with consumer items and the activity of shopping, creating a powerful ambience. Richard Hamilton's painting "Just what is it that makes today's homes so different, so appealing?" depicting a domestic interior that is an assemblage of consumer products, was produced in 1956, the same year Gruen's Southdale opened. Hamilton's collage is a critical prefiguration of a landscape and cultural milieu that continues to be dominated by new forms of consumption. In his picture, the "brands" of the objects create "identity"; if the products and advertisements were stripped from the picture, the two figures would be naked, and the space empty.[56] For Gruen, the shopping mall's internal court represented a new type of public space: "the community's living room." Yet for his clients, merchandisers, and the first generation of consumers, it became a select stage for collective display and individual representation of new consumer products and styles. Of course, the best city streets had always been that–but much more–they were part of the unlimited public space of the city. To adapt a concept from the mythology of late 1920s Soviet revolutionary culture, architects were called upon to provide "social condensers" out of which the new Soviet man would emerge. In the U.S. from the 1950s, especially once the "public" spaces were enclosed, the regional shopping center became a cultural condenser of its own–a laboratory of retail consumption that more and more joined consumption with entertainment.

The optimistic premise of Gruen's early regional shopping centers had been that, in the automobile age, the community center did not need to be a residential cluster but might well be a shopping cluster, and that with a balance of mixed uses, the attractive power of the traditional urban center could—after a limited fashion—be created in the new, dispersed suburban landscape. The ideal person to create this new urban-suburban hybrid and manage its production, orchestrating the many different interest groups, was the architect-planner. The best examples of regional shopping centers were pioneer achievements not only from the standpoint of planning but also for their design quality at every level from the largest structures to the signs, lighting, landscaping, and, especially in Gruen's early centers, the works of art, for which he had fought particularly hard. To critics such as Jane Jacobs and Grady Clay, Gruen's first full-fledged regional shopping center, Northland, indeed seemed to demonstrate a new spatial strategy that could mediate the interests of private business with the collective venture of making a new kind of public space.

In the dense mixed-use environment of the historic core of Vienna that had modeled so much of Gruen's thinking, commerce, culture, and all other human activities were woven together. As architects lost their leading role in shopping-center development, however, Gruen believed that subsequent projects were stripped of their social and cultural functions, transformed into a formula by developers and their institutional investors, and then replicated countless times across the American landscape. Far from identifying and serving the needs of an existing community, developers knew that people would flock to the giant shopping center, whether it had social and cultural facilities or not, and no matter what the distance to existing communities.[57]

By the late 1960s, to the embarrassment of his partners and clients, Gruen rejected paternity of the shopping mall. A decade later, in an article in the *Los Angeles Times*, he said, "I refuse to pay alimony for those bastard developments."[58]

An architectural ambience. Mother and child at Eastland, Detroit 1957.

Despite Gruen's protestations, though, he could hardly claim innocence; in 1960, together with Larry Smith, he had published *Shopping Towns U.S.A.*, which for a time was the "Bible" for shopping-center developers. While Gruen had concentrated on the architectural and planning aspects, Smith, the brilliant real-estate economist, laid out the parameters for an efficient income-producing operation. Furthermore, the Gruen shopping centers, after the typological and programmatic experimentation of the early projects, began to repeat themselves; even the shopping centers that VGA produced, after the triangular layout of Randhurst (1962), became formulaic. Gruen himself admitted some of his principal failures, "we have not succeeded in making the walk from the parked vehicle to the building cluster . . . anything better than sheer drudgery. Worse, on ground parking creates an environment which repels good residential–and other–development in the area" (*Centers for the Urban Environment,* 39, 91-2).

Having returned to Vienna in the late 1960s, Gruen wanted to prevent these practices from wreaking the same havoc on the European city, which could hardly bear the land wastage associated with the American regional shopping-center model. Gruen's success as a shopping-center planner, however, haunted him in Europe as well. He sought unsuccessfully to create a European shopping-center model with a more varied functional mix and more positively integrated into its context. In 1969, he was asked to design a large regional shopping center, the Shopping City Sued, just beyond Vienna's southern boundary near Voesendorf. Gruen had learned from his experience in the U.S. that regional planning had to carefully coordinate the commercial renewal of a downtown with developments on the periphery; otherwise either or both would be unsuccessful. Now, having warned the city about the misapplication of the new American building type, he turned down the Shopping City Sued commission, claiming that its influence would extend beyond local shopping areas even to the urban core–at the time, he was working on a planning study for the historic center. In articles and public speaking engagements, Gruen attempted to throw doubt on whether the Shopping Center Sued would survive economically, but he knew perfectly well that, given Vienna's suburban expansion, the metropolitan area's first regional shopping center would prove successful.

In 1978, Gruen was invited to speak to developers and investors at the Third Annual European Conference of the International Council of Shopping Centers in London on the topic "The Future of Shopping Centers." Gruen, who had doubtless been introduced as one of the "pioneers," proceeded to state that the shopping center in its conventional meaning had no future at all. He argued that the legitimate answers to these questions had existed more than 20 years earlier, but that both questions and answers had been "washed away in the deluge of mostly indiscriminate shopping center development in North America" that now spread to the rest of the world ("Shopping Centers, the why...," 8-9). He could even, to his dismay, now refer to the giant American-style shopping center that stood half a kilometer outside the southern city boundary of Vienna, and the deleterious effects this development had on not only the historic core but all of the other 23 districts.[59]

57 Peirce, "The Shopping Center and One Man's Shame." This a shortened version of: Gruen, "Shopping Centers, Why, Where, How?," *Zentrum fuer Umweltplanung.*
58 Gruen, "The Sad Story of Shopping Centers," 351.

By 1978, Gruen had been out of the U.S. for 10 years. Despite his personal spin on the history of the shopping center, other architects were nevertheless creating new images and opportunities. Three years after Cherry Hill, the architectural firm of Wurster, Bernardi and Emmons, together with Lawrence Halprin & Associates, transformed a disused chocolate factory in San Francisco into Ghirardelli Square, a tourist destination with a variety of shops and restaurants, and an early conversion of inner-city industrial buildings by adaptive reuse. A major breakthrough came from James Rouse, who, more than anyone else, was to take up where Gruen had left off, transforming the urban shopping center into the festival marketplace, a hybrid that relied on tourism, small stallholders, food courts, and entertainment–a retail planning strategy that would become a new starting point for reviving downtowns.

Shopping Towns USA

The Planning of Shopping Centers

Reinhold
Progressive Architecture Library

by Victor Gruen
and Larry Smith

59 Georg Frankl, author interview, Vienna, 1998. Frankl left Victor Gruen International to build the Shopping Center Sued.

60 For example: "New Thinking on Shopping Centers," *Architectural Forum*, 122; and later, "Downtown Needs a Lesson from the Suburbs," *Business Week*, 47.

A Lesson for Downtown

The large new suburban market had come to life through government interventions—the FHA and the Interstate Highway System—and the rise of the industrialized merchant builder. Together these provided the means and the image—the suburban house on its lot—to satisfy both the American myth of the homestead and the desire to escape the city's "problems," a codeword for poverty, crime, and racial friction. The regional shopping center, in turn, arose to meet this market's needs. Having mastered retail planning at smaller scale in the late 1940s, and having, from the outset, invested retail architecture with a specifically urban function, Gruen had believed in the varied roles the regional shopping center should play: as retail center, regional subcenter, community-planning instrument, and even civil-defense station.

The commercial success of his early shopping centers led to Gruen being called upon by business, civic, and academic communities to testify about the new building type. Yet even before Northland opened, the conclusion to many of his lectures turned not on the shopping center as a suburban phenomenon but rather as an "experiment" with significance for the city.[60] The importance of the shopping center for the suburbs was clear, but what was its significance for the downtown? In the December 1953 *Women's Wear Daily*, Gruen wrote, "I am convinced that many of the lessons learned in the planning of large shopping centers for the suburbs can be successfully applied to our downtown urban shopping centers." But the lesson for downtown was that people wanted a well-managed, up-to-date shopping experience that was spacious, safe, accessible by car or public transit, and nearby other popular functions. Gruen's contribution to the development of the regional shopping center belongs to the first generation of both suburban and urban centers, yet he could never have imagined the enormous impact the shopping center would have on his next goals: reviving the dilapidated centers of America's cities.

"The motor has killed the great city. The motor must save the great city." Le Corbusier[1] *The American City . . . . one can't get into it; one can't get around in it; once in it, one can't park; one can't get out of it . . . . (The Heart of Our Cities, p. 12)*

Despite the drama and innovation of the shopping centers, for Gruen they were merely the means to get at what he considered the most serious problem of the day: the deterioration of American downtowns, which he ascribed, above all, to their inability to deal with the automobile and lack of coherent planning. The automobile's power to destroy the quality of city streets and public places had long enraged him; indeed the overwhelming presence of automobiles and trucks in the downtowns had already been an issue in the 1920s. As early as 1922 even Henry Ford suspected that the car spelt the death of downtown[2]; and in 1925 Le Corbusier could write that "to leave your house meant that once you had crossed the threshold you were a possible sacrifice to death in the shape of innumerable motors" (*The City of Tomorrow*, xxiii). By 1927, almost 26 million cars and trucks were on America's roads. (The increasing use of trucks to distribute the output of mass production was just as significant as the presence of cars.) The city street, at one time the everyday public environment for pedestrians and the principal space for understanding the urban landscape for those in private or public conveyances, became a venue for congestion and carnage–32,500 deaths in 1930 alone.[3] Clay McShane describes what the rule of cars meant for public space in America:

[I]n their headlong search for modernity through mobility, American urbanites made a decision to destroy the living environments of nineteenth-century neighborhoods by converting their gathering places into traffic jams, their playgrounds into motorways, and their shopping places into elongated parking lots. These paving decisions effectively made obsolete many of America's older neighborhoods.[4]

Without planning, and with accelerating patterns of consumption and mobility in the postwar years, the problem was only intensifying. Whether and how the city would survive universal car ownership and the demand for convenient mobility and access was the question that Gruen set himself. Something had to give: automobile use or the form and function of the city. For Gruen it was above all an issue of planning, and the principal planning question was simply, how much space to give the car in the city?

Through success with the regional shopping center, VGA had by 1956 become a large corporate office with a network of expertise, and Gruen would now turn this elaborate instrument to downtown development and urban renewal projects. Although the common belief is that the suburban shopping center killed downtown, in fact it was in his first shopping centers that Gruen found some of the most effective solutions for his urban projects. The fundamental design components that he would, in his many projects from 1956 to 1968, transfer from the shopping center to downtown involved two primary pairs of relationships: buildings and spaces, and streets and traffic. First, buildings grouped in a cluster would yield new public spaces. Second, public, private, and service traffic would be separated, and streets would be qualified by use. Central to all his downtown projects were the qualification of streets and the management of traffic: one of Gruen's great contributions to the American cityscape was his insistence that these infrastructural matters, normally the province of engineers, should be no less important to the architect-planner than the design of buildings–to say nothing of the paramount importance of public spaces.

Protecting Shopping from the Automobile

The conflict between increasing automobile traffic and existing patterns of buildings and spaces in American towns and cities had reached such a point even before U.S. engagement in WWII that various solutions had already been proposed. Although closing a city street to allow safe and leisurely shopping free of moving vehicles was considered radical, the concept developed parallel to the shopping center and drew ideas from many of the same projects. Even before the end of the war, some European cities had been planning to modernize their centers in this way. When, for instance, the center of Coventry was destroyed by the *Luftwaffe* in 1940, the city immediately planned a new central area with a pedestrian shopping center, residences, and a ring boulevard to distribute incoming traffic.[5]

How likewise to transform the American "Main Street" from a thoroughfare to a pedestrian mall was the starting point for *Architectural Forum's* "194X" issue of May 1943–the same issue in which Gruen and Krummeck defined a postwar model of a neighborhood shopping center. The *Forum* editors proposed that the Main Street of a typical small city (using the example of Syracuse, N.Y., with a population of 70,000), be converted to a pedestrian area. The mandate for so pronounced a change, the editors asserted, stemmed from the increasing use of cars, which had made shopping "a hazardous and nerve-racking enterprise for the pedestrian (70-1)." Even by 1943, traffic congestion was identified as a primary factor driving customers–followed by merchants–from established business districts, and the restructuring of the city center to accommodate the automobile and the pedestrian shopper was emerging as a significant question for planning. The principal elements of the *Architectural Forum* proposal were the pedestrianization of 11 blocks of Syracuse's main shopping street, Erie Boulevard; construction of a two-way perimeter road around the center, from existing streets; and provision of plenty of

1 Le Corbusier, *The City of Tomorrow*, 277, n. 1.
2 "Henry Ford's Page," *Dearborn Independent*. Qtd. Gallion and Eisner, 102. "Plainly, so it seems to some of us, that the ultimate solution will be the abolition of the City, its abandonment as a blunder . . . . We shall solve the City problem by leaving the City."
3 Scott, *American City Planning Since 1890*, 361. As Kenneth Jackson pointed out in *Crabgrass Frontier*, in 1925 Ford was turning out nine thousand cars per day; by 1927, there were almost sixteen million "Tin Lizzies," and total automobile registrations in the U.S. had reached twenty-six million, one motor vehicle for every five people in the country (168).
4 McShane, "Transforming the Use of Urban Space." Qtd. Jackson, *Crabgrass Frontier*, 168. The steady growth of the automobile is well described in Chapter 9, "The New Age of Automobility," 157-171.

5 Buchanen, *Traffic and Towns*, 171. Buchanen described the successive plans for rebuilding the center of Coventry, which were published as early as 1941. "When, in the early planning, the magnitude of the potential growth of motor traffic was realized, the pedestrian area was enlarged with additional parking on the rooftops of buildings. Inside the center surrounding beltway, which has a diameter of less than a mile, a bus loop road (diameter half-a-mile) serves the buildings and pedestrian areas." Buchanan concluded however that the central area was too large for exclusively pedestrian traffic and that, given the chance to start again, planners and designers should permit a higher level of motor car usage. (171). For Coventry, see also *Architect and Building News*, March 21, 1941; and Sert et al, *The Heart of the City*, 134-5.

off-street parking, where possible, adjoining the perimeter streets. These logical measures would be adapted by Gruen in his own projects a decade later. Around the same time, Ketchum, Giná and Sharp produced a plan for Rye, N.Y., which proposed closing the main street and converting it to a grass-covered mall, a linear "New England village green," which was a strategy similar to what they would soon propose in their first shopping-center projects. They would retrofit storefronts with arcades to frame and protect shoppers from the weather, and join streets immediately around Main Street to form a perimeter route giving access to parking areas behind the stores. In an extension of his argument, Morris Ketchum proposed that the central business district of Rye be understood as a single retail cell—or shopping unit—which could be part of a major city. In *Shops and Stores*, he wrote, "By multiplying such cells in size and number, and locating them between larger areas of up-to-date housing, adding parks and through-highways, one would get a glimpse of what might be the future pattern of American cities." Ketchum's speculation would be taken up some years later in Gruen's project for the Cellular Metropolis of Tomorrow. Although the plan for Rye, published in the August 1946 *Architectural Forum*, was rejected by the citizens and never carried out, it would prove influential (281).

A Nation on Wheels

During WWII, Detroit's automobile factories were devoted to producing military vehicles, but in the 1950s, automobile production regained momentum, and the conflict between the car and the city became a new focus of debate in the city-planning community. Catherine Bauer, who in 1934 had called automobiles one of the dominating features of American life, by 1956 wrote,

Our old way of figuring density by so many persons per square mile has now become irrelevant. The crucial figure for U.S. planning is now density of cars . . . . Since 1946 we have added 24 million humans and 20 million automobile registrations. By 1976 we should have more than 56 million more people and conservatively figured, 50 million more passenger cars in use. Traffic and all it means is the key factor in urban renewal . . . .[6]

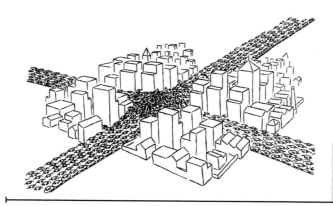

Suburban drivers converge on the downtown. *The Heart of Our Cities*, 100.

---

6 Bauer, "First job, control new-city sprawl," 103. 22 years before, Bauer had written with Clarence Stein, "The automobile has been one of the dominating features of American life for more than twenty years." Stein and Bauer, "Store Buildings and Neighborhood Shopping Centers," 185.

"The crucial figure for U.S. planning is density of cars."
Architectural Forum's forecast that by 1976 there would be 100 million autos.

great land-eater, the auto, faces a
future: by the start of 1976, US pas-
cars may reach the 100 million
double their number today. This
a FORUM projection of current data,
the average household will have
again as many cars as it has now.

76 annual auto passenger miles will likely be 1 trillion (1,000,000,000,000)

Sources: US Census Bureau
Automobile Mfgrs. Assoc.
ARCHITECTURAL FORUM estimates

The trouble was that American downtowns had been built before the automobile, and there had been little building and investment in most American cities between the Depression and the end of WWII. The strongest interest for rebuilding downtown came from business and merchant associations, who were increasingly concerned about the disappearance of their market. As with the Housing Act of 1934 and Veteran's Administration Act of 1944, which were so pivotal in building out the suburbs, a group of acts from 1949 would have great impact upon the cities: the Housing Act of 1949 and its amended versions in 1954 and 1961, and the Highway Act of 1956. I will discuss these later. The urban projects in Part 3 are variously described. I have used "revitalization," a word often used in the 1950s, as a general term. "Downtown redevelopment" designates projects that were predominantly private, although they may also have drawn on public funding. "Urban renewal" projects were originally launched by the federal government to address the problems and costs of producing affordable housing in inner city neighborhoods. As I will explain later, with successive revisions of the Housing Act, the scope of urban renewal was extended to other forms of development.

To revitalize the downtowns, and especially the shopping area, Gruen believed two conditions needed to be addressed: the physical deterioration of the downtowns themselves and the intensifying traffic. Any concept of revitalization, however, must start with the separation of different kinds of traffic to restore the public space of the street. Yet the idea that cars should be banned from city centers was always a shock to downtown merchants, who wanted customers to drive up to the entrance doors. In his speeches to business and trade organizations, Gruen used his trademark ironic storytelling to make his point:

[At first] . . . . a romance between the merchant and the automobile developed . . . . [but then] the retailer realized his affections had been misdirected . . . . the retailer's true love belongs not really to the automobile but to the female customer sitting in it. No car–not even the most elegant Cadillac–has ever bought a dollar's worth of merchandise.[7]

What the regional shopping center clearly demonstrated proved difficult for downtown department-store owners to accept and impossible for private drivers to believe–that automobiles took up an enormous amount of space: 200 square feet at rest, 600 square feet at 30 miles an hour, 1200 at 60 miles an hour, etc. (*Heart of Our Cities*, 239). These figures, set against the actual numbers of automobiles coming into cities, were the basis for numerous cartoons showing cities turned into parking lots, highways running through cathedrals, and so on.

Although extremely critical of its misuse, Gruen accepted that the automobile was here to stay and would flourish; after all, as a resident of Los Angeles in the 1950s, he used his car as much as anyone. The goal was not to fight the car but to adapt cities to the automobile age without compromising the qualities of urban culture. The core area of American cities could never be renewed without finding the right balance between access for cars and trucks, adequate parking, and generous public space. This meant making profound infrastructure changes that would help the automobile achieve the mobility for which it was designed.

The Street: New Form, New Program

Changes to infrastructure and automobile use needed to resolve two glaring problems. First, the city street was programmatically overloaded: it was both the main public space of the city and the venue for all forms of traffic. What was through-traffic doing on local streets? Why should public streets be used as service alleys and public sidewalks as loading platforms? Why were cities, in an effort to maintain indispensable traffic flows, forced to build new through-freeways at tremendous cost, with the consequence—to be tragically demonstrated in the Bronx in New York, or the center of Boston—of splitting up their urban communities? The street wasn't "dead" as prewar modernists had imagined; in the postwar city, it would have to be requalified: typologically, programmatically, and formally. This would require a "use classification" for streets, which would allow specific spaces, equipment, and ambience to develop according to the nature of traffic.

The second problem was the increasing misuse of the automobile for mass transportation, or as Gruen would describe it, a "mass of individuals" each in his or her own car, which was the obvious reaction by consumers to the decreasing standard of public transport. Any new urban-planning philosophy would have to realize that movement to and from core areas must rely to a large degree on public transportation. In a jibe at technology, Gruen asked why it was that fantastic progress was being made in all technological fields but public transportation.[8]

To maintain its role as the functional and symbolic center of the city and its metropolitan area, the American downtown therefore faced a simple dilemma. On one hand there was a growing demand for mobility and access for vehicles, so realistic space must be made for traffic and parking; on the other hand, cities had to be made safe and attractive for pedestrians, so more public space must be made. To solve this dilemma, Gruen would look to the regional shopping center. The decisive infrastructural gesture there had been to create specific areas for private, public, and service vehicles. This had yielded the public spaces, equipped with their own architecture, landscaping, and art. These were the two planning principles that, for the shopping center, could support different configurations of department store(s) and store buildings. For Gruen, they were not merely devices that would be adapted for downtown, but the starting point for all his urban and planning design.

7 Gruen, "Retailing and the Automobile," *Architectural Record*, 199. This article was adapted from Gruen and Smith's recently published Shopping Towns U.S.A., and discusses automobile traffic with respect to shopping in suburban and urban centers. In the meantime, Gruen and his former client, Jack Strauss, Chairman of Macy's, were carrying on their own debate about traffic in Manhattan in the daily papers, each accusing the other of being the "gravedigger of the city." They were able to put their case to the public in a half-hour ABC News feature on the paralyzing effect of New York traffic in 1962, "Do Not Enter," Bell & Howell Close Up, directed by Nicholas Webster.

8 Gruen's harangue against the use of automobiles as "mass transportation," and the lack of new forms of public transit, see, for example, Gruen, "The Present Pattern," 126, 128; and "Cities in Trouble-What Can Be Done," (Interview with Victor Gruen) *U.S. News and World Report*: 86-90. "It's absolutely unbelievable that, in an age in which we have invented jet planes and rockets, we should not have one new idea about rapid transportation. There is no doubt that we can build a rapid-transit system that is faster, more convenient, and quieter—one that would persuade even the most enthusiastic auto driver to prefer rapid transportation." See also *Heart of Our Cities*, 239.

The Heart of the City: Modern Architecture Discovers the Center

Gruen was hardly alone in his ideas about revitalizing downtown by creating attractive shopping areas and separating foot and car traffic. In 1952, *The Heart of the City: towards the humanization of urban life* was published, edited by Jaqueline Tyrwhitt, an English planner and member of MARS (Modern Architectural Research Group); Josep Luis Sert, the Catalan architect, planner, and president of CIAM; and the Italian architect Ernesto Rogers. *The Heart of the City* documented the 8th CIAM conference in Hoddesdon, England.[9] Whereas the prewar meetings of CIAM, dominated by Le Corbusier, had focused on the functional planning of the city and new forms of social housing, CIAM 8 proposed projects for "recentralization": the creation of new urban cores with a mix of commercial, retail, and civic functions and separate foot and vehicular traffic. In "Summary of Needs at the Core," the editors proposed that there be only one core for each city and that the core be an "artifact"—a designed built ensemble secure from automobile traffic; cars would be parked at the periphery. Artworks and media should animate the public space itself (6, 164). The discussions at Hoddesdon about the "core" anticipated the debate that would soon follow in the U.S. about the role and form of public space in both suburb and city.

Downtown Needs a Lesson from the Suburbs

By the early 1950s, then, architects, planners, city administrations, and research institutes were forming a consensus on what a healthy American downtown might be like. As an editorial in the *Architectural Forum* put it, "Shopping centers were so far ahead that it was time for Main Street to begin borrowing back," 122. The question for established downtown shopping districts was precisely how, and not whether, to intervene in their declining business.[10] What distinguished Gruen was the position he was in, by way of his extensive work in the regional shopping center, to interpose. In a series of articles, culminating in 1954 with "Dynamic Planning for Retail Areas" published in the *Harvard Business Review*, Gruen made explicit the link between the regional shopping center and downtown. Eager to apply what he had learned in the suburbs, he upbraided frightened downtown merchants for doing nothing about their shopping areas since the war. He was sure that he had the solution: not just the organization and separation of traffic as the basis for the pedestrian shopping areas, but, more crucially, the "Gruen team's" scientific method to determine the conditions for planning a new kind of urban center, applied from its extensive experience with shopping centers. This included merchandising and feasibility studies and the analysis of the flows of people, goods, and traffic.

In "Dynamic Planning," Gruen challenged private business groups, city planners, urban-renewal officials, and city residents to take responsibility for the welfare and prosperity of the city. Criticizing both dilapidated downtowns and the suburban strip—the double blight on the American urban landscape—he argued for well-planned retail areas in the city center as well as the suburbs, and cautioned against accepting that the downtown and suburbs were in conflict with each other. "This conflict between downtown and the suburbs is a phony. The two are complementary parts of a whole." [11]

The problems of downtown were not due to suburban-urban conflict, but to a lack of creative and thorough planning. Instead of reacting defensively to problems, city officials, planners, business leaders, and retailers needed to join together to redevelop their downtown shopping districts and reimagine the downtown as the heart of their metropolitan area. The starting point, though, would be the "unscrambling" of pedestrian, automobile, and service traffic.

Gruen illustrated the article with his sketch project for the small Wisconsin city of Appleton, one of the office's first proposals for downtown redevelopment, in which he adapted the traffic organization and pedestrian spaces outlined in the "194X" issue of *Architectural Forum*, with the economic and space-planning strategies that he had developed with Larry Smith for the regional shopping center. He summarized these measures, which would become well known by the mid-1950s: 1) provide a one-way perimeter traffic artery around the business and retail district, using existing streets as far as possible; 2) clear all non-conforming and obsolete buildings within this perimeter; 3) use this cleared land to provide off-street parking for all day visitors; 4) create a series of super-blocks by closing all but two or three local streets; 5) create a landscaped pedestrian mall to provide a pleasant and safe atmosphere for shoppers; and 6) provide space within the perimeter for expansion ("*Dynamic Planning for Retail Areas*," 59). Gruen went on to cite the many cities that had started preparing renewal plans, among them Pittsburgh's "Golden Triangle," Philadelphia's Penn Center office developments, and the Back Bay project by the Boston Center Architects, which included a three-story shopping center, four office buildings, hotels, and a convention center.[12] Yet he warned his readers that these efforts often met strong resistance, especially from the large merchant homebuilders operating in the suburbs, who opposed diverting investment to the inner cities, and the National Parking Association, which supported surface parking lots in place of buildings in city centers. Against these and other negative factors, not the least of which was the weakness of statutory planning processes, Gruen repeated that only a unified effort would be effective.

9 Sert, had emigrated to the United States and would be appointed Dean of the Graduate School of Design at Harvard, where he would initiate a program of urban design.

10 In *Chain Store Age*, Gruen repeated the argument for his trade audience in "The chain's stake in planning the center," 41. "The threat to downtown is a bugaboo . . . .The question for chain store men in urban areas is not whether to establish suburban stores but how to establish them. Fortunately, retailers exist who are not only spearheading the planned shopping center in the suburbs, but who are trying to do something about downtown.´ Projects underway in some of our major cities indicate the planned shopping center need not be an exclusively suburban phenomenon."

11 Gruen, "Dynamic Planning for Retail Areas," 53-4. In the early 1950s, it was still believed that the growth of suburban centers was due to an increase in population in the areas they served and the resultant rise in purchasing power there and not to the flight of businesses to the suburbs. Higher quality shopping facilities would draw customers away from their present downtown shopping only if it was becoming more and more inconvenient. In his 1948 article

"Some Projects in the Northeast," for the *Journal of the American Institute of Planners* (JAPA), Kenneth Welch reminded his readers that the regional shopping center was not an instrument of decentralization but rather recentralization; it would be the attractive power of the centers that would ensure their commercial success and their interest. If they weren't urban in themselves, they needed to generate–despite their limited program–the attraction, variety, and spirit of the urban (7).

12 "proposed Back Bay Center development - for Stevens Development Corporation," *Progressive Architecture*, 73-85. PA described the award winning project as a "shining new core for the old metropolis." Hotel, offices, and convention center were all anchored by a huge department store and a multi-level "shopping promenade" with a roof of glass. A one-way ring road system served a parking garage with spaces for 6000 cars enabling the complex to be largely pedestrianized. A visionary project that incorporated many design and planning elements that Gruen used at Fort Worth, and especially Mid-Town Plaza, the Back Bay Center was unfortunately not built.

Indeed the complexity of interrelationships between urban redevelopment, road and traffic planning, and demands from such groups as the parking lobby—together with the impending Highway Act of 1956, which would have an enormous impact upon the urban and suburban landscape—were taken up at several national conferences by representatives of the civic, business, and design communities. At the Urban Traffic Forum conference of 1953, the *Architectural Forum* argued hopefully that future roadbuilding and traffic planning should start not at the State Highway Engineer's Department but at the mayor's office and city-planning departments. Following the same logic, a municipal parking agency should coordinate parking, and citizens' groups should participate on behalf of the entire community.[13]

In 1956, following several previous attempts, Congress finally passed the Federal-Aid Highway Act, which would initiate to be the largest civil-engineering project in history. The Act could potentially support the belt highways that Gruen would urge cities to build as the mediating structure between regional traffic patterns and a redeveloped downtown. If this system were not subject to planning, however, it could have a disastrous effect on urban communities, exacerbating rather than relieving traffic conditions in the cities and accelerating the flight to the suburbs.

At two conferences in 1957, the impact of the Highway Act on the American cityscape and landscape was taken up in urgent discussions: the Act had passed quickly, state highway engineers were being granted extensive powers, and there had been almost no public discussion on either subject. In his article "Main Street 1969" (summarizing the first conference, held in Little Rock, Arkansas), Grady Clay, the real-estate editor of the *Louisville Courier-Journal*, commented that the Federal Highway program in America would require regional planning on a scale for which few regions and fewer cities were yet equipped. The second conference, sponsored by Connecticut General Life Insurance Co. and entitled "The New Highways: Challenge to the Metropolitan Region," included among its speakers Victor Gruen, Lewis Mumford, Edmund Bacon, Gordon Bunshaft, Wilfred Owen, and Ladislas Segoe. Mumford declared that, instead of planning motorcars to fit into our life, we were fitting our life to the motorcar; Segoe urged that we realize the futility of trying to meet the traffic problem in our cities by building more and greater-capacity highways.[14] In his paper, "Highways and the American City," Gruen demanded

13 "Urban Traffic Forum," *Architectural Forum*, 111-119. Under pressure of World War II, Congress enacted the Defence Highway Act of 1941 which designated certain highways for troop, war material, and supply movement. The 1944 revised Act called for a national system of interstate highwways. Finally, in 1956, the Federal-Aid Highway and Highway Revenue Acts (Public Law 627) passed, enabling the funding of a 41,000 miles of interstate and defence highways, including 6,000 miles of urban freeways to be completed by 1972. Under the 1956 Act, the responsibility for location and design was assigned to the State Highway Departments. Grady Clay reported that the text of the Act carried virtually no mention of regional and urban planning. The goal was to connect all major cities with a population above 50,000. The Federal Government would pay 90 percent with the remaining 10 percent paid by the states themselves. The total federal contribution was envisaged to be 50 billion dollars, although at the Little Rock Conference, Grady Clay reported it to be some $106 billion.

14 "What people said at Connecticut General's symposium on highways," (Excerpts), *Architectural Forum*, 206. See also, "Symposium in a Symbolic Setting," *Life*, 53-4. The September Symposium "Highways and the American City," was held at the new Connecticut General Life Insurance Headquarters building by SOM (Gordon Bunshaft) and Isamu Noguchi in Bloomfield, Connecticut. Though left out of the decision-making process, the interest of designers and planners in the potential of the highway system continued throughout this period. In books, articles, and projects, Christopher Tunnard, Lawrence Halprin, and Kevin Lynch demonstrated the link between the individual, movement, perception, and urban form.

that the multi-billion-dollar highway program be made subject to, and not master of, a bold new planning philosophy for shaping both regional and urban environment. In the open country, highways could be integrated with topography and landscape, he said, but in cities, their effect was too often socially and visually destructive. "Why shouldn't this tremendous investment be coordinated with regional planning goals to create a more beautiful American cityscape and landscape?" Some of the recommendations for dealing with traffic congestion discussed at the conference were congestion pricing, selective decentralization, separation of trucking traffic in time and space, and encouraging the use of mass transit. Although these ideas may seem obvious enough to us now, despite their appearance in progressive urban-design projects, they were neither incorporated into the Act nor taken up in the following years.

In 1955, Gruen began to refer in articles and lectures to a new project for "City X," which would demonstrate how an entire city center could be both technically modernized and given a more urbane and humanistic setting. "City X" would also show how to exploit the federal government's support for highway building to integrate urban and regional traffic systems. Gruen was poised to offer a new model of the city in the automobile age. The new project would be the first of many, whose fate would hang not merely on the ability of the architect-planner to coordinate the many consultants, but his ability to communicate with, and manage, the conflicting aims of political, economic, and community groups.

In 1956, Victor Gruen Associates' "A Greater Fort Worth Tomorrow" offered a new image of the city in the automobile age—a specific concept for how to reconcile the American city and Americans' use of the automobile. In early 1955, J. B. Thomas, head of the Texas Electric Co., the largest utility company in Fort Worth, had been considering future investments and energy demands in the area. After reading "Dynamic Planning for Retail Areas" in the *Harvard Business Review*, he invited Gruen to Fort Worth to discuss how to rejuvenate the downtown business center to keep it competitive with both its own growing suburban areas and Dallas, its ambitious neighbor 30 miles to the east.[15] Thomas' own business concern reflected the fundamental dilemma facing many American cities in their role as service-providing entities. In the city center, where a service grid already existed, under-used buildings and empty lots meant that the system was less and less able to sustain itself. The impetuous expansion of the suburbs, on the other hand, would require expensive new service installations.

In Fort Worth's past, George Kessler, in 1909, and Harold Bartholomew, in 1927, had both made plans that included loop roads around the downtown. Nothing had come of these ideas, though, and by the early 1950s, Fort Worth was choked by some 300,000 vehicles a day. The accelerating growth of the surrounding area, together with the worsening traffic, placed the future of retail and office development downtown in a precarious position relative to sites in the suburbs where land cost less. Thomas realized that the current city administration and population had little experience of planning issues, and he wanted to provoke a discussion about the future of Fort Worth's downtown.

---

15 Gruen, *Traeumer*, 217. Gruen's account in his autobiography is corroborated by Jones, "A Greater Fort Worth Tomorrow: Victor Gruen's Vision Revisited." Thomas had emerged as a leader in the region after having launched a water resources study that led to the construction of lakes and resevoirs in previously dry west Texas cities (4, 6).

Fort Worth Press

Weather: Partly cloudy, colder today; near freezing tonight.

FINAL
HOME
EDITION
PRICE 10 CENTS

VOL. 85, NO. 140   FORT WORTH, TEXAS, SUNDAY, MARCH 11, 1956   80 PAGES

Presenting Your
FORT WORTH
OF TOMORROW

The Gruen Plan: Pages 18-21, First Section

ere's What a Plan Could Do to Seventh Street

is Seventh St., of the future as Gruen Plan de-
see it. Cars are gone—stored in six parking
'te in upper right. Street l- ' 'caped.

park-like mall. Landmarks remain among the new
buildings. Medical Arts Bldg. is at left center, far
background. The fabulous plan was presented to

Fort Worth business men yesterday. No definite
action has been taken on it. It's the first city
dream plan designed in the United States.

Before and after: Fort Worth as it might have been. Above, aerial view of Fort Worth in 1955; and below, with the Gruen plan. The Texas Highway Department had already planned to build raised highways accessing the downtown and cutting off the railroad station. Note the large areas of railroad yards separating the downtown from the inner suburbs.

In February 1955, Gruen's team began an extensive analysis on the future performance of the downtown, based on the market-research and traffic- analysis techniques developed with Larry Smith for their regional shopping center projects. How much office, retail, and parking space would be needed if Fort Worth were to reach its projected population of 1.2 million by 1970? Gruen projected the need for 9.6 million square feet of retail, and a traffic flow of up to 150,000 cars daily. The street area required was 16 million square feet, three times the existing capacity. At the same time, the team carrying out a building-condition survey concluded that a substantial area for redevelopment already existed in the form of sites that were empty or occupied by one- or two-story buildings, some of which were used by polluting industries. The traffic analysis indicated that a radical change would have to be made, and the building survey suggested that space was available.

After a number of unsuccessful schemes, Gruen proposed the radical idea of making the entire downtown a pedestrian zone, surrounded by a beltway. "A Greater Fort Worth Tomorrow" proposed that by 1970 the heart of the city be made into a mile-square (1639 acres), mixed-use, traffic-free shopping and business "oasis." The plan was structured by four interventions. The first was the belt highway, to be built on grade, which would gather traffic from the arterial roads and define the boundary of the downtown. The second intervention was six four-story parking garages, each holding 10,000 cars, to be located just off the beltway ramps. In order to shorten walking distances, the garages were arranged perpendicular to the beltway so that they penetrated into the downtown. The result was that the farthest distance between any building and the nearest parking garage would be 600 feet–about the same distance as that between Fifth and Sixth Avenues in New York, or between Hudson's department store and the middle distance of the parking lot at Northland. The garages would serve as gates to new mixed-use districts, organized by an interrelated grouping of plazas and malls. The third intervention was the transformation to a fully pedestrianized downtown. Commuters and shoppers, after parking, could either ride electric mini-buses or simply walk to various districts. The spatial structure within the new core area would modify the historic street grid by incorporating empty lots or using different building setbacks, thus creating a varied system of public spaces. The renovation and redevelopment, district by district, would let the entire project be achieved by phased reconstruction. Fort Worth's underdeveloped office market was to be expanded not by concentrating in a single CBD but by building smaller office clusters, which was part of Gruen's strategy of creating self-sufficient districts. The commercial viability of the plan was especially important because Texas, eschewing federal "handouts" or oversight, would not participate in the Federal urban renewal program. By eliminating automobiles and trucks from the city's streets, 4.4 million square feet of road surface would become available, about half of this space being converted into landscaped and paved public areas, and the remainder open for new buildings. The land made available for building would represent a value of about $40 million, which was enough, Gruen claimed, to cover the cost of the fourth intervention, underground service tunnels for buses, taxis, and goods and service deliveries, as well as for utility lines in easily accessible installations.

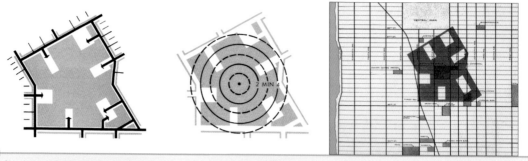

Circulation diagrams, parking garages and loop drawn over aerial photo; and a comparison in scale: downtown Fort Worth superimposed over Midtown Manhattan. Inner highway loop and large scale parking terminals as essential new urban infrastructure and building types. Gruen's sketches showed the roofs of the terminals used alternately as heliports, parks, and sports clubs. Adjoining each of the garage terminal buildings are an access road, and public plaza(s) that become the center of their respective district.

With these interventions, Gruen was convinced that downtown Fort Worth could again serve as the primary social and cultural center for the city, as well as its new suburban areas. A masterplan was necessary, he believed, because small-scale local actions were no match for the social, economic and cultural forces affecting regional settlement. The plan was the instrument to build public and private consensus for change, because neither government nor private enterprise alone could overcome urban problems.

Catalyst

On Saturday, March 10th, at the Petroleum Club, Victor Gruen and Edgardo Contini staged a dramatic, three-hour presentation before 200 leading citizens invited by J. B. Thomas, who cautiously introduced the project as "A Plan for Fort Worth not THE Plan." In this presentation (and the many that followed), Gruen made clear that the plan would not be easily accomplished but would require "a unanimity of public and private efforts rarely achieved in our time." He described the plan not as a fixed building project but a catalyst to private and public discussion and a realistic and achievable program that should be a basis for planning activities for many years ahead; and he said that, despite the depth of analysis and detail, it was a preliminary study, in order to allow for the widest possible latitude of subsequent development. Having sponsored the plan and staged its presentation, Thomas declared that to renew Fort Worth's downtown would take "guts, money and inspiration." He then announced that he was bowing out and would leave the question to be settled and advanced by the public.[16]

Local media and numerous slide shows disseminated the plan to thousands of interested citizens—creating the unusual situation of a public educated on the problems of city planning. In the weeks after the presentation, *The Fort Worth Star-Telegram* carried almost daily stories of the plan.[17] Much as Thomas had hoped, a citizens' steering committee formed "The Greater Fort Worth Planning Commission," which included working groups to deal with the parking garages, belt highway, land acquisition, and city-county matters. VGA were to remain design consultants but not undertake any subsequent private commissions.

As had been the case with Northland two years earlier, strong support for the Fort Worth plan came from Jane Jacobs, writing first in the *Architectural Forum* and again the following year in her article "Downtown is for People," in "The Exploding Metropolis" issue of *Fortune* magazine. Jacobs recognized the project's debt to the type of planning developed for the regional shopping center and commended it as a framework for later detailed development. She applauded its retention of existing buildings and the inclusion of a wide public through the many presentations, but pointed out that it had no chance of acceptance unless an effective city-county planning commission was formed.[18] Jacobs was interested not so much in Gruen's proposals for the

---

16 Jones, "A Greater Fort Worth Tomorrow: Victor Gruen's Vision Revisited," 7.
17 Various editions of the *Fort Worth Star Telegram* in the Victor Gruen Papers scrapbooks LoCVGP OV 22. For example, Pershing, H., "Daring Plan for City has Roots in Old World," "City Leaders Throw Solid Support Behind Futuristic Municipal Plan," and "More About Design for Future City," all from March 11, 1956. The presentation and subsequent debate over the plan appeared daily in the Fort Worth newspapers and soon thereafter in an ever wider circle of publications. Thousands of Fort Worth citizens had already had the scheme explained to them at the Home Show or in slide-tape talks supplied by the committee. Gruen remarked that there must be more citizens—especially more leading citizens—in Fort Worth who understand what city planning is about then in any other U.S. city.

A new urban promenade: arterial highway, parking terminal approach, and entry into new district plaza. The undeclared thesis behind this traffic infrastructure model was that the coordinated design of urban highways and entry sequence into the city will render the complex urban landscape legible and present urban space as unfolding narrative.

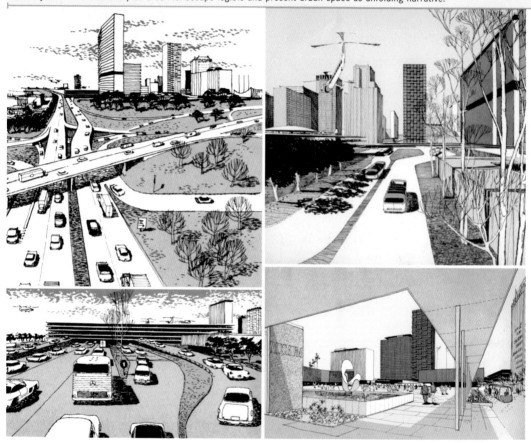

18 "Typical Downtown Transformed,"*Architectural Forum*, 147. Jacobs wrote, "The plan reflects the shopping area model transformed, its biggest debt is to the shopping center type of study. The close analysis of the plan's effects on the interests of everyone involved. This is something new for city planning. . . . The way the planner's part is conceived: the plan provided a strong skeleton but the fleshing out would be left to the city's users. Remarkably little of what exists would be interfered with . . . . The way in which the plan was presented; there was no attempt to force it over or finagle it backstage. No mincing of the fact that the citizens must assume responsibility for it future. See also, Jacobs, "Downtown Is For People," in Whyte (Ed.), *The Exploding Metropolis*, 157-184.

beltway, parking garages, or even the pedestrian area, but rather in the reincarnation of the street as a place of varied spatial and functional qualities enlivened with variety and detail. She would later be the harshest critic of modernist masterplanned urban renewal projects, but with Fort Worth, the extent and variety of the functions and spaces of the street made this modernist plan acceptable. Rather than being eliminated, the city's streets were to be returned to the pedestrian; in "Downtown is for People," she wrote:

The Gruen plan . . . will interrupt the long, wide gridiron vistas of Fort Worth by narrowing them at some points, widening them into plazas at others. It is also the best possible showmanship to play up the street's variety, contrast, and activity . . . . and it is excellent drama to exploit the contrast between the street's small elements and its big banks, its big stores, big lobbies, or solid walls. (Jacobs, 165)

Sketch for public areas. The set back of new buildings would be varied to create a complex spatial (pedestrian) streetscape. The surface would be enlivened with gardens, covered areas, art, and kiosks–the "salt and pepper" of a city.

We Don't Got no Harness Marks on us: a City Unprepared for Planning

Jacobs was right: there could hardly have been a city as unprepared for radical redevelopment as Fort Worth in the 1950s. The original plan met not only expected snags but also others for which Gruen was totally unprepared. Besides the generally conservative business environment, there was no ready mechanism in the community for carrying the plan into effect, and, despite the space in the published plan devoted to implementation–a cost analysis and phasing diagram had been made for each part of the project–without an existing civic decision-making structure, an enormous gap remained between intention and execution. Although the city had a small planning department, planning in Fort Worth had been largely ceded to private enterprise, with private corporations underwriting redevelopment of blighted areas. The city had previously been run by one man, Amon S. Carter, Sr., publisher of *The Fort Worth Star-Telegram*, and his death in 1955 left a leadership vacuum that would not be filled until the 1960s.

The Fort Worth Plan lived and died on issues of mobility and access–restructuring movement and parking relative to the vested interests of downtown landowners. Ironically, despite the intensive studies of parking and traffic, parking-lot and garage owners helped defeat the project. In addition, the plan would require directing investment to the city center, which ran against the momentum of suburbanization, which the city was actively supporting in the form of annexation. The annexation of suburbs spread the tax base and made it logical for business to seek locations away from the center–which the Gruen plan specifically tried to limit. Residents in the newly annexed towns and suburbs always voted against inner-city investment projects. In "Whatever Happened to Fort Worth," Jeanne R. Lowe quoted George Thompson, Jr., a powerful local businessman, on the subject of the proposed pedestrian mall and plaza plantings: "People like to do business where there are people and traffic, and where there is the sound and appearance of commercial activity. I don't want to do business in a botanical garden."

The most important component of A Greater Fort Worth Tomorrow? Critics claimed the city had no structure to carry out the project, yet Gruen offered this organization plan for its implementation. In the center a committee, constituted as a non-profit corporation, representing citizens-, governmental- and commercial groups.

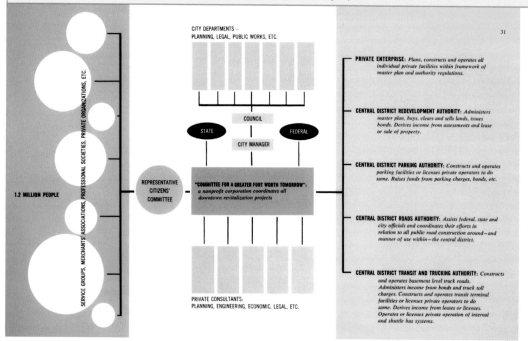

31

CITY DEPARTMENTS –
PLANNING, LEGAL, PUBLIC WORKS, ETC.

SERVICE GROUPS, MERCHANTS' ASSOCIATIONS, PROFESSIONAL SOCIETIES, PRIVATE ORGANIZATIONS, ETC.

1.2 MILLION PEOPLE

REPRESENTATIVE CITIZENS' COMMITTEE

COUNCIL
STATE   FEDERAL
CITY MANAGER

"COMMITTEE FOR A GREATER FORT WORTH TOMORROW": *a nonprofit corporation coordinates all downtown revitalization projects*

PRIVATE CONSULTANTS:
PLANNING, ENGINEERING, ECONOMIC, LEGAL, ETC.

PRIVATE ENTERPRISE: *Plans, constructs and operates all individual private facilities within framework of master plan and authority regulations.*

CENTRAL DISTRICT REDEVELOPMENT AUTHORITY: *Administers master plan, buys, clears and sells lands, issues bonds. Derives income from assessments and lease or sale of property.*

CENTRAL DISTRICT PARKING AUTHORITY: *Constructs and operates parking facilities or licenses private operators to do same. Raises funds from parking charges, bonds, etc.*

CENTRAL DISTRICT ROADS AUTHORITY: *Assists federal, state and city officials and coordinates their efforts in relation to all public road construction around–and manner of use within–the central district.*

CENTRAL DISTRICT TRANSIT AND TRUCKING AUTHORITY: *Constructs and operates basement level truck roads. Administers income from bonds and truck toll charges. Constructs and operates transit terminal facilities or licenses private operators to do same. Derives income from leases or licenses. Operates or licenses private operation of internal and shuttle bus systems.*

The American downtown core as an "Oasis": a dense but spacious urban environment activated not merely by the diverse functions of the buildings themselves, but also by a flotilla of stands, kiosks, and pavilions animating the public spaces. The charm of the image is supported by the separation and control of traffic as demonstrated at Southdale, and serviced from below at a scale only Disney could have imagined.

What was radical about the Fort Worth Plan was the notion that inner-city areas might one day have better environmental conditions than the suburbs—better air quality, more traffic safety, and the kind of security that one finds in a public space—so that the city could once again become a privileged living area. It was one of the earliest comprehensive redevelopment plans for an American downtown and anticipated drawing together resources made possible by the Housing Act (1949, 1954) and the Highway Act (1956). What seemed new at the time was the method of evaluation and the criteria applied to a city center in the automobile age. In "Typical Downtown Transformed," the *Architectural Forum* commented, "this seems to be the first city for which actual dimensions for the problem have been calculated and faced. The method shows up usual traffic planning for what it is—pursuit of expedients to solve an unmeasured problem" (147). Sam Bass Warner, in his introduction to the revised edition of *The Exploding Metropolis*, recalled that the plan offered a vision of a social and active downtown. He added that, during the following 30 years, central Fort Worth continued to lose its affluent white customers, so that by the early 1970s, it had become the home of the poor and nonwhite (x, xiv).

Even if political power had been on his side, the Fort Worth plan would have been a massive and long-term undertaking—the wholesale makeover of a city center for pedestrian and automobile. As Reyner Banham later wrote, "Its scale and absoluteness were stunning; the first of the 'business districts-on-a-podium' projects that inspired megastructuralists; widely published, it set a standard of detailed elaboration and sheer vastness of ambition that all later projects had to match if they were to be taken seriously" (*Megastructure*, 42). Yet it is possible to look at the plan in another way, not as a megastructure, but as six partly self-sufficient urban districts. Similar to the main railway stations with their plazas in European cities, Gruen's parking garages were fronted by a public open space—a plaza around which old and new buildings could be clustered. This would function as the core of the new district, with streets leading to the surrounding neighborhoods.

Sketch model of parking garage, district plaza, and building cluster. The great incursion of massive parking garages used to create new public open space and new building program.

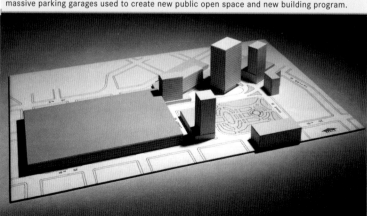

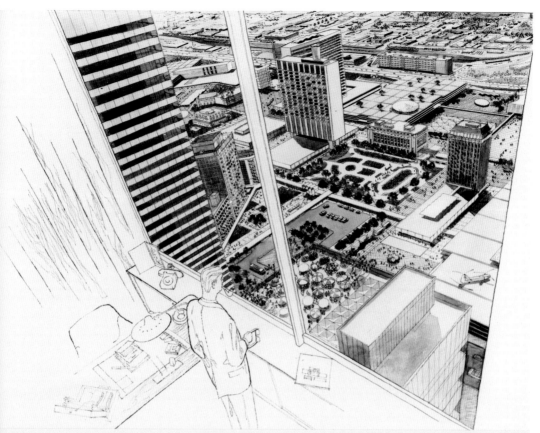

A day in the life; two scenarios from A Greater Fort Worth Tomorrow. Fourteen years after the plan, a businessman looks down from his office, and a suburban housewife strolls through the downtown on a shopping and leisure trip.

A new visibility and legibility of the city would be given by the sequence of movement from freeway, to garage, to public plaza, and back. Gruen took pains to explain that the plan would be carried out in phases, perhaps over many years, that business and community groups would be partners in decision-making, and that other architects and planners would carry out the execution. The beltway was a formidable barrier between downtown and inner suburbs and would have required very strong connections such as land- or public-space bridges. The restriction of service traffic to underground tunnels, when it could have been organized to take place out of hours or in a system of service alleys (as Gruen would himself propose for Fresno), would have been awkward and expensive. Fully excluding the automobile from the public realm removes an important part of contemporary urban experience, and we know now that there are various methods for allowing reduced automobile traffic to move slowly through the city in a way that is compatible with pedestrians. Yet the sheer clarity and completeness of the bird's eye perspective "photo" of the completed project—actually a painting montaged into a photograph—contributed to the belief that entire central areas could be made over under a single plan.

Yet despite the failure of the city to go further, America now had a new image of the city: a starting point for the resurrection of city life and urban culture. What it would be like to shop and work within a pedestrian ambiance would be demonstrated on a more modest scale in two smaller cities with more established planning departments and more civic-minded business communities: Kalamazoo, Michigan, and Rochester, New York.

The Burdick Street Pedestrian Mall, Kalamazoo, Michigan
Wouldn't it Be Wonderful to Be the First City to Do it?

In 1957, in the wake of the publicity of the Fort Worth Plan, a group of business and property owners in the central business district of Kalamazoo invited Gruen to prepare a planning study and report on the potential for redeveloping their downtown. Kalamazoo, lying between Chicago and Detroit, had a population of 57,700. Its shoppers were driving to the new outlying regional shopping centers, which was bad enough news for local downtown merchants, but what alarmed them most was the decrease, in 1955, of over $1 million in the reassessed valuation of the central business district. Gruen argued that development of the suburbs could not be stopped, but a renewed downtown would stimulate growth to offset it.

At a public meeting in March 1958, Gruen unveiled "Kalamazoo 1980," modifying the measures developed for Fort Worth for a smaller city and phasing the plan for a long-term evolution from the city's relative low-density to a higher-density downtown. The first stage was to create a one-way perimeter road using existing streets. Inside this perimeter, 180 acres would be cleared of nonconforming uses to provide parking fields so that visitors, shoppers, and workers could park no more than a few minutes' stroll from their destinations. Using state and federal highway funds, the second stage would relocate and transform the perimeter road into a low-speed, limited-access beltway, deflecting through-traffic away from the center while enlarging the future downtown. The third stage was to gradually build out the center, replacing the parking fields with parking garages and releasing land for development. The final, most visible phase of the

New American townscape. Burdick Street Pedestrian Mall, Kalamazoo, MI (1959).

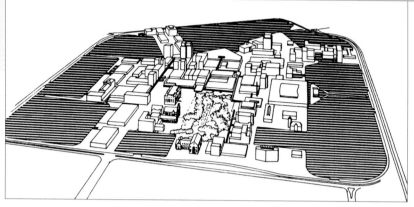

Bird's eye view. "Kala-mazoo 1980." In the first phase, the downtown is reconceived as a regional shopping and civic center.

project was to pedestrianize Burdick Street, Kalamazoo's main shopping street. Gruen likened the proposed interventions to his most successful shopping centers, and the report showed not only the plan of Kalamazoo overlaid on the plan of Northland, but an oblique view of central Kalamazoo looking, after the first stage of redevelopment, more like a regional shopping center complex than a small midwestern city. Perspectives of the final phase of the project showed a "compacted" central pedestrian area focused on Burdick Street with the pedestrian bridges linking the upper floors of the parking decks, and Burdick Street Mall itself transformed into a year-round, roofed, and air-conditioned shopping plaza. The center of Kalamazoo would become a downtown regional shopping center surrounded by an existing and redeveloped town.[19]

Although the plan was accepted "in principle," the city soon realized that it lacked the money to purchase and clear the land for parking lots and rights-of-way for the second-stage perimeter beltway. But, to show that progress was being made despite financial limitations, in June 1959 the downtown Kalamazoo City Planning Commission undertook at its own initiative the pedestrianization of two blocks of Burdick Street. Two months later, the Burdick Street Mall, which featured gardens, water fountains, pavilions, bus stops, and even a revolving stage for fashion shows, was officially opened.

Burdick Street Mall, the nation's first downtown pedestrian shopping mall, brought a casual, leisurely, suburban atmosphere to midtown and was immediately popular. But to the surprise and dismay of his clients and the townspeople of Kalamazoo, Gruen publicly criticized the execution of the project, contending that a pedestrian mall without the infrastructural elements–perimeter road (or beltway), street improvements, parking areas, and support for mixed-use development–was, by itself, merely a gimmick and should only be the final, most visible element in a downtown-restructuring program.[20] Gruen's concern was based not only on the "reverse" sequence of planning in Kalamazoo, due to lack of funding, but on the failure in other towns of

"Wouldn't it be wonderful to be the first city to do it?" (Epigram) Gilmore, "Plan Stirs Curiosity, Wins Praise."
19 "Ray Dykema remembers when: the making of the mall," Encore, 28-32, 64-66. Also "Kalamazoo, 1980, A Planning Study by Victor Gruen Associates and Larry Smith & Company, 1958." Appendix A-5. Was Gruen lucky that Kalamazoo only executed part of the plan?

The "Northland-ization" of a small city would have been a drastic solution, isolating the retail area from the surrounding urban fabric. See also "The Kalamazoo Mall," City of Kalamazoo 6.
20 Bradford, "Gruen's Mall Visit Mends Some Fences."
21 "Downtown Gets Uplift," Life; "Can Cities Save Downtown Areas?," U.S. News & World Report, 74.

temporary mall experiments, where the mall was not part of a larger renewal project and only created traffic jams elsewhere in the city.

Despite Gruen's protests, though, the Burdick Street Mall proved that a vehicle-free shopping street could spark a downtown revival, and over the years, through the city's careful addition of further development projects, Kalamazoo became one of the relatively few cities in the Midwest to avoid a drastic deterioration of its central business district. 1959, in fact, became the year of the downtown pedestrian shopping mall: in October, *Life Magazine* reported that 55 other cities had plans similar to Kalamazoo, and in the following month, *U.S. News and World Report* wrote that 100 cities were following the same idea.[21] Gruen may have been disappointed with Kalamazoo, but it had simply undertaken what was practicable for a small city and no more.

For the second time, Gruen found the process of executing an urban redevelopment project fraught with political and financial problems. The regional shopping center was a quintessential modern project: it was the result of rational demographic and financial calculation, it would be built on virgin land, and its functions were clearly separated. The linear progression of decision making and project stages that characterized his successful regional shopping centers projects was much harder to achieve in an urban context. After the "success" of the Burdick Street Mall, Gruen was at pains to explain that pedestrian malls by themselves could not overcome inadequate urban transportation systems, obsolete buildings, a poor functional mix, or a lack of civic, business, and political leadership.

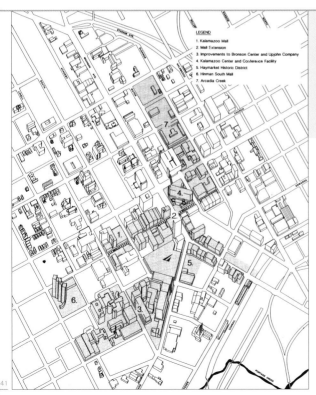

LEGEND
1. Kalamazoo Mall
2. Mall Extension
3. Improvements to Bronson Center and Upjohn Company
4. Kalamazoo Center and Conference Facility
5. Haymarket Historic District
6. Hinman South Mall
7. Arcadia Creek

Attoe and Logann's axonometric diagram of downtown Kalamazoo showing how the city used the original Burdick Street Mall and its extension as the fulcrum for future urban development projects.

Left, metropolitan area highway plan with planned outer loop and link to the New York State Throughway; and diagram of the planned inner loop with the Midtown Plaza site (2) framed by the loop and the city's main crossing streets.

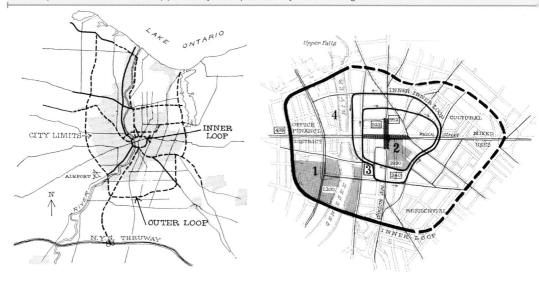

Before and after: existing cityscape and Midtown Plaza as built.

22 "The Planning of Midtown Plaza," *Architectural Record*, October, 1961, 135.
23 "Rochester Brings Them Back From the Suburbs," *Engineering News Record*, 30. Also Ann Taylor, City Planner, author interview, 1999.

Among the business and civic leaders were the mayor Peter Barry; c manager Bob Aex; municipal committees, which were dominated by some fifty individuals representing the old business families; planne Ladislas Segoe; and the two department-store families.

If the city of Kalamazoo was simply too small to undertake large-scale, long-term restructuring, Rochester would demonstrate how a city must be prepared and organized to pull together such a project. In December 1956, as the Fort Worth Plan was being debated, Gruen traveled to Rochester to meet with the owners of two competing downtown department stores who were troubled by the deterioration of their center city and wanted a long-term evaluation. Gilbert J. C. McCurdy of McCurdy's Department Store and Fred S. Forman of the B. Forman Co. Store believed their business was falling off due to the lack of downtown parking and to new developments in the suburbs. They were unsure about opening suburban branch stores, but "if not suburban stores," they said, then what?[22] Gruen visited the outlying shopping centers but thought that no real market existed in the suburbs, either, and that the problem was the deterioration of downtown Rochester itself. But unlike McCurdy and Forman, Gruen doubted that there was too little parking: from an airplane, he said, the center of Rochester looked like nothing but a big parking area rendered inefficient by some remaining buildings (*Heart of Our Cities*, 303).

The conditions for undertaking a downtown-redevelopment project in Rochester couldn't have been more unlike those in Fort Worth. Since 1936, the city had been operating under stringent financial restraints to reduce its debt, and by 1951 it had achieved a Triple-A credit rating. A progressive and ambitious group of business and civic leaders were interested in change, and these were people "who could back up their ideas."[23] The city had set the stage for redevelopment by securing funding from the New York State highway program to construct a new inner ring-road, additional arterial streets, and an above-ground 500-car municipal parking garage to stabilize the city's central area and attract new investment to the downtown core.

After meetings with McCurdy's and Forman's, VGA and Larry Smith made their analysis of the city and metropolitan area in early 1957. Smith agreed with Gruen that the suburban market was not large enough to justify McCurdy's and Forman's expansion into the suburbs. To avoid driving up land prices, McCurdy and Forman, with advice on land acquisition based on the Gruen-Smith parking and property survey, began to assemble the site secretly. With $11 million borrowed from the New York State Teachers Pension Fund, they set up dummy corporations to acquire the 17 pieces of land that would make up the redevelopment parcel. Only the mayor and the city manager knew of the plans.

Gruen then set about integrating his plans for the project, to be named Midtown Plaza, with the city's planning for a downtown core. He proposed that instead of the planned 500-car parking garage, the city build a three-level underground garage with 2000 parking places. Public bus routes serving both the edges of the city and the inner area should be brought together in a new regional station at Midtown Plaza. Finally, to make a direct link between the project site and the new inner loop, Gruen proposed that the city build a new principal-access street. The acceptance of these measures ensured that the evolving renovation of downtown and the development of Midtown Plaza would support each other.

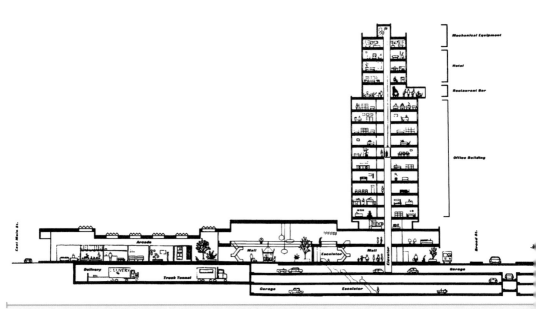

Midtown Plaza; the long section runs from Main Street (left) to the bus station area. The underground parking garage is offset. The lane leading from Main Street has its own space and is also toplit.

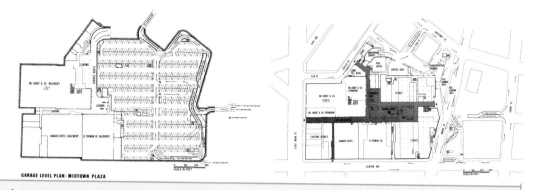

GARAGE LEVEL PLAN · MIDTOWN PLAZA

A new town square with urbane qualities? Midtown Plaza, street level plan. Access to the central interior plaza was by escalator from the parking garage below, and four lanes leading to the surrounding streets. Southdale revisited?

By September 1958, after taking more than a year to assemble its site, the Development Corporation publicly announced the project: Midtown Plaza would be a cluster of existing and new buildings, combining the compactness and mixed function of a downtown with the atmosphere, amenities, and convenience of the newest shopping centers. Although the basic program of an urban pedestrian shopping center with offices, hotel, bus station, and underground parking garage had been agreed by the January 1958 sketches, the project was otherwise in a state of continuous revision and expansion: Midtown Tower, for instance, which would be the first "skyscraper" in Rochester in 30 years, was enlarged from 10 to 18 stories; and, the four-story pavilion of the Telephone Company arrived late, replacing a third department store. Where the Fort Worth Plan integrated several districts, each clustered around its parking garage and together making up an entire metropolitan core covering 639 acres, Midtown Plaza demonstrated how a single, compact, mixed-use complex, covering seven acres, might work.

Contracts were let in 1960, and throughout 13 months of construction all existing buildings remained open and operating. The complex, more than half of whose activities did not involve retailing, would be built according to what Gruen called "the podium principle." The entire development was to be constructed on top of the 2000-car, three-level parking garage, which measured 608 by 504 feet and extended part of the way under Broad Street. The garage itself was equipped with the new automatic circulation and environmental systems. The two department stores (one new and the other renovated), the office tower surmounted by a restaurant and hotel, and a new office building for the telephone company were all organized around a central pedestrian mall, measuring 295 by 106 feet and 60 feet in height–roughly the size at Southdale. The two levels, surrounding the mall, were to contain restaurants, commercial agencies, and some 60 shops, many of which were open-fronted and were selected by Gruen and his clients to attract a sophisticated audience. The indoor plaza included a sidewalk cafe that would seat 130 people, kiosks, exhibit spaces, and a large totem pole, all recreating in an urban setting the environment that had proved so successful at Southdale.

View as built, and interior plaza view (1962). The hotel, occupying the upper part of Midtown Tower, is clad in pale yellow pressed metal panels. The interior view shows shoppers and visitors gathered around the Clock of the Nations at 12 noon, when all of the stages open and revolve.

Midtown Plaza opened on April 10, 1962, and the pessimists who had predicted it would be impossible for an inner-city project to win investors were surprised to see 10,000 people at the opening and every space let. Used at all times of day, especially in bad weather and through Rochester's harsh winter, the indoor plaza became the main public space for the city. As at Southdale, the space was divided by an escalator-bridge. A cantilevered winding stair with fountain linked the plaza to an adjoining public area. Daylight filtered through a louvred ceiling. "We wanted to create a town square with urbane qualities," Gruen said in the *Architectural Forum*. "At the same time the plaza is important as a setting for cultural and social events—concerts, fashion shows, balls and those activities one connects with urban life" ("Center for Rochester," 112).

The focus of the indoor plaza was the 28-foot-high Clock of Nations, a hand-made mechanical ornamental clock in "baroque" 1950s style, a reference to the town clocks in European city centers such as Munich and Prague. To many of Gruen's colleagues (and no doubt for many architects today), the cheerful Clock of Nations was architectural kitsch. For Gruen, though, the clock itself and its enormous appeal confirmed his opinion that "architecture could be informed not only by serious intent, but also by humor, emotion, and fantasy" (Traeumer, 230).

Clock of the Nations

Having lectured and written on the subject for 10 years, Gruen now believed that Midtown Plaza proved that one could transform the planning strategies of the regional shopping center for American downtowns. Unlike the practice at the new regional shopping centers, whose "public spaces" remained in private ownership, the central indoor space and the arcades leading to it at Midtown Plaza were taken over by the city and remained accessible to everyone. Likewise, the vast parking fields that surrounded all suburban shopping centers and formed too great a barrier to be combined with peripheral development had, at Midtown Plaza, been compressed in section into the three-story underground parking garage, enabling Midtown Plaza to function within the city's street network. The program of the regional shopping center, which was becoming both limited and repetitive, was here augmented by office towers and hotel. Where at Northland and Southdale the bus stations would play an ever-decreasing role, Midtown Plaza also functioned as a public-transport nexus: platforms for up to 20 local and inter-regional buses located at the southeast corner ensured maximum accessibility for public as well as private transport.

In his autobiography, Gruen claimed that in Midtown Plaza, "a soul-less CBD became transformed into a real 'city center,' with which even the outlying residential areas could identify" (230). To city mayors he described the project as America's first executed downtown renewal plan, whose importance lay in the coordination between public and private investment. Midtown Plaza was indeed one of the early successes of commercial inner-city redevelopment, being one of the first projects undertaken fully by private investors but integrated within the framework of Rochester's publicly supported urban-renewal plan. The initial investment in the transportation infrastructure by federal, state, and city government, particularly the underground parking garage, gave private investors the impetus to raise the money for the rest of the building project. Although Gruen considered himself the principal actor in the planning and building of the project, from the point of view of Rochester's planning consultant, Ladislas Segoe, Midtown Plaza—a private redevelopment—was not the result of Victor Gruen's genius, but the result of more than 10 years of municipal planning and was precisely the kind of project that had been envisioned.[24] Both men were right. Certainly Gruen was perfectly positioned to do it. Urban public space, surrounded by (private) commerce, in a mixed-use complex, equally accessible to both public and private transport, was a demonstration of everything he believed a downtown center should be.

24 Ladislas Segoe in an undated letter following an article in the *Urban Land*, June 1962, 2-5. Segoe wished to clarify how far both traffic planning, parking garage and the desire to create a new shopping area had evolved before Gruen was brought to the project. Segoe himself had declined to make plans for a shopping center because he felt that as city planner it would have constituted a conflict of interest. See also Aex, "Rochester Unveils America's First Midtown Bazaar," 175

At Midtown Plaza, private development alone would never have risked so much capital without the beltway and garage, which, together with the connecting street to Rochester's inner loop, made it possible to travel to the interior court from anywhere in the region. The attraction of a new kind of center combined with a smooth system of access for an increasingly mobile population meant that for a short while a suburban public would travel into town to shop comfortably and conveniently. Writing in *Plymouth Traveler*, Diane Wharton reported,

The garage approaches are hooked in with a series of new limited access highways. I tested them, found you could get to the shopping center (Midtown Plaza in the center of the city!) from a residential area seven miles away in less than ten minutes. You park easily, ride escalators up to a beautiful air-conditioned mall with shops on two levels . . . . Midtown Plaza may turn out to be a shopping center landmark. It enables families who have homes with attached garages to go shopping without ever stepping outdoors. As long as our lives are tied to our autos that's fairly close to the ultimate.

This euphoric testimony to shopping downtown without experiencing the city is striking evidence of a gap between Gruen's intentions and the different reception of the project by central area residents, the business community, and the suburban public. In "Downtown Core is Revived," James P. Wilmot, Sr., a local shopping center developer claimed Midtown Plaza was no ordinary shopping center—it wasn't going to get the everyday business of the ordinary housewife—it was an "event," and no woman was going to shop there "without dressing up." Wilmot's comments hint at the future confluence of shopping and entertainment, which would change the role of downtowns.

Midtown Plaza was clearly a new attraction for nearby residents and, for downtown business boosters, stimulated the building market. Over the next few years, the Xerox Corporation, for instance, abandoned its finished plans for a head office outside the city and instead erected a tall office building connected to Midtown Plaza by a footbridge; in a separate development, the city began planning a $50-million civic center across the Genesee River, to be completed by 1970. Yet choosing Midtown Plaza over one of the outlying shopping centers merely confirmed in the minds of suburbanites the idea of the downtown as a place for special activities, and not an integrated living and working environment. Gruen's mixed-use commercial projects were too rarely accompanied by new residential development directly adjacent, or within convenient walking distance, to the commercial core. Not until his downtown redevelopment projects of the mid-1960s—such as the Central Area Plan for Boston or the dense center planned for the new town of Valencia—were residential and commercial planned together. With few exceptions, there has been no market for this kind of integrated city building until very recently.

Almost a decade before Midtown Plaza opened, the *Architectural Forum* had predicted that "the enclosed shopping center [was] bound to influence other kinds of public buildings ("New Thinking on Shopping Centers," 122). Gruen had indeed synthesized the new suburban structure of the regional shopping center into the downtown core. As he would later write, the project had "served commerce without being dominated by it" (*Traeumer*, 227). After the publication of the Fort Worth Plan, Victor Gruen Associates were entrusted as planners or advisors on about 50 downtown-redevelopment projects. Certainly the office had a rough method to use as a starting point, later to be modified to suit individual conditions. Still reflecting the aims of CIAM 8's *The Heart of the City* and his initial adaptation of his shopping-center method, Gruen outlined his seven steps for the American city at the annual Conference of Mayors in 1960. To address the most immediate conflict of an increasing number of vehicles in a fixed area of streets, one must 1) separate human and vehicular traffic and provide areas for pedestrian use; 2) build concentric ring streets or highways with adjoining high density parking; 3) create new performance specifications for streets, to reflect not just their traffic loading but also their local context; 4) improve existing and develop new forms of public transport; 5) construct new low- and medium-density housing; 6) abandon or avoid the strict separation of functions advocated by the early CIAM; and 7) urge local governments to create new forms of federation to better address metropolitan-scale problems.[25] These steps may seem simple today—even rudimentary—but that is only evidence of their fundamental quality. Gruen had long claimed that a dense, lively urban core could be both the heart of the city and the representative public space for the region. In Fresno, he would be able to translate what this homily could mean with an extensive planning project.

25 Gruen, "Urban Planning for the 1960s," Speech C 72. U.S. Conference of Mayors, Chicago, IL. May 13, 1960. Reprint. LoCVGP box 81.

VGA's "Comprehensive Plan for Fresno, California" was an extensive project that effectively operated at three scales simultaneously. First, by a series of peripheral freeways, it established an edge to the city, connecting Fresno with future regional movement patterns; second, it defined the different functional areas in the central area; and third, it offered a network of public spaces that could link commercial with civic and other functions in the old downtown core. The breadth and scope of the project involved a wide variety of consultants in all aspects of planning: traffic infrastructure, the creation of legal instruments, and negotiations with state and federal agencies. Due to the slow-moving urban-renewal process, which I will describe later, the project took six years. By the time the Fulton Street Pedestrian Mall opened, changes in politics, demography, and development goals created obstacles for the long-term effectiveness of the project.

Fresno, established in 1872, was the regional center of the fertile San Joaquin Valley, halfway between San Francisco and Los Angeles and, by 1954, the leading county in the U.S. for farm products. As the population of the city and county grew, however, the historic downtown became less able either to serve or to match this growth. Facilities for traffic and parking were inadequate, areas adjacent to downtown were deteriorating, and Fresno's city center was threatened by new development in the suburbs. A vivid enough sign in 1956 was the departure of Sears & Roebuck from Fulton Street–Fresno's main shopping street–for a new location in a suburban mall. Once before, in 1918, Fresno had been far-sighted enough to commission a plan for the city by the San Francisco architect Gilbert Cheney, and it was the unearthing of Cheney's plan in 1956 that started the city administration and business community on the course toward planning their future.

Comprehensive Plan for Fresno, CA (1958-64). Central area plan with highway interchanges. The central area, bounded by a beltway, encloses the core "fringe," itself defined by a ring boulevard. A further loop road serves the pedestrianized core area.

A. OUTER COMMERCIAL
B. INNER COMMERCIAL
C. INDUSTRIAL, WHOLESALING AND WAREHOUSING
D. CIVIC CENTER
E. CONVENTION HALL
F. MEDICAL COMPLEX
G. INSTITUTIONAL COMPLEX
H. RESIDENTIAL

COMPREHENSIVE PLAN FOR THE CENTRAL AREA
Fresno, California

VICTOR GRUEN ASSOCIATES   ARCHITECTURE · ENGINEERING · PLANNING

January 1960

Core area plan (core superblock) showing parking garages on the Southwest perimeter. The main cross axis running SW-NE, crossing the Fulton Street Mall, crosses the park and leads to the new city center.

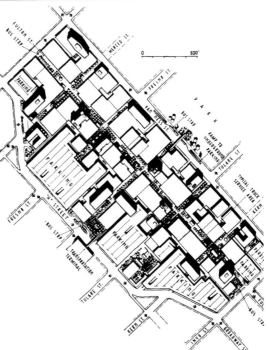

"Life on the Mall," Perspective. At Fresno Gruen and Contini built this image. The image was repeated innumerable times by other draughtsmen, for other projects, other architects. Everyone is white and middle class, precisely the people who chose in the mid-1960s, rather than remaking and reinhabiting the city, to leave it.

"Three in One": Integrating Planning for the Region, City, and the CBD

In the summer of 1958, Gruen and Fresno worked out a unique three-part contract that would relate immediate development problems with the question of long-term growth of the city in its region. Gruen and Edgardo Contini, who was partner in charge of the project, concluded that if the three entities—City, downtown Redevelopment Agency, and CBD merchants—would cooperate and indeed jointly carry financial commitment for a revitalization study, the chances of action would rise greatly. Recalling the problems at Fort Worth, where the lack of early participation by the city government had proven one of the major obstacles, VGA were eager to involve all parties from the beginning.

The first of the three projects called for a comprehensive plan for the entire central area of Fresno, over 1,850 acres. The main feature was a new freeway loop, which would connect the city to planned regional highways. The second called for a more detailed study of a 65-acre "Core Superblock" area, surrounded by an inner traffic loop. As at Fort Worth, VGA proposed that the Core Superblock be entered directly from parking structures along its perimeter, but rather than an expensive system of service tunnels, a system of one-way alleys would serve the superblock, providing access for service and fire equipment. The third project was to be a detailed plan for the 36.5-acre "Central Business District Project One," which was to include the pedestrianization of several blocks of Fresno's main shopping artery, Fulton Street. The new pedestrian mall would not be merely a linear space but also include crossing streets, principally Mariposa, which would lead to a new planned civic center and courthouse. At the edges of the mall would be 10.5 acres for off-street parking–a gain from 1,600 to 7,400 spaces, which, in future phases, could be developed with parking structures. The mall design would be a joint effort by VGA and Eckbo, Dean & Williams of San Francisco.

Throughout the development process, Gruen and Contini kept the public and the business community informed and involved. Many different interest groups were to join in the consultation and planning, which proved that often-fractious components of the community, such as the State Highway Department and local neighborhoods, could work together. By keeping everything out in the open, VGA could integrate the wishes and requirements of different parties with proposals for the city and metropolitan area.

An important precedent was the ability of VGA and the city to persuade the state to adopt Gruen's freeway-loop system. Contini claimed that the feature that would most forcibly shape the entire downtown area was going to be the alignment of the three regional freeways that would someday converge in Fresno:

The first thing we studied was the proper location for the freeways. Twenty years ahead of their construction we established the freeway routes in the central area. Never before had a city gone to the California division of highways and said, 'we must know now where your freeways are going. We want them here, because we need so much area within the freeway loop to accommodate our growth and so much perimeter to transfer the traffic volumes that we anticipate in 20 or 30 years. ("Fresno Mall Gives Small City A New Heart," 38)

The location of the freeways and most of the land-use recommendations were followed. The planning process, which went further than those required by the Urban Renewal Administration, created new legal and financing tools in the State of California, such as those necessary for transforming a working street into a pedestrian mall. In early 1960, the same year that the Gruen plan was accepted by all parties, the state legislature passed the Pedestrian Malls Act, and, in the following year, the city created an assessment district to finance about 30 percent of the $1.9-million total cost–Federal Urban Renewal funds made up nearly all the rest. The legal authorization of the mall design and approval from the Urban Renewal Administration took two years, and ground was not broken until 1964. In September 1964, the opening ceremony took place, and Fresno's Fulton Street Mall became as busy as a bazaar.

Aerial view of Fulton Street Pedestrian Mall

26 Taper, "The City That Puts People First." Republished for a wider audience as Taper, "A City Remade for People." Reader's Digest, 146.
27 Contini, Edgardo, "The Renewal of Downtown Fresno: A Case Study," 19. See also: Contini, "Notes on Fresno," 1970, LoCVGP; *Progressive Architecture* (Observer) Jan. 1965, 184, 186; and "Downtown – Fresno's Future."

Life on the Mall

Once again the popular press responded to the new image of city life offered by the pedestrianization of Fresno's main shopping street. In "A City Remade for People," Bernard Taper wrote,

I am sitting contentedly, a cool drink at my elbow, right in the middle of Fulton Street–the main street of Fresno, California . . . . What I am doing now is simply a part of a new pattern of life this bustling city of more than 150,000 has adopted: one starting from the premise that downtown is for people . . . . Where there once were traffic jams, fumes and the standard ugliness of the American city's downtown, there are now gardens, fountains, pools and numerous pieces of handsome sculpture.

The large area of the pedestrian mall (nine blocks of former city streets yielding some 330,000 square feet) was planned to be broken up into a series of interrelated spaces by varying the building lines of subsequent projects. Garret Eckbo designed the public spaces to be as compact as possible to conserve high-value land, minimize walking distances, and increase the feeling of intense activity. He added pavilions, garden structures, and, especially because of the dry climate, varied water features. Both paving patterns and the placement of objects–trellised sitting areas, planting beds, and artworks–were made to create diagonal cross-axes in contrast to the rectangular block structure. By breaking up the long street space, Eckbo created a hybrid urban landscape enriched by varied forms, bright colors, and water. The different mall spaces were accented with sculpture, lighting, and sound equipment.[26] "Pedes-trains," similar to those at Disneyland and World's Fairs, ran the length of the mall and let passengers off where they chose. As in the early Gruen shopping centers, the mall was well visited day, night, and on Sundays, when many of the businesses were closed.

The effort of VGA, which masterminded the process that created the different plans, was complemented by the work of Garret Eckbo, who could concentrate on the detailed design of the public spaces. Neither Gruen nor Eckbo, however, was able to exert–to the same degree as in Gruen's own shopping centers–control over the signs of businesses along the Fulton and Mariposa Malls. For some critics, an uncontrolled montage of individual storefronts and advertising signs marred the clarity of Eckbo's design for the public spaces.[27] Controlling the architecture was, however, less crucial for Gruen, who believed that the most important ingredients for the success of the mall were the people who used it. They did use it, and they shopped: in the mall's first year, the average gain in retail volume was nine percent.

Many cities sent delegations to see the symbol of Fresno's dedicated community effort and to learn how it was accomplished. Louis H. Jacobsen, chief engineer of Rotterdam's Department of Town Planning, said of the Fresno project, "(It is) by far the most satisfying sense of human scale and human values of any project I have seen in the U.S. . . . In other American towns I visited, the people were arguing about one-way streets. It was splendidly stimulating to find them in Fresno arguing for the merits and demerits of their artworks" ("A City Remade for People," 150).

Fresno was one of the first regional plans for a city in California. The interdependence of the three plans persuaded federal redevelopment officials, for the first time since the Urban Renewal Program had been in effect, that pedestrian malls were valid expenditures in rebuilding downtown areas. As at Rochester, the high aims of public and private agencies matched the intentions of architects and planners. As the commercial planning mantra went, redevelopment spending would be the necessary spark for future private investment. By 1965, the project had stimulated a further $800,000 for remodeling and $19 million for new construction in the central area. Three other redevelopment projects also started, including housing and a new civic center.

The collaboration between VGA and Eckbo, Dean and Williams, together with the three city agencies, received a *Progressive Architecture* Design Award in 1965. Three years later, the project received a U.S. Department of Housing and Urban Development (HUD) Award for Design Excellence, and VGA produced a 21-minute public-service documentary film, "A City Reborn," about which Secretary of the Interior Stuart Udall declared, "The rejuvenation of the central core of the City of Fresno, CA, and its conversion into a highly enjoyable urban environment is a model for American cities. All Americans interested in the future of our urban centers and in what President Johnson calls the 'New Conservation' should see 'A City Reborn'." [28]

Despite the enthusiasm of critics and government officials, however, within a few years Fresno's renewal project became a casualty of the war between the suburbs and the downtowns. While Washington helped Fresno with urban-renewal funds, the city, Gruen said, showed a "schizophrenic" attitude by simultaneously placing new federal offices in Fresno's suburbs, not downtown. In addition, pressure from shopping-center developers and their investors resulted in the building of two shopping centers in the near suburbs. This misalignment of public and private investment, which was usually to the detriment of the downtowns, was a pattern that would be often repeated across the nation.

Up Against Urban Renewal

In describing the transformation of American regional settlement patterns, Gruen often referred to the "push-pull" phenomenon. The suburbs pulled people from cities; but the cities themselves pushed them out. The highway system expedited this physical, economic, and above all social transformation. Yet, while the traffic debate unfolded, from the 1940s through the 1960s, the discourse about the fate of the city and the viability of the central business district hinged on two codewords: slums and blight.

"Slums," referring to deteriorating residential communities, was fused with race and crime; as Robert Beauregard wrote, "The overcrowded tenement was a dominant image of the industrial city of the early twentieth century and a fact of life for the many foreign immigrants and rural migrants

28 Stewart Udall. Qtd. in a flyer for "A City Reborn," LoCVGP. Excepts from the documentary are on a videotape in the AHCVGC. In 1999, a copy of the film remained at Gruen Associates, Los Angeles.AIA Citation for Excellence in Community Architecture, 1965; and "HUD Award for Design Excellence," Fulton Mall, Fresno 1968.
29 Seligman, "The Enduring Slums," 111.
30 Crawford, "Daily Life on the Home Front," 134-5.

who took employment in large factories and innumerable sweatshops" (Voices in Decline, 36, 112). Already by 1940, the census found that more than one-third of the population was occupying substandard housing. Daniel Seligman, writing in the influential book, *The Exploding Metropolis*, referred to the irony of the enduring slums in the second decade of postwar prosperity: "Today some 17 million Americans live in dwellings that are beyond rehabilitation–decayed, dirty, rat-infested, without decent heat or light or plumbing. . . . The problem . . . is most severe in the biggest, richest, most industrialized cities."[29]

"Blight" referred to the condition of the areas immediately surrounding central business districts, characterized by dilapidated buildings, junk yards, vacant lots covered with cinders, and once-impressive mansions that had been converted into funeral parlors, etc. (Greer, "Is Your Town Fit to Live In?," 50). A typical aerial view showed empty lots and disused or underused buildings, many of them single-story structures housing unsuitable industries.

Considering that there had been little investment in American cities since the Depression, the task of renewing them was daunting. But the real test of new inner-city community development involved race. While more and more white working- and middle-class families were leaving the cities, a corresponding counter-migration was taking place: changes in agricultural practice in the rural South drew many African Americans, from about 1940, to the cities of the Northeast and Midwest in search of industrial jobs. Despite the robust urban industrial economy, which had brought the U.S. through the war, however, the lure of cheap land, tax breaks, and a new model of single-story factory served by truck instead of railcar led to massive deindustrialization in the cities from 1941. For newly arrived African Americans, there would be fewer and fewer industrial jobs. The magnitude of this migration, some five million between 1940 and 1970, created social and economic stresses that continue to drive municipal, state, and federal policies. This flood of newcomers, which Nicholas Lemann called the "largest migration of a single people in our history," encountered a culture of ignorance and denial through the 1950s (*The Promised Land*, 6). The problems and conflicts that would come to questions of housing, jobs, and social equity would render many aspects of urban renewal and reform ineffectual. Rioting before the opening of the Sojourner Truth Housing Project in Detroit in 1943 had been a portent of things to come.[30] Although the federal government would create the instruments for affordable housing in the inner cities, the implications of America's racial transmigration remained unrecognized by politicians and ignored by academics, increasing neighborhood conflict, which resulted in white city dwellers taking the new opportunities to flee the city.

The Housing Acts: only Government Intervention Can Level the Playing Field

The fundamental difference between developing an unbuilt site and developing one downtown were the site-preparation costs. In the suburbs, after purchasing the land, one planned, designed, and built. In the city, beyond questions of ownership and higher land values, one often had to demolish, and especially with former industrial sites, remove polluted soil. Renewing existing buildings was also considerably more expensive than building new. To protect the historic investment of existing commercial, shopping, and residential areas, to provide new development land, and to renovate old infrastructure, or build new infrastructure, required some sort of government intervention and support. To make development downtown more attractive and open to a broad spectrum of developers, public authorities would have to take over site-preparation costs. Private developers could then undertake individual buildings or a building ensemble. The National Housing Act of 1949, often referred to as the Urban Renewal Act because of its focus on subsidizing new rental housing in designated parts of cities, was amended in 1954 to include rehabilitating older housing in those urban-renewal areas. In the amended Housing Act of 1961, President Kennedy aimed to further interest private development by reorienting the Urban Renewal Program away from clearing slums and toward rejuvenating industrial, commercial, and cultural areas, including middle-income housing, mass transportation, and urban open spaces, so that city centers could again be the nerve centers for their expanding metropolitan areas.[31] Gruen's belief in precisely this goal—that downtown could again represent the city and region— meant that it was natural for VGA to expand from private downtown-redevelopment projects and exploit the opportunities provided by the Urban Renewal Program. The 1954 Act confirmed the importance of planning by requiring cities and towns to produce a comprehensive development plan including administrative structure, a finance plan, and a citizen-participation program. Within a few years, these new legislative tools, together with the success and publicity of Midtown Plaza, enabled VGA to undertake city-center renewal projects for around 50 cities.

31 For the Housing Act of 1949, see *Congress and the Nation* Vol. I, 478. The National Housing Act of 1949, Title 1 (Senator Howard Taft), was the enabling Act for the Urban Renewal Program. The Act provided two-thirds of the money needed to subsidize planning, start-up costs, property acquisition, demolition, and relocation for federally approved urban renewal projects. Local government had to pay the remaining one-third. The intention of Congress was to attract private developers into the business of redeveloping federally approved urban renewal areas by sharply reducing the risk of failure. The Act provided city governments with the power of eminent domain (compulsory purchase) to insure that they would be able to acquire sites from owners who were unwilling to sell. The Amended Housing Act of 1954 introduced further changes among which was federal mortgage insurance that covered up to 95 percent of the cost of new and, importantly, rehabilitated housing in urban renewal areas. The opportunity for architects and planners arose from the fact that every community receiving urban renewal assistance was required to have a *workable program* for community improvement, including a comprehensive plan, which was required to include: (1) a land use plan, (2) a thoroughfare plan, (3) a community facilities plan, (4) a public improvements program, (5) a zoning ordinance, and (6) a subdivision ordinance. Garvin, The American City..., 465; also, *Congress and the Nation*, 1969, 189; and Gruen, von Storch, and Ehrlich, "Urban Renewal," 10-18, 21-26.

32 David Rosen, author interview, Los Angeles, 1998, 2000.

33 In the 1850s, Gratiot was the destination of German immigrants and by the mid-twentieth century it had been populated by African-americans from the south seeking industrial jobs. The current residents of Gratiot occupied many houses without running water, central heating, indoor baths, or toilets. A Citizens Committee for Redevelopment was set up by the Detroit Common Council in the spring of 1954. Gruen and Walter Reuther, President of the United Auto Workers, met with the leaders of the African-American community over residential mix, agreeing on a roughly 60 percent white-40 percent African-American. Garvin (1996), p. 209-10; and, Gruen, "The City in the Automobile Age," 50-1. See also "Redevelopment f.o.b. Detroit," *Architectural Forum*, 116-25.

VGA were one of only a few architecture firms to restructure themselves to undertake urban-renewal projects, setting up a Renewal and Urban Redevelopment division. While the Highway Act would enable city redevelopment agencies to get funds for new roads, the amended Housing Act provided federal insurance on mortgages for a wider market of new or rehabilitated housing in cities, thus interesting private investors in urban redevelopment. While the architects and planners working with Gruen could design the projects themselves, the role of Gruen's Renewal and Urban Redevelopment division was to undertake exploratory feasibility studies, assist in pre-application and applications for federal grants, make field surveys and relocation plans, and coordinate the efforts of other consultants.[32] Looking back at the urban-renewal projects of the '50s and '60s, however, highlights two difficult questions: what are the necessary conditions for a successful partnership between government and private developers in carrying out large-scale urban development; and to what extent can architects design community, especially in a difficult and rapidly changing social, economic, and demographic context? In the early 1960s these questions would find few satisfactory answers.

Gratiot Community Redevelopment, Detroit, Michigan

Detroit will Replace a Slum with a Mixed Income and Mixed Race Suburb

One of Gruen's early attempts at large-scale inner-city redevelopment was in Detroit, where Northland's success had projected VGA into the forefront of the architecture and planning scene. In 1954, Gruen, collaborating with Oscar Stonorov of Philadelphia and Minoru Yamasaki of Detroit, would use the cluster-planning idea, developed at Northland, for residential community design. The masterplan for "Gratiot," a large, mixed-density residential development, was sponsored by a Citizen's Committee for Redevelopment led by Walter Reuther, President of the United Auto Workers, which had obtained rights to a 142-acre site just north of downtown, near the Wayne State University Medical School.

The intention at Gratiot was to replace the inner ring of substandard dwellings that had grown up to serve nearby industry with a modern residential community organized around neighborhoods. By offering "the advantages of a suburban lot—rest and quiet—with the desirability of being close to a big city center," the new community would only rehouse the local population, but, as a mixed-income project, also attract back to the heart of the city the middle classes, who otherwise were settling in subdivisions outside. Similar to the regional expansion plan of the J. L. Hudson Company, Gratiot was conceived by the Citizens Committee (which indeed included Foster Winter of the J. L. Hudson Company) as a prototype for a regional-development strategy that aimed to create 25 similar-sized neighborhoods around the downtown business district, thus replacing the "ring of choking slums." [33] The plan, which would ultimately house about 4,000 families, consisted of three self-sustaining "superblock" neighborhoods, each surrounded by a perimeter street, thereby leaving the residential area free of traffic. Each neighborhood would contain a mix of dwelling types, together with schools, playgrounds, parks, food markets, and service facilities.

The collaboration with Stonorov and Yamasaki worked surprisingly well, and in 1955 the project received a *Progressive Architecture* First Design Award for Town Planning and Redevelopment. Despite qualifying for $4.3 million in federal subsidies, no suitable developer was found and the project developed no further. A year later, however, after the Housing Act of 1954 came into effect, Herbert S. Greenwald of Chicago, together with his partner, Samuel N. Katzin, assembled a smaller development package of 78 acres for the Gratiot site. Greenwald and Katzin, with their architect Ludwig Mies van der Rohe and the planner Ludwig Hilbersheimer, built Lafayette Park, a project combining slab apartment buildings and row houses.[34]

It is unfortunate, though, that Gratiot was never built as Gruen, Stonorov, and Yamasaki had conceived it: mixed-use residential neighborhoods that would accommodate the existing social and racial mix, rather than the purely middle-class development built by Mies and Greenwald. Would such a social experiment have worked, and could liberal architects have created a physical form in which a diverse community could thrive? The vision of an integrated community for Gratiot was probably too optimistic; more telling was the inability to find a developer and financing, a problem that would dog the urban-renewal program until the end.

Gratiot urban redevelopment (project). Gruen, Stonorov, and Yamasaki's ensemble of neighborhood clusters combining row houses, courtyard apartments, and high-rise. What, more than typological variety and generous outdoor spaces, could architects provide for the rehousing of a mixed-race inner city community?

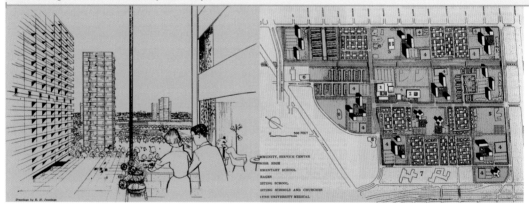

34 "Urban Redevelopment, Detroit, Michigan," *Progressive Architecture* (Awards) 100-105; *Traeumer*, 318-19; Garvin, *The American City* (1996), 209-10.
35 Plotkin, "West End Development, Another Boston New Look,"; S. Pierre Bonan was, in 1960, working on Title 1 (urban renewal) projects with Kahn & Jacobs in New Haven; I.M.Pei at Society Hill, Philadelphia; Harrison & Abramovitz in Brooklyn; and, again, with VGA on a $100 million project in Stamford. For Bonan, see "People," *Architectural Forum*, June 1960. reprint, LoCVGC.
36 "Urban Design, Award Citation," *Progressive Architecture*, 112. Charles River Park was illustrated in Shopping Towns U.S.A. (1960) in the Epilogue: The Future of Shopping Centers. Gruen, however did not include the project in *The Hearts of Our Cities* (1964).
37 Attorney Jerome L. Rappaport, acting on behalf of the developer, blamed Federal Housing Administration for the slowdown on the project. The developers wanted the F.H.A. to drop some of the safe-
guards that were holding up the loans, but the F.H.A. wouldn't back the following loan until previously constructed housing units proved their marketability. The conflict occurred during completion of two of five residential parcels, and the Boston Redevelopment Authority faced a $100,000 penalty for default against delays. See, Yudis, "Is West End Project Due for a Long Slowdown?"
38 McQuade, *Fortune*, 135. ". . . but the large essay of the Hynes administration into actual renewal had been a disaster. The West End, an entire neighborhood, 38 blocks, 41 acres, and 9,000 residents in the middle of the city had been wiped out–a low-rent, low-rise Italian tenement section . . . The area was ruthlessly cleared to make way for a cluster of high-rise, high-rent apartment houses, a banal grouping of blunt balconied towers on a treeless plain–and a bitter warning to all of the timeworn Boston neighborhoods of what renewal might mean to them too . . ." See also: Garvin, *The American City* (1996), 82, 222.

In 1958, the builder-developer S. Pierre Bonan, who was carrying out urban-renewal projects in several East Coast cities, gave Gruen the commission to plan and build "Charles River Park" in Boston's West End. The site was part of the West End Italian community, an area that had been declared a "slum" in 1953. The $50-million project would be developed on 46 acres overlooking the Charles River Basin and was conceived as a synthesis of "country come to the city," but with "big city advantages: a six- to eight-minute walk downtown, easy access to public transportation, and nearby attractions." [35]

In order to create local identity and comfortable scale and avoid problems of repetition and anonymity associated with large developments, Charles River Park adapted the Gratiot cluster-planning model, dividing the site into five neighborhoods, each with its own access from the surrounding streets and each containing between 400 and 500 families. The neighborhoods, free of internal traffic, were to be linked by a continuous park–the new "common." Schools, churches, shops, and a cultural area would also be accessible both from a pedestrian walk and a loop road, which was accessed from the surrounding streets.

In 1959, before building contracts had even been let, *Progressive Architecture* awarded Charles River Park an "Urban Design Award Citation." [36] Despite starting well, however, the project ran into problems. From Gruen's point of view, negotiations between the developers, the Federal Housing Administration, and the city deteriorated, leaving the architects in limbo. [37] But the real problems at Charles River Park were twofold: first, an urban-renewal project was going to replace a working-class community with a middle-class one; and second, little preparation had been made for rehousing the existing residents and finding new premises for business owners. A "Committee to Save the West End" argued that while the buildings in the old neighborhood might need repairs and apartments were overcrowded, the area was still a good and safe place to live, and home to many small businesses. But the community never formed an effective front against the forces of redevelopment, and, between 1958 and 1960, 38 blocks covering 41 acres were demolished, and some 9,000 residents were dispersed all over the metropolitan area. Walter McQuade, writing in *Fortune*, described the ruthless clearance as "a bitter warning to all of the timeworn Boston neighborhoods of what renewal might mean to them too." [38] The West End, the community that disappeared in preparation for the Charles River Park project, became a national symbol of the effects of urban renewal on people.

An urban-renewal project could fail for many reasons. Besides the usual economic problems, conflicts could arise between all parties: developers, city and federal government, and the local community. The legal structure and planning procedure ensured that projects took an exceptionally long time; after demolition, building sites were inactive, often for many years. An architect focusing merely on design and construction had little control because the forces were too external. The most damning problem of the urban-renewal program was that there no adequate financial or organizational measures existed to support the relocation of residents and businesses from areas slated for renewal. As Herbert Gans wrote in his 1962 book *The Urban Villagers* (which made the "West End" project infamous), after their eviction, few former residents could continue in their previous jobs, and most were paying higher rents. Rather than a detail, the relocation of tenants into better and more integrated accommodations should have been a priority. James Rouse, who was involved in drafting the amended Housing Act of 1954, believed he had written in sufficient provision for the renewal of existing neighborhoods through a combination of renovation, new-build, and if necessary relocation to a new area as a homogenous neighborhood.[39] The chance to demolish and build anew at large scale, however, was too attractive to politicians and developers, not to mention architects. The importance of

Charles River Park. Birds eye view, and Perspective view from apartment window. The idea was to lure suburban dwellers back to highrise apartment neighborhoods with generous apartments, public open space, convenient parking, and services.

39 At the time, James Rouse described the task of urban renewal as "to create clean, livable, cared-for neighborhoods out of the vast sprawling stretches of filth, congestion, and disorder that mark most of the inner city." He believed that the large slum areas needed to be broken down into identifiable "human-sized" neighborhoods, which would be much more practicable to work with. Though he was always the optimist, Rouse's definition shows how differently politicians, developers, and their architects understood the powers granted by the Housing Act. (*Better Places, Better Lives*, 68)

40 Contini, "The Renewal of Downtown Fresno," 14. See also Contini, "Urban Renewal, Performance and Prospects," 3-7. Contini wanted the best of both worlds: eminent domain for the city's part, and for the community in question, adequate support and relocation. The ULI declined to support Contini's views on the city's right to public domain.

41 Doxiades. Qtd. Beauregard, *Voices of Decline*, 176. Doxiades remarks were cited in "Can today's big cities survive?" *U.S. News & World Report*, 56.

preserving neighborhoods and rebuilding communities was often entirely ignored (*Better Places, Better Lives*, 44, 126). Worse, as Frieden and Sagalyn have shown, facts about the level of support for relocation were often misrepresented (*Downtown, Inc.*, 31-2). Later Rouse realized that it was simply neither acceptable nor possible to demolish a whole community, and that planners would have to develop the techniques to transform blighted areas, step by step, into sound, healthy neighborhoods. This as well as other weaknesses proved fatal. Many urban-renewal projects directly confronted the vast social, economic, and demographic changes that were taking place in American cities. The very slums to be improved were predominantly immigrant and especially African-American communities. The repeated destruction of these neighborhoods by urban-renewal or highway projects led leaders of those communities to call federal programs not urban renewal but "negro removal" (Downtown, Inc., 51).

Redeveloping existing residential areas was, in contrast to commercial redevelopment projects, clearly a social undertaking. Gruen's partner Edgardo Contini later noted that one could measure the success of central-area renewal far more in the complex terms of social problems and social benefits than in the more simple modernist planning goals of slum clearance and economic performance.[40] The Greek planner Constantin Doxiades put it more explicitly: "The problem of the cities which started as a structural problem turned into a problem of succession of economic and social classes, and finally has turned into a racial problem."[41] Writing his autobiography years later in Vienna, Gruen felt freer than in his contemporary speeches and articles to comment on U.S. racial-social problems and their relationship to architecture and planning. With the benefit of hindsight, he commented that "the 'WASPS' could not be lured back, merely with the promise of parking places, to the deteriorating, unsafe and traffic jammed city centers, exclusively inhabited by discriminated against racial-ethnic groups (sic)," (Traeumer, 212).

It is impossible to say whether the liberal vision of Gratiot, which imagined that the ethnic and racially mixed population could be rehoused in a new form of community, would have been successful without the kind of citizen-participation process that would not even begin to be developed until the 1970s. Certainly the use of eminent domain to evict a community was soon found to be unacceptable. The epic changes in demography and settlement were too much for slowly evolving technical planning, which relied on blunt planning instruments, insufficient process and participation, and a scale of development that was too large. For all his talk about the architect's authority and his role as "team leader," Gruen himself never engaged these problems personally. Yet, in 1966, as he devoted his time increasingly with masterplans for new town and international projects, his New York office began a large-scale rehabilitation program of row houses in Brooklyn. And a decade later, James Rouse would begin to devote more and more of his time to renovating row houses in African-American neighborhoods in Baltimore.

What Can We Learn From Gruen's Urban Planning Projects?

In his many masterplans, Victor Gruen recast the old downtown shopping street into a mixed-use, partly pedestrian shopping district. He brought back from the suburbs the retail mix, public spaces, and sense of security. The generous access roads and parking places of the regional shopping center reappeared as belt highways and underground parking garages.

The Fort Worth Plan remains a comprehensive vision of how to recast a downtown as a cluster of urban districts, each organized by its principal public space. What is regrettable is that despite the project's reputation as a monumental and total vision, it should have been practicable for the city, together with private investors, to start one of the district projects (parking garage, public space, new buildings) as a first step.

Burdick Street, Kalamazoo, reputedly America's first downtown pedestrian mall, was never a great work of architecture, yet improved vehicular access and sufficient parking made it a convenient and compact shopping environment, enriched with a calender of local events. The mall has survived not only because it has been periodically renovated and extended, but because over the years the city has supported a chain of further development projects followed that extended to the entire downtown.[42]

Midtown Plaza is the most literal case of the popular energy and economic power of the first regional shopping centers being transferred and adapted to a center-city site, and it was a high point in the work of VGA. After its opening in 1962, the city of Rochester claimed that $150 million was spent on construction of new buildings and rehabilitation of old ones as a direct result of Midtown Plaza. A marked difference between Midtown Plaza and typical shopping-center practice was the public ownership of its interior space, showing that the exclusionary practices in the suburbs were perhaps not necessary. Forty years later, Midtown Plaza remains open, but barely. Both department stores are gone, and a later generation of shopping centers finally drew out the middle classes from the city. Like Kalamazoo, the significance of the project was always greater than the sum of its parts, each of which today seems forlorn and a little ugly. At the time, the project faithfully rendered Victor Gruen's ideas about introverted architecture, but today, the plain exteriors of the inward-directed complex give no visual support to the underused streetscape around the center. A new project integrating interior and exterior cityscape is required.

Four years passed before the federal government released urban-renewal funds for Fresno's Fulton Street Mall. In 1961, urban renewal legislation had been broadened to include commercial projects, which enabled the entire "core superblock" to be brought into a single urban renewal project, and allowed consistent design and development control. Yet, the delay proved to be crucial. In 1964, when the Fulton Street Mall opened, Fashion Square Shopping Center also opened in the north suburbs, four miles from the center of town, and immediately began to

---

42 In *American Urban Architecture*, Attoe and Logann describe a series of downtown development projects, which were to follow the building of the Burdick Street Mall and illustrate the cumulative and mutually reinforcing effect of multiple projects carried out over many years rather than a single, much larger urban renewal project, 148.

draw consumers from downtown. Simultaneously, white working- and middle-class residents were leaving the residential areas southwest of downtown and being replaced by Hispanic- and African-Americans, transforming the area economically and culturally. The ability of a market to support consumption sites is not unlimited. As Lizabeth Cohen observed, the market segmentation that resulted from the proliferation of shopping centers outside the center cities created a situation where no amount of revitalization could make a city, whose population was becoming increasingly minority and poor, attractive to suburban white middle-class shoppers ("From Town Center to Shopping Center," 1067). Despite its exemplary community decision-making process, Fresno lost the battle between the suburbs and city center.

Gruen learned from these projects that, despite his authority and skill as an entrepreneur and planner, and despite the merits of his goal to return residents as well as cultural activities to the city center, the social, cultural, and planning context needed different tools and strategies:

From the unrealized Fort Worth Plan we learned that planning activity without the willingness of the administration came to nothing. Soon thereafter, we discovered that projects developed solely in collaboration with official authorities would be suspiciously judged by the citizens, and could then, through citizens' initiatives and critiques in the mass media, be blocked. Success would only be achieved in those cases, in which we had formed a client-consultant structure that coordinated existing federal and state administration, representative citizen's committee, and the city administration. At the same time, a program of extensive public relations became necessary with the mass media. (Traeumer, 222)

Despite the breadth of a project's representation in the community, the people themselves would have to grasp the economic, ethic, and aesthetic aspects of urban and suburban space. Very little could be achieved unless a community was ready to participate in and accept planning and, especially, controlled land use. In "The City in the Automobile Age," Gruen wrote, "To bring about this kind of urban order through planning on a nationwide scale . . . . we need, above all, a consensus of an enlightened public—men and women who realize the causes and effects of the ills of our present-day cities and who will demand that their living environments be places of physical, moral, and spiritual health." By the nature of his profession, the architect-planner was caught in the middle of this engagement between narrow interests and broad consensus. Yet Gruen would argue that to be in the midst of this conflict was also a strategic position if architect-planners would act at all levels. If, however, they absented themselves from this challenge, they would simply become marginalized to the point of being exterior and interior decorators (Charter of Vienna, 17-18).

Planning is the Activity; Cooperation is the Method; the Region is the Field of Action

Gruen believed that the problems of downtowns did not stem from the conflict between suburb and city, but from a lack of creative and thorough planning. In the mid-1950s, he focused on the unequal shopping standards between the planned regional shopping center and the downtowns, a condition that was aggravated by traffic problems. Ten years later, with the first generation of his downtown redevelopment and urban renewal projects behind him, Gruen learned that this "creative and thorough" planning must encompass the larger contexts of the region, the complexity of social equity, and the new processes of participation. Later he also had to accept that the competition between the new regional shopping centers and downtown shopping districts was genuine; his work in Fresno had been severely affected by new shopping centers built at the edge of the city.

Gruen's work designing new towns, which he would begin by 1960, would lead him to call for even more extensive planning that could operate from the scale of a neighborhood to the scale of the entire region. At that larger scale, new highways had to be laid out in a way that would frame—not destroy—existing landscape and settlement. Equally important would be the networking and balancing of the relationship between the historic center and new suburban centers. How to achieve these goals? Planning was the activity; cooperation between city officials, business associations, and the community was the method; and the metropolitan area—the region—was the field of action.[43]

In "Cityscape-Landscape," Gruen distinguished for the first time what he saw as the role and task of the architect-planner in the emerging regional city:

Architecture today cannot concern itself only with that one particular set of structures which happen to stand upright and be hollow "buildings" in the conventional sense. It must concern itself with all man-made elements that form our environments, with roads and highways, with signs and posters, with outdoor spaces as created by structures, with cityscape and landscape (18).

It was not enough to focus on the clustering of buildings in a way that would offer a system of public spaces, already an ambitious task; the architect-planner should incorporate and appropriate streets, roads, highways, and their immediate surroundings into his field of operation. In consolidating his view of how the role of the architect-planner, Gruen and VGA would once again be able to exploit federal legislation to move into a new area of work.

Under Presidents Hoover and Roosevelt, federal monies had been used by a new breed of person: self-declared "planners." In the early 1950s, as mentioned earlier, as part of an amendment to the Housing Act of 1949, President Eisenhower had formed a Subcommittee on Urban Redevelopment, Rehabilitation, and Conservation to establish the federal government's role in determining the fate of cities. One result of the Subcommittee's work was to require cities seeking federal assistance for urban-renewal projects to make an official plan. Eisenhower had wanted planners, and the Housing Act of 1954 legislated planning as the means by which American cities would be renewed.[44] The Fort Worth project had forced VGA to adapt the research, analysis, and planning methods developed for the regional shopping center to the making of an urban plan. With this experience behind them, VGA were ready to meet the need of American cities for comprehensive plans.

Merchants Will Save the City?

At Fort Worth, Gruen had realized that many businessmen were suspicious of planning, so he argued not for its theoretical but for its practical results. It was the key to the city's survival, and was thus beneficial to the business community in particular and to America generally. Business should be the most important ally of planning; after all, it had been Oscar Webber of the J. L. Hudson Co. who understood the need both to develop a regional marketing strategy and to create centers of the highest quality. In an interview in the *New Yorker*, Gruen went so far as to say that "it was the effort and interest of the merchants and trade organizations that would save the city."[45] In trying to persuade clients about the benefits of planning, Gruen would claim with frustrated irony,

Americans are excellent planners. We plan our suburban homes, our kitchens, and our assembly lines; our department stores are a marvel of planning. But only rarely does planning in America step outside the boundaries of the individual structure. Too rarely does it attempt to integrate various individual entities with each other and concern itself with an overall concept . . . .
("The City in the Automobile Age," 49)

According to Gruen, however, the obstacles were many: conflicting authorities; the dominance of quantitative thinking exemplified by powerful State Highway Engineers; the "frontier mentality," which led to the exploitation of the land; and lack of traditional professional involvement in urban design, represented by the weakness of the American Institute of Planners.[46]

As mentioned above, in 1961, President Kennedy was reorienting the urban-renewal program from slum clearance towards the revitalization of industrial, commercial, and cultural areas: how could cities be reshaped as more effective nerve centers for expanding metropolitan areas? Gruen agreed: the renewal of a city center must be coordinated with planning for the entire metropolitan area, yet it wasn't just a question of physical planning, planning for the metropolitan area meant planning for all social groups. Otherwise, Gruen and others could indeed revitalize the downtown business and shopping districts, and the same business groups that supported

43 In "The Emerging Pattern," Gruen wrote, "Planning accomplishes in the physical sense, what legislation does in the moral realm," (162). The aim of planning was not to limit personal liberty, but quite the opposite, to give it the greatest possible opportunity. Alexander Garvin described planning as guiding change: encouraging desirable change, and minimizing undesirable change. Successful planning is "a public action that generates a desirable, widespread, and substantial private market reaction." (xi, 3, 8) Rem Koolhaas drew an important distinction between what architects and planners do: whereas architects must consume opportunity (to create a singular building), planners must create opportunity, or as Garvin put it, "planners must concentrate on increasing the chances that everyone else's agenda will be successful."
44 Olsen, *Better Places, Better Lives*, 63.
45 Gruen, *New Yorker*, (reprinted in *Charette*, August 1956),

Reprint. "What Northland teaches us is this—that it's the merchants who will save our urban civilization. 'Planning' isn't a dirty word to them; good planning means good business . . . . As art patrons, merchants can be to our time what the church and nobility were to the middle ages." In "The City in the Automobile Age," Gruen wrote, ". . . very few businessmen consider the most important factor of all: how the community is planning now for the future. No community stands still . . . the businessman should determine what the environment will be like in 20 years . . . all industries must think of creating conditions to lure higher types of employees. Also, they should be reasonably sure of how the community will handle its growth so that the features that brought them there don't change or possibly reverse themselves." (49)
46 "City Planning." In "Reminiscences," dated May 17, 1974. LoCVGP, Box 20.

Redevelopment Plan and perspective for the Core of Stamford, CN (1960). Despite the intelligence of Gruen's project, for example, the pedestrian core area buffered from the elevated highway by light industry and office buildings, it's legal status was merely as a land use plan.

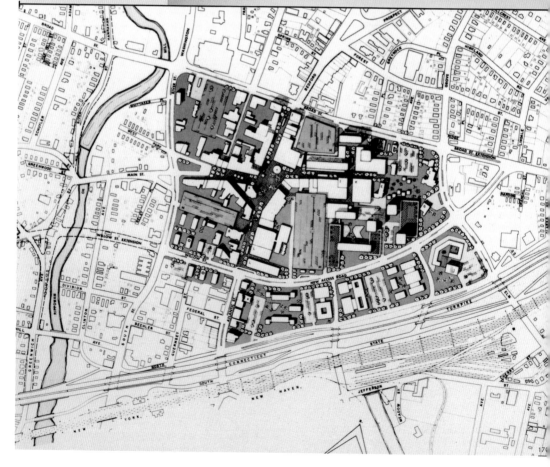

this work were eager to support their investment downtown by replacing the old inner-ring, working-class residential communities with middle-class housing; Charles River Park was a perfect example. But to replace one class with another without regard for where the displaced residents and their businesses would go was socially unsustainable. Gruen acknowledged that, in the worst cases, urban renewal was not removing slums but just moving them elsewhere. The problems of American downtowns, aggravated by ethnic and denominational prejudices, brought him to the conclusion that single or local measures could never create a just and harmonious balance in the city; both the scope and the process of urban renewal would have to be far more inclusive ("Urban Renewal," 15). Jane Jacobs' withering critique on the work of planners and the urban-renewal program, published in her 1961 book *The Death and Life of America's Great Cities*, cast a pall over the efforts of planners, the idea of the masterplan, and the ability of government and private industry to remake cities. Yet Gruen would remain convinced that a far broader planning instrument, one that could balance local issues in the context of a regional concept, could work.

Masterplanning: Success or Failure Can only Be Judged over a Long Period of Time

The statutory requirement that cities produce comprehensive plans to qualify for federal urban-renewal dollars was the impetus for the many masterplans produced by VGA and others; from the late 1950s until Gruen's retirement, VGA developed more than 50 such plans. But what was the result of all this work? A masterplan is a framework enabling a chain of decisions and actions to follow. Its development strategies must be robust enough over the long term so that subsequent development could be implemented by others. Thus it must allow for time and other plans, and it requires the skillful and fortuitous bringing together of individuals. There needs to be a positive economic climate and political will. And we now know that a masterplan cannot address deep-seated social problems. Without the participation and consensus of all interested and directly affected parties, a masterplan will probably fail. Looking back, we have trouble remembering or believing in the optimistic plans made in the decades after World War II, but, as Alexander Garvin argues, the disillusionment with urban planning is far from justified: innovative projects in a host of cities have become obscured by the many projects that were unsuccessful or never completed (The American City, 1–2).

The success or failure of a masterplan can only be judged over a long period of time, perhaps 25 years, during which the plan, architecture, urban design strategies, and development practices will evolve. Politicians will come and go, and in the best instances, the affected communities will find their voice and productively join the process. Two examples of Gruen plans subsequently altered, carried out, or revised by others are his Plan for Stamford, Connecticut (1960), and "A Revitalization Plan for the City Core of Cincinnati, Ohio" (1962).

The authors of *New York 1960* described the process well if not critically in their summary of VGA's plan for Stamford. In the late 1950s, the Connecticut Turnpike (now Interstate 95) cut through part of the old downtown core. In 1960, the city signed a 60-acre urban-renewal project planned by Gruen, with S. Pierre Bonan, the developer at Charles River Park, as developer.

While basically following the principles of his Fort Worth project, Stamford retained two business streets and related side streets within the pedestrian area. Also, by 1960, Gruen was calling for the rehabilitation of many of the older buildings. The project was delayed because of property disputes and relocation of existing tenants, and by the time construction began in 1966, a new architect had been appointed. By 1974, Stamford, despite all the problems of urban renewal, had become a destination point for jobs and services. Two decades after the Gruen plan, a downtown shopping mall opened, making the center of Stamford, formerly a provincial town at the edge of the New York metropolitan region, a "sanitized corporate dreamworld" (1089). That was hardly the intention behind Gruen's original plan. If the image of the downtowns in the Gruen perspectives is a period cliché, the architects and planners building in the 1970s and 80s created no satisfactory replacement image.

The centerpiece of Gruen's masterplan for the 475-acre core area of Cincinnati was a transportation interchange with offices on the city's main square. Local and regional buses would enter the core at a lower level direct from the beltway. Perimeter parking garages would allow, rather than a completely pedestrianized downtown, a gradation of traffic on city streets according to a "zoning plan" for different types of traffic. An important innovation in Gruen's thinking was his transferral of the system of "use classification," conventionally used for private land, for public streets. He proposed several classifications–from the most restrictive (pedestrians only), to specialized (public transportation and service vehicles only), to "permissive" (sic) (all types of vehicles) (Upgrading Downtown, 178). Gruen's plan for Cincinnati, with its focus on a central public space adjacent to a new transportation center, was not carried out because it was too expensive, certain elements wouldn't have worked, and other elements would have been blocked by the local community. As Alexander Garvin pointed out, two years later a new plan by RTKL made changes and improvements, yet basically brought forward the framework of the Gruen plan ("Unbuilt Cincinnati," 25).

Unlike the buildings that remain as evidence of the architect's work, evidence of a specific masterplan is hard to discern. I have included the plans for Stamford and Cincinnati as two examples of the fate of a "typical" Gruen masterplan. There are many others: St. Paul, MN (1958) and Green Bay, WI (1958) and incorporated waterfront into their plans, while the Central Business District Plan for Boston, MA (1967) proposed that the central area be organized by a series of pedestrian nuclei as a way of linking business, shopping, and historic structures; and the Masterplan for Teheran (1967) proposed to enable that metropolis to modernize by two measures: a subway system to create an alternative to worsening traffic, and the implementation of a system of district centers each with its own bazaar.

Revitalization Plan and perspective for the City Core of Cincinnati, OH. (1962). The Gruen plan combined aspects of the Fresno and Midtown Plaza, Rochester projects. The generous network of pedestrian malls, created for Fresno, was combined with the three-dimensional planning at midtown Plaza, including a city and regional bus station and an urban shopping center.

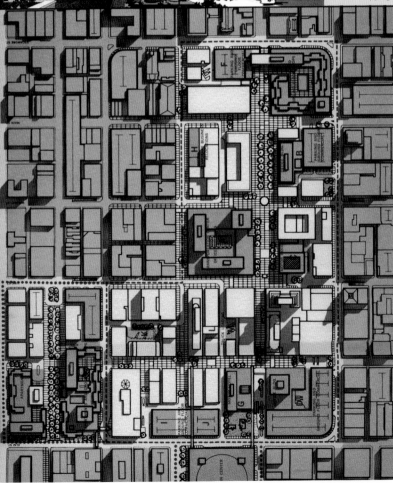

Gruen recognized the clash between the car and the city early; the need to contain the automobile set the tone for everything he did, but his object was to exploit it intelligently. As Wolf von Eckardt, Gruen's long-time booster, wrote, "The task then is not to indulge in idle fantasies about abandoning cities or automobiles, but to try to find, through planning and design, a *modus vivendi* for their coexistence" ("Escape from the Automobile," 18). The 1956 Highway Act could have provided that opportunity. If design and planning professionals didn't recognize it as such, big-city politicians saw the chance to relieve traffic congestion and increase mobility and access by means of urban highways. Yet once the mayors had successfully secured highway miles for their cities, the interstate system affected the American cityscape and landscape in ways its supporters never anticipated. Instead of facilitating movement, many new highways simply became choked with traffic. Instead of linking neighborhoods, urban highways isolated and even obliterated them. Rather than reinforcing downtowns, the beltways, built farther out partly for defense purposes, would later become the new "main streets" of America's city-regions. The intersections of beltways with highways radiating outwards from city centers would be the prime locations for, first, shopping centers, and, later, "Edge Cities," which became regional subcenters. But most of all, the effect of the Highway Act, as its planners had intended, was to disperse factories, stores, and people; in short, to create a revolution in living habits. The failure of urbanists and planners to become partners to decisions on the location and design of the freeway system led Gruen later to claim that the chance to integrate highways and urban planning had been lost:

The main tool we've had—the freeway system—we've thrown away . . . . this system could have been designed in a way that would have stressed and supplied clusters of dense activity . . . . by surrounding them and then connecting them with the downtown area. But, in designing the system, no thought was given to the city planning approach. It was purely engineering . . . . the shortest route between two given points.[47]

---

47 Gruen. Qtd. in Herbert, "Rebirth of Nation's Cities Owes a Debt to Victor Gruen," 14.
48 Cedric Price. Qtd. Gruen, "Approaches to Urban Revitalization in the United States," 190-1.
49 Qtd. Smithson, A. (ed.), "Team 10 Primer," 574. Texts date from 1960. See, for example, Patterns of Growth, Mobility, and London Roads Study: ". . . a comprehensive system of urban motorways is the only thing capable of providing the structure for a scattered city." Alison and Peter Smithson had argued for the urban motorway as an essential structuring element that would increase the legibility of big cities. Mobility was a key not only socially but also organizationally in town planning and they sought in their projects to give it a more representative form than a highway buried in the urban fabric. It would seem however that the highways planned in their projects would have divided the city no less than the urban highways planned by American traffic engineers.

Urban Highways, Perception, and Regional Form

In "*A Greater Fort Worth Tomorrow*," a series of perspective drawings showed how the revitalized city center would be perceived from specific points along the journey from suburb to the arts and shopping districts downtown. The first drawing shows the journey from suburb to beltway, with the silhouette of the city center in the distance; in the second drawing, having exited the beltway, we approach one of the great parking garages–a helicopter is landing on the roof; in the third, we are emerging from one of the museums in the arts district–we look across a plaza surrounded by varied new buildings, our parking garage stands in the distance; and the fourth portrays a lively pedestrian mall at the heart of the city. This standard presentation technique reveals an aspect of modernist–and contemporary–citymaking that architects and planners have only barely begun to exploit. Gruen is showing us that highways can be so designed that the downtown can be seen and understood as a whole, and its different districts identifiable. It is a narrative in which the "view from the road," to use the title of Kevin Lynch's 1964 book, would contribute to a new kind of urban comprehension in which motion, perception, and the relationship between building and ensemble would become part of an everyday urban experience. It means that highways, and indeed automobile use, when carefully integrated into regional and city planning, and urban design, can be part of a concept of urbanity.

Gruen's often overwrought criticism of the car, and his insistence that the city center was irreplaceable as the basis for urban culture, suggests that he refused to acknowledge both how people wanted to live and the irreversible trends of dispersal and increasing automobile use. Yet the Fort Worth perspectives, and the spacious layouts of his new town and new city plans shows that good planning could accommodate both dense urban environments and generous space for the automobile. When urban highways were cut destructively through cities, and when the car was used indiscriminately as an instrument of "mass transportation," he would become sarcastic.

In 1962, at a lecture Gruen delivered at the Architectural Association in London, Cedric Price challenged Gruen's negative views of the car and the city:

To talk about the car as a wicked weapon. . . . is to ignore the fact that the motor car is wholly an extension of human faculties . . . . One's whole range of activity, of social intercourse, human contact and pastimes, is extended to an immeasurable degree . . . . I would suggest that the heart of the city is no longer valid and it is very questionable whether we should be using words like 'town' and 'city' anymore. The new freedom that we have through extra leisure and through eventually 100 percent mobility means that as long as the architects do not stop us and the planners do not stop us, the pattern of life and the fullness of life and therefore the resultant civilization patterns can be free and multi-directional.[48]

In a similar vein, architects such as Alison and Peter Smithson argued for the urban motorway as an essential structuring element that would increase the legibility of big cities. Mobility was a key not only organizationally but also socially in town planning, and they sought in their projects to give it a more representative form: "Mobility has become the characteristic of our period. Social and physical mobility, the feeling of a certain form of freedom, is one of the things that keeps our society together, and the symbol of this freedom is the individually owned motorcar."[49]

Whatever the arguments that Gruen and others might lodge for or against the car, the continued build-out of suburbia simply demanded it. By the 1960s, spatially and functionally dispersed development was a fact; one had to keep driving to live—mobility was indeed, to a large extent, "enforced mobility," as Gruen put it (Heart of our Cities, 213). As cities spread out, the increasing number and use of motor vehicles of all kinds was becoming the major instrument of typological change. The demand for personal mobility given by the car and the need for efficient distribution and delivery by the trucking industry meant that the structure of the city would have to be reconsidered altogether.

Disappearing off your Screen: the American City

At the peak of his work in urban-redevelopment projects, Gruen was engaged with a city for which Americans showed tremendous ambivalence. In Southern California, the myth of mobility, freeway culture, and then the Watts riots of 1965 doomed the idea of compact planning, density, and investment in public transport. Even in the Midwest and East Coast cities, despite the examples of Burdick Street Mall, Midtown Plaza, and projects by others in cities such as Philadelphia, Pittsburgh, and Baltimore, the inability of city governments and the federal urban-renewal program to respond to changing economic and social developments doomed the urban reforms of the Kennedy and Johnson administrations. Gradually through the late '60s and early '70s, the American city was allowed to become, as Robert Beauregard described it, "the site for society's contradictions" (Voices of Decline, 244). In his autobiography, Gruen bitterly remarked that perhaps the American center cities didn't have that much to lose and for some time had offered people little more than traffic jams (Traeumer, 213). A few years before, in an article titled "Why we want our cities ugly," Phillip Johnson claimed that Americans would never accept anyone else's vision for a beautiful city and a sustainable environment until they had changed their values—Johnson used the German word Weltanschauung—or, more simply, until they exchanged their preoccupation with their private realm for an interest and trust in the public realm. He quoted the Secretary of Defense, Robert McNamara: "Building or rebuilding our cities is not a question of money. We can afford to defend our country and at the same time rebuild it beautifully. The question is one of the will of the American people." McNamara was wrong; unfortunately, the Vietnam War and inner-city riots precipitated a long winter, when politicians dared not mention the word city because of its negative associations. The downtown-redevelopment projects of Victor Gruen and others, built in the 1950s and 1960s, would be left for America's newest citizens and remaining inner-city communities to fathom. Those who could afford it left the city behind in pursuit of a different utopia—insulated, homogenous, and anti-urban, and brought into existence by the automobile.

Buildings, streets, parking lots: the texture of the American downtown (Rochester, NY around 1958).

Toward New Urban Forms

Gruen spent the second half of his American career fighting the continued dispersal of the American city, but his work was beset by contradictions. More than once, he found himself torn between competing opportunities—his office was asked by a city for a downtown-development or renewal project, and at the same time approached by development groups eager to build a shopping center outside the city boundaries. He tirelessly campaigned for the renewal of America's downtowns, yet the completion of the Interstate Highway system, the continuing expansion of the suburbs, and the proliferation of shopping centers, robbed downtowns of shoppers and investment. Critics would later claim that Gruen never came to grips with the role of cities versus suburbs.[50] His redevelopment projects brought downtown the more generous suburban spatial standards developed for the regional shopping center—acknowledging the expectations of a new generation who would not go back to pre-World War II space standards. This was the first step in a process that continues today whereby the traditional civic, religious, and economic function of the historic downtowns are partly, or wholly, replaced by tourist, consumption, and "experience" activities. Yet this new suburban scale would prove difficult to integrate with existing urban context. While suburban development continued to spread the American city into its region, Gruen searched for the opportunity to create a new urban form that could accommodate the automobile and low-density community planning, while, at the same time, offering attractive and dense mixed-use central areas. In seeking a new settlement pattern, Gruen looked for a structure that would allow contradictory forces of decentralization and concentration to coexist. While VGA's shopping-center and urban-redevelopment divisions continued to work in the suburbs and downtown, Gruen was drawn by a new interest, the opportunity to create new towns; an American counterpart to the experiments taking place in Britain, Scandinavia, and France.

Alternatives to Sprawl: Gruen's Theory of Citybuilding

Sprawl versus Utopia

From Cluster Planning to new Cities

Are New Towns and Cities Possible?

Sprawl versus Utopia

Between the late 1950s and the late 1960s, a toxic collection of factors stimulated architects and planners to create altogether new images of the city. These factors were sprawl, the disappearance of the natural environment and its degradation thanks to poor development practices, and the seemingly unsolvable problems of the inner city. In Western Europe, the problems of sprawl were only beginning to make themselves felt. The impetus for new city models there was the failure of late modernism to furnish images, spaces, and forms with which people could identify.

Sub-Cityscape

In America, the pace and extent of suburban expansion meant that the real-estate industry, private development, and municipal authorities, who were bound to provide roads and utilities, were barely able to keep up with growth. Few of these actors were considering what the consequences of rapid and dispersed growth would be for the future of city and region. The problem was not growth itself, but the inability of metropolitan areas to cope with the rising population in any other form than sprawl. In 1955, Gruen had been invited to speak about Northland at the International Conference on Design at Aspen, Colorado. Instead he presented a paper entitled, "Cityscape-Landscape," which referred to the diverse and dispersed city fabric that was stretching far beyond the city into the metropolitan region and was, as Gruen described it, "tightly woven here, loosely woven there–forming an overall weave often a hundred miles in every direction." "Just as landscape was an environment in which nature predominated and of which there were many different varieties, so too," he wrote, "were there many types of cityscapes, including traditional buildings, blocks, avenues, and squares. But, unfortunately, many other new '-scapes' were becoming ever more prevalent." Gruen defined these, in his characteristically battered English, as "technoscape–the detritus of technology," consisting of automobile graveyards and industrial waste dumps"; "transportationscape–the tinny surfaces of miles of cars and acres of parking lots"; and "suburbscape–the parade ground of the mass housing industry." All of these combined to make "sub-cityscape," and the quintessence of sub-cityscape was the commercial strip "clinging like leeches to all roads." The agent of sub-cityscape of course was the private automobile, misused as mass transport. Because of sub-cityscape, city planning became obsolete before it even had the chance to become effective, and so would have to be replaced by a new regional planning ("Cityscape...," 18).

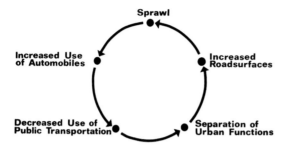

Sprawl

Increased Use
of Automobiles

Increased
Roadsurfaces

Decreased Use of
Public Transportation

Separation of
Urban Functions

The suburban labyrinth, or "Enforced mobility." The suburbanite condemned to unlimited automobile trips merely because of separated single-use development. In our time, the "soccer mom" as chauffeuse.

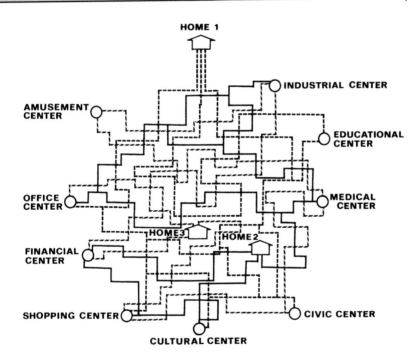

HOME 1

INDUSTRIAL CENTER

AMUSEMENT
CENTER

EDUCATIONAL
CENTER

OFFICE
CENTER

MEDICAL
CENTER

HOME3   HOME2

FINANCIAL
CENTER

SHOPPING CENTER

CIVIC CENTER

CULTURAL CENTER

At the time, Gruen's evolution from shopping center designer to planner of urban-redevelopment projects—Fort Worth was in design—gave him an overview of the conflict and symbiosis between suburb and downtown. In contrast to the assiduous multidisciplinary planning required for the regional shopping center, Gruen claimed the sprawling development along roads and highways was the result of short-range economic thinking, political accommodation, and a lack of regional planning. With sprawl, infrastructure and services were being stretched to the breaking point, at increasing cost to municipalities. By the time Peter Blake published *God's Own Junkyard: the Planned Deterioration of America*, in 1964, the build-out of the suburbs had reached far beyond the early postwar subdivisions that Gruen had been describing. Blake fumed over Eisenhower's tax and depreciation incentives, which encouraged development on new greenfield sites. Able to write off a building's value in a short time, developers of strip centers or regional shopping centers could build cheaply, cut maintenance costs, and then sell out. This strategy soon resulted in a bewildering duplication of strip centers and shopping malls, the proximity of Gruen and Rouse's Cherry Hill and Moorestown malls being one example. From the point of view of architectural, urban-design, and regional-planning quality, changes in tax law discouraged long-term investment in buildings and their surroundings.[1]

As critics of sprawl, Gruen and Peter Blake followed a first generation in the 1930s, including Lewis Mumford, Catherine Bauer, and Carl Feiss, who reacted to the implications for traffic, roads, and community design of the large number of automobiles produced in the 1920s. What were the instruments for a new planning that could bring legibility to the relationship between the old downtowns, inner-ring industrial areas, open space, and the automobile-dependent suburbs? What pattern, or form, should new development take? Was there a planning model or development strategy that might control, guide, or at least mediate the contemporary urbanization?

1 Blake, *God's Own Junkyard*, 28. See my note 10, Part 2: Hanchett, "U.S. Tax Policy and the Shopping Center Boom of the 1950s and 1960s," 1082-1110.
2 Hays, *Beauty, Health, and Permanence*, (12, 528). Samuel Hays describes the importance of the quality of one's environment as a direct reflection of the aspiration for a better life: what is achievable for "oneself, one's community, and one's society." See also, Rome, *The Bulldozer in the Countryside – Suburban Sprawl and the Rise of*

American Environmentalism, xi.
3 Lear, Afterword, in Rachel Carson, *Silent Spring*, 259-60. and Melosi, "Lyndon Johnson and Environmental Policy," in Robert A. Divine (Ed.), *The Johnson Years*, 140. As Linda Lear pointed out, part of the force of Carson's book, which caused President John F. Kennedy to order an examination of pesticide misuse, was its appearance at the height of the cold war, shortly after the Cuban Missile Crisis, and against a backdrop of nuclear testing and stockpiling.

A corollary to sprawl that would prompt new thinking about development was the increasing effect it was having upon the natural environment. "America's Suburban Revolution" had brought almost immediate consequences to the air, water, and landscape. A paradox of massive suburbanization was that from the start, not only were there technical problems, such as septic tanks leaking into the water table, but there was a clash between continuing suburbanization and the interest and demand for open space, recreation, and the preservation of wild lands. The natural amenities, one of the attractions of the suburban dream, became threatened as more people moved away from the city. As one subdivision joined another–filling valley floors, climbing up the slopes of foothills, or eating into forestland–open space disappeared and, paradoxically, led to a greater interest in outdoor recreation, especially in the State and National Parks; landscape began to be understood as an essential part of human habitation. As people related naturally to where they lived and worked, this aspiration for a better environment was infused with a sense of place: home, region, and the wider world.[2] In 1962 Rachel Carson published *Silent Spring*, chronicling the environmental consequences of the use of persistent chemical pesticides in industrialized agriculture, and opened the public consciousness to the interrelations between humans, nature, and technology; soon concern about congestion and pollution eclipsed the previous focus on the loss of wilderness. The natural environment and the built environment were becoming understood as finite entities, and this realization would be the starting point for the idea of the Sustainable City.[3]

"The masked builder strikes again."
Cartoon by Virgil Partch from
Gruen's *Heart of Our Cities*.

While middle-class Americans were discovering that the suburbs had their own problems, the deteriorating physical and social conditions in the inner cities and older industrial areas precipitated an urban environmental consciousness at the highest political level. In his "Great Society" speech, President Lyndon Johnson made a plea for the city, issues of social sustainability, and civic vision. The Great Society would be "a place where the city of Man serves not only the needs of the body and the demands of commerce but the desire for beauty and the hunger for community . . . . It is a place where men are more concerned with the quality of their goals than with the quality of their goods."[4] Johnson's commitment to the city and to the environment, together with the contribution of his wife, Ladybird Johnson, was unusual and in stark contrast to subsequent administrations, which have seldom uttered the four-letter word "city," a code for poverty, race, and an endless drain of tax dollars.

In 1965, Gruen was asked to be part of Ladybird Johnson's White House Conference on National Beauty, her goal was to improve the appearance and quality of life of Washington, D.C., beautify the highway system, and raise concern for the "environment." While apparently superficial, Ladybird Johnson's role was valuable; "beautification" directed popular attention to the appearance of the public environment and improvement of the quality of life in towns and cities. In his autobiography, Gruen described his involvement with the committee at first with irony–Washington at the time had large areas of poverty and unemployment. Thirteen years before the Environmental Protection Act, Ladybird Johnson's interest inspired environmentally minded individuals and groups to become involved in shaping government programs. Her goal to "leave this splendor for our grandchildren" effectively defines one of the key concepts of sustainability (Gould, 172).

4 The "Great Society" speech. President Lyndon B. Johnson, 22 May 1964, University of Michigan, Ann Arbor, in: *Congress and the Nation* Vol. II, 1969: 188. Johnson also said, ". . . many of you will live to see the day, perhaps 50 years from now, when there will be 400 million Americans; four-fifths of them in urban areas. In the remainder of this century urban populations will double, city land will double, and we will have to build homes, highways and facilities equal to all those built since this country was first settled. So in the next 40 years we must rebuild the entire urban United States . . . ." See also, Melosi, "Lyndon Johnson and Environmental Policy," 122,139.
5 Wright, *The Disappearing City*. Broadacre City was described further *When Democracy Builds* (1945), and *The Living City* (1958). Broadacre City, which imagined the urban population dispersed into a landscape of single-family houses, accepted mass use of the automobile, and required the roadside market and community center for social, commercial, and cultural activities. Wright's vision was a synthesis of the department store and a county fair, and in *The Disappearing City*, he described it thus: "vast amusement parks, commercial spaces standing alongside the road and made up of enormous and splendid buildings, will be designed for the sale not only of commercial products but also of cultural productions . . . ." He described the community center as an "attractive automobile objective," an entertainment center that should include a golf course, zoo, and art gallery. See *The Living City: Markets*, 168 and *Community Centers*, 174.

Urban Utopias

The search for new city form recurs in the history of architecture, and in the early and mid-1960s it stirred an active debate with widely divergent views and sometimes fantastic proposals. Architects and planners sought a new type of city that, in contrast to the 19th-century industrial metropolis—with its cramped living quarters, lack of green space, and social division—offered easy access both to nature and to local and regional centers, besides accommodating increasing automobile traffic. If the dream of the 20th-century consumer was a house with a garden, then the century started with Ebenezer Howard's Garden City in 1902, which proposed satellite towns of about 30,000 inhabitants around a metropolitan core. Howard's theories were soon put into practice at Letchworth (1904) and Welwyn (1919), both outside London, and they were taken up across the Atlantic by the Regional Planning Association of America. In 1930, RPAA members Clarence Stein and Henry Wright opened the first phase of Radburn, New Jersey, "the first suburban subdivision for the motor age." The Radburn "superblock," which synthesized Garden City ideas with the best American subdivision practice, utilized a cul-de-sac to separate pedestrian from automobile traffic, a logical measure given that, by 1927, 26 million cars and trucks were on American roads. Although never completed, Radburn was a highly influential precedent that Gruen and many other architects and planners would take up.

Besides Howard's planetary Garden City model, the most persistent images for architects were Le Corbusier's *Ville Contemporaine*, which Gruen had seen in Paris in 1925, and Frank Lloyd Wright's Broadacre City, an infinitely expandable settlement pattern that was continually modified from the 1930s to the 1950s. For traditional urbanists, Wright's arguments for Broadacre City were particularly hair-raising. In 1932 he wrote that "the future city will be everywhere and nowhere, and it will be a city so greatly different from the ancient city or any city of today that we will probably fail to recognize its coming as a city at all . . . . "With the aid of the automobile and the telephone, it would erase the distinction between urban and rural and thus make the great industrial cities redundant. In a prescient remark hinting at the future ambiguity of the architect's role, Wright stated that America would need no help to build Broadacre City: "it would build itself, haphazard." [5]

Writing in the September 1956 *Architectural Forum*, Catherine Bauer argued in "First Job: Control New-city Sprawl" that none of these examples, all conceived in the early part of the century, could be appropriately adapted to the circumstances of the contemporary American city. She believed that Howard's reduced density and Wright's decentralization would be the kiss of death for city and country alike; as for Le Corbusier, his towers and slabs were too easily stripped of their innovative features, recast as mass housing, and isolated from their surrounding communities. A new concept was needed to sort out problems of traffic, infrastructure, and the symbiotic relationship between the old city centers and the new expanding suburbs (106-9).

By the early 1960s, three new ideas for city development had appeared that accepted the *laissez-faire* nature of American development patterns and sought to acknowledge the importance of mobility: "Megalopolis," an analysis by the French geographer Jean Gottman of the slowly coalescing urbanized northeast corridor between Washington and Boston; "Dynopolis," a progressively expanding linear city model developed by the Greek planner Constantine Doxiades; and, from Melvin Webber, "Non-place Urban Realm," which was not a city model but a prediction of the urban lifestyle of the future, where communication and professional association, not spatial contiguity, were the qualitative factors. Each of these theses represented a serious analysis of trends in settlement pattern and lifestyle, but they were anathema for Gruen.

However accurate a term for a continuous multicentered regional city, Gottman's "Megalopolis," as Robert Stern pointed out, frightened and irritated traditional urbanists almost as much as it did the public at large. In the case of New York, it implied a gradual loss of distinction for both city and region.[6] Would cities, by growing together, simply lose their identity as entities in a regional urban landscape? Doxiades' "Ekistics," the science of human settlement, was not so very far from Gruen's ideas about environmental planning. Both shared the view that the architect-planner should seek to balance all forms of the development within its region. Doxiades' "Dynopolis" project, developed for Washington, D.C., and illustrated with machine-like diagrams, showed the city expanding exponentially southwards along the Potomac River, with urban centers at regular intervals. The city would be organized into superblocks scaled to automobile speeds, rather than traditional urban streets and blocks. Through-traffic was restricted to the perimeter of the superblocks, except for slow-speed *cul-de-sac* access to the residential neighborhoods. The central area of the superblocks was reserved for pedestrians. Where Gottman merely gave a name, "Megalopolis," to a developing superregional urban form, Dynopolis would presumably need a strong political and legal framework to coerce development to follow a linear pattern. Gruen agreed with Doxiades' adaptation of the superblock, yet called his Dynopolis project "More Miracle Miles," believing that the downtowns were already much too large and loose; "the job is to tighten up this inner sprawl not eat up more and more land by elongating the city core," he said.[7]

The most radical theory–for the dissolution of the city, or rather, the evolution of an urban lifestyle that could take place in just the sort of dispersed individualized landscape imagined by Frank Lloyd Wright–came from the planning theorist Melvin Webber, whose reaction to the

6 Stern et al, *New York 1960*, 25. See, Gottman, *Megalopolis: The Urbanized Northeastern Seaboard of the United States*, 1961. Gottman defined Megalopolis physically as "an almost continuous stretch of urban and suburban areas from southern New Hampshire to Northern Virginia and from the Atlantic shore to the Appalachian foothills . . . and functionally as "the cradle of a new order in the organization of inhabited space" (3). In Megalopolis, despite the apparently "continuous" development, relatively little of the area is developed to urban densities. For Gruen's view, see *The Heart of Our Cities*, 181-2; and Gruen, (Interview), "Cities in Trouble-What Can Be Done?," *U.S. News & World Report*, 84-93. He described Megalopolis as, "the phenomenon of many city areas growing together into one tremendous, disorganized and

amorphous 'over-city', which has lost many of the characteristics which a true city should have" (86). Ten years later, Peter Hall described three great Megalopolitan concentrations in the United States, Boston to Washington (39 million), Chicago to Pittsburgh (over 20 million), and San Francisco-Los Angeles-San Diego (over 25 million in the1980s); see Hall, "Anonymity and Identity in the Giant Metropolis," 44.
7 Doxiades, *Architecture in Transition*, 106-9. Gruen discussed Dynopolis briefly in *The Heart of Our Cities*, 181-2; and in Ehrenkrantz, and Tanner, "The remarkable Dr. Doxiades," 115.
8 Webber, "Non-place Urban Realm." *Explorations into Urban Structure*, 89. See also his, "Order in Diversity: Community without Propinquity," 30, 49.

expansion of cities into their metropolitan regions led to his theory of the "Nonplace Urban Realm," precisely the kind of city that Victor Gruen would fight against. Webber believed that the spatial patterns of American cities were going to be considerably more dispersed, varied, and space-consuming than ever–whatever metropolitan planners or anyone else tried to do. Mobility and communication were more important than traditional attachment to "place." The amount of communication and interaction between diverse social interest groups were the indicators of a new kind of density in a spatially unbounded urban realm. The very aspects of the city that Gruen was trying to "fix" were for Webber redundant and simply a hindrance to the emerging idea of a "post-city," yet urban age. What was at issue was the size and nature of "centers." For Webber human interaction, or appropriation, qualified a place as "central," but centrality need not be bound to fixed built spaces.[8] For Gruen, the experience of suburban and urban shopping centers simply demonstrated that people needed and wanted to be drawn to central places, to visit them frequently, and to stay for some time.

New city forms

Jean Gottman's 1961 diagram of the urban region between Washington, D.C. and Boston. Gottman's thesis has since become fact, the region is commonly known as the "Northeast Corridor."

The Dynopolis model applied to Washington, D.C.

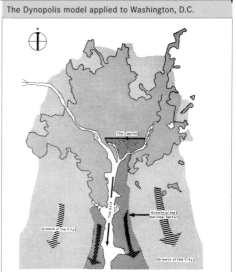

Doxiades' diagrams for Dynopolis. Planning would some-how steer development towards progressively expanding directional growth.

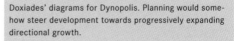

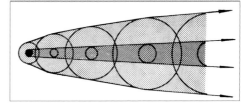

The American city, which had spread out along railroad lines in the 19th century, was now growing along the new highways. The planned interstate highway system became in practice, in city planning theory, and in the popular press a backbone structure for development leaving cities. In the 1950s, at the height of the Cold War, the idea of decentralizing cities along the lines of the highway system as a dispersal strategy against nuclear attack was taken up by the planner Ludwig Hilbersheimer and illustrated in his 1949 book, *The New Regional Pattern*. Rather than dispersing settlement according to Garden City principles, as Clarence Stein and the architects and planners associated with the Regional Planning Association of America were proposing, Hilbersheimer's project was radically abstract and modernist. The idea that linear "cities" could follow the highway network appealed to the popular press, which seized upon the idea of infinitely expanding highway cities; *U.S. News & World Report*, for example, published several articles with titles like "Cities As Long As Highways–That's America Of The Future" (1957) and "Sprawling Strip Cities–They're All Over U.S." (1961).

The concept of the endless city, the ability for both parents to be constantly driving, and the potential of technology to enable a virtual community offered no answer to the question of local identity, or the value of a collective civic culture, which was what concerned Gruen above all in his concepts for a new city. When Cedric Price claimed that it was perhaps cities and centers that were the problem and not sprawl and the automobile, Gruen could only reply in exasperation that "in the end boy doesn't meet girl over the television set."[9] Gruen would seek to create limits and spatial distinction within the expansion that the Gottman, Doxiades, and Hilbersheimer models simply accepted. In contrast to Webber's idea of "virtual" urbanity, Gruen believed that physical public space was the vessel of urban culture. If Webber seemed to be describing daily life in metropolitan Los Angeles, Gruen's reference point, if not Vienna, was the urbanity of the Rockefeller Center in New York or downtown San Francisco.

Strip versus cluster. The city as a function of traffic and road design. Strip cities are the result of local traffic, and the potential of cluster cities is based on the widely spaced access points along the interstate highway system. The Architectural Forum saw these latter as "the potential nuceli of really organizable new cities (1956)."

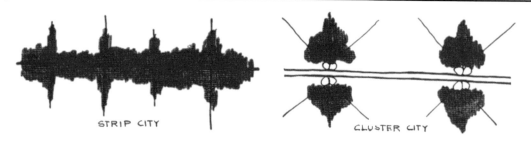

STRIP CITY   CLUSTER CITY

9 Gruen and Cedric Price. Qtd. Gruen, "Approaches to Urban Revitalization...," 190-1.

Gruen's Theory of Citybuilding: Cluster Planning

Gruen's theory of citybuilding evolved from four concepts: first, a network of public spaces, second, the cluster as the principal planning element; third, the city as a regional yet finite entity; and fourth, the architect-planner as the key figure to manage the increasingly complex process of guiding development on a regional scale.

The principal leitmotif within Gruen's urban-design and planning theory was public and semi-public space—its scale, program, and meaning. Its evolution from a design element to key component of Gruen's humanistic philosophy of cities and urban culture may be traced in his development from shop designer, to architect of shopping centers and planner of downtown shopping districts, to a planner of new towns and new cities. The arcade spaces that Gruen developed for his shops enabled a potential customer to step from the pedestrian flow and the noise of traffic into an urban room that was part of the street. Later, this intermediate zone between street and interior was reiterated in the malls, lanes, and arcades of his first shopping centers, restoring to shoppers—even in the privatized world of the suburbs—a collective "public" realm. When the spaces of the shopping center were brought downtown, either as indoor "community living rooms," as at Midtown Plaza, or through the extended pedestrian mall system at Fresno, Gruen named this "environmental planning." In the early '60s, Gruen used the term "environment" to mean the structure of urban public spaces—the setting for the social and cultural life of the city—won away from the encroachments of the automobile.

In the early open-air shopping centers, but especially downtown, public space wasn't to be understood merely as a singular entity—a square or plaza—but as a series of urban settings, a spatial and built ensemble where people and activities came together. Taking the idea of a livable pedestrian environment one step further, Gruen wrote in "On Architecture and City Planning—A Yale Report," that the city should be like a large outdoor living room where activities could be publicly enjoyed together with many others—"something," he claimed, "which we have nearly forgotten." In Gruen's city, architects and planners would exercise one of their noblest tasks: shaping open spaces. Public space animated by human activities, not the architectural object, was the building block of cities.

If the structure of public spaces formed an armature for public life, how were buildings to be arranged? "Cluster planning" was an idea Gruen had discovered around 1952 in the transition from the first Eastland project—a linear form closed into an ellipse—to the design of Northland, where the tenant-store blocks were clustered around the Hudson's department store, creating a series of open spaces; Northland was a group of five buildings. In contrast to the spaciousness without space of standard subdivision planning practice, or the towers and slabs set in a "park"—the often dysfunctional model of modernist planning—cluster planning was a flexible design instrument that ensured urban public space as the core element of any development form; it could be superimposed and expanded or contracted to fit existing conditions. In support of his thesis, Gruen claimed that these kinds of places already existed in the American landscape, and entirely new ones were being developed in the mid-1950s. The traditional American college campus was proof that an ensemble of buildings with limited automobile access was attractive; Gruen argued that the best regional shopping centers represented equally successful planning experiments: cluster planning worked ("The Emerging Urban Pattern," 132). Once he had achieved the spatial composition of the cluster, Gruen was sure he had found an organizational form not only for a shopping center but for a city. In "Modern Architecture," he wrote,

The answer seems to me to lie in the creation of human activity nuclei or clusters, based on the scale of acceptable walking distance within each unit. Each cluster will be separated from the next by neutral areas of varying width, which may be devoted to agriculture or recreational purposes. Constellations of clusters will form communities, constellations of communities towns, and a galaxy of towns a metropolitan area around a compact and vigorous, cultural, social, administrative and economic center, the metropolitan core. Between these nuclei within the neutral areas, there will be ample space for the traffic carriers of the future.

The organization of the regional shopping center thus yielded a spatial and programmatic structure not only for revitalizing downtown shopping districts, but also for recentralizing the emerging city region. In his article "The Planned Shopping Centers in America," written for the inaugural issue of the international journal *Zodiac*, Gruen described the recentralizing agency of the planned shopping center in its regional context and linked the potential of his new cluster system with the reality of the emerging American regional city:

As a planning concept, it (the regional shopping center) is a formula of the new order to come within our entire urban pattern, and in this term I include not what we usually refer to as cities but the entire sprawling fabric of suburbs and metropolitan towns. As a planning concept . . . it is the forerunner of the nuclear or cluster or, as some people call it, the cellular approach for regional planning.

---

10 Team 10, *Arena*, June, 1965, 13. Qtd. Jencks, *Modern Movements in Architecture*, 305. See especially, Alison and Peter Smithson, *The Charged Void*, 19,30.
11 Maki, "Investigation into Collective Form," 22. Maki studied at Cranbrook and Harvard, and taught at Washington University in St. Louis between 1956-63. Like Gruen, he criticised the over reliance on technology and believed it must not dictate urban form. Both Maki and van Eyck criticized the vast structures of the *avant garde*, such as the Tokyo Bay project of Kenzo Tange.

Space and Identity

The idea of cluster planning, whereby the city would be articulated by many centers of intensity instead of just one–the historic core–appeared more or less at the same time in Europe and North America. As Gruen evolved his ideas, younger architects and planners associated with CIAM, inspired by a more social and popular vision, were seeking new urban forms that created spaces for identity, place, and community. With the goal of re-establishing urban identity in a mobile society–"The feeling that you are someone living somewhere"–Alison and Peter Smithson offered two design strategies: establishing hierarchies of urban roads, and replacing Le Corbusier's four functions (living, working, recreation, circulation) with a hierarchy of human associations: city, town, village, and homestead.[10] The Smithsons used the word cluster to mean "a specific pattern of associations, to replace such group concepts as street, town, city . . . which are too loaded with historical overtones." With regard to urban structure, they were more specific; desribing their Berlin Hauptstadt project, they wrote that "present-day cities have a scattered urban structure and patchwork urban form–that is, the characteristic urban form is the *cluster*" (*The Charged Void*, 30).

Fumihiko Maki, an early member of both Team 10 and the Japanese Metabolist groups, published "Group Form" in 1960. Maki's interest in the need to design for a mass society and his idea of the city as a living organism, subject to growth and change, led him to similar ideas of organizing urban space. He sought the "smallest organizational structure," which was a cluster or ensemble of buildings and spaces, which he called "Group Form." Like Gruen, Maki believed that the investigation into group form would inevitably lead to a new regional planning, or as he put it, "regionalism in collective scale."[11]

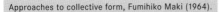
Approaches to collective form, Fumihiko Maki (1964).

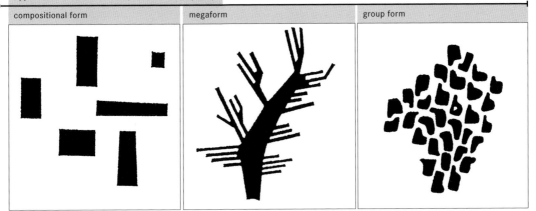
compositional form   megaform   group form

Gruen's third main concept in city-building was his belief that the city was a finite entity: when a city grew to more than 1.5 million people, it needed more than a single center; it would also need the organization of strong urban subcenters. Gruen proposed three options to manage growth but resist sprawl: recentralize by creating new "urban cores," build new towns beyond the greenbelts, and build new cities from scratch; each option worked, ultimately, with the cluster model.[12]

The immediate option was the first, to establish centrality and identity within existing sprawl by creating new cores. Gruen proposed that the regional shopping center, which had initially attracted residential and commercial development away from existing centers, should now, through better spatial and programmatic integration with its surrounding community, become a key component in the fight against sprawl. Rather than the agent of decentralization, the regional shopping center should become an agent of recentralization. New urban cores could be "accelerations" of the regional shopping center model that were better integrated and more densely developed and had a greater variety of functions. Yet better integration, in the case of Northland, for example, would be hard to achieve. The shopping center cluster of buildings was surrounded by its parking fields and buffer zone, and this isolation was merely exacerbated by the parking areas serving the medical center and office buildings that were built nearby. Years later, the "dense" suburban cores described by Joel Garreau as "Edge Cities" would be bedeviled by the same fundamentally anti-urban problem. There were no streets; you had to drive across parking fields or back onto the local highway to get to each function. In both *The Heart of Our Cities* (1964) and *Centers for the Urban Environment* (1973), Gruen acknowledged this mistake and further declared, apparently forgetting the unrealized intention to create an integrated development at Southdale, that the full potential of the regional shopping center, especially as an "urban core," had never been achieved, due to the omission of a closely planned residential community.[13]

In contrast to programmatic acceleration of the regional shopping center, the longest-term intervention, and the most radical in terms of scale and intention, would be to build self-sufficient new cities. These would be located far from existing urban centers to promote a better balance in national and regional development. Many new cities had been laid out in America's past, with both new urban structure and new social and political arrangements being the goal. Such a program, however, would have to be planned and sponsored at the highest political level. Between these short- and long-term strategies for mitigating sprawl, Gruen proposed developing smaller new towns, which would be built near existing metropolitan centers.

12 Letter, Victor Gruen to Ada Louise Huxtable, January 8, 1964. Letters File. LoCVGP.
13 Gruen, *The Heart of Our Cities*, 202; Gruen, *Centers of the Urban Environment*, 90–92.

Spaciousness of 516-acre Whitney estate would be preserved . . .

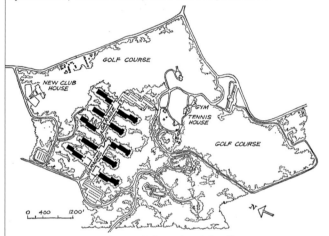

GOLF COURSE

NEW CLUB HOUSE

GYM

TENNIS HOUSE

GOLF COURSE

0   400   1200'

N

by clustering 247 town houses at the center of the site . . .

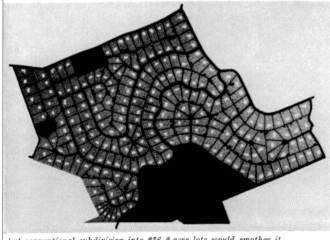

but conventional subdivision into 236 2-acre lots would smother it.

Town Center, Vållingby New Town (Stockholm), Sweden (1954). The poster child of European new towns, Gruen, Rouse and and everyone else made the pilgrimage. A mixed-use center, surrounded by apartments, with convenient pedestrian access to immediately adjacent lower density "villages," and all served by rapid transit from the city center. Still a model for today's Transit Oriented Development.

The Case for New Towns

Since the end of WWII, several European capital cities had been planning a system of new towns to address both housing shortages in their centers and the demand for increased space per family. Gruen was well aware of these from the annual trips he made to Europe, touring, lecturing, and hunting for clients, and he referred in articles and speeches to the progress of these projects, especially Vållingby, near Stockholm (1954); Tapiola, near Helsinki (1953); and Cumbernauld, near Glasgow (1962). American developers and planners were following suit with well-publicized projects for Irvine in Orange County (1963), designed by William Pereira with a new campus for the University of California; Reston, Virginia (1962), developed by Robert E. Simon; and Columbia, Maryland (1964), developed by James Rouse; the latter two to be planned in the sprawling Baltimore-Washington region.

In "The Case for Building 350 New Towns," the critic Wolf von Eckardt, writing in the mid-1960s, anticipated that by 1990 the population in the U.S. would increase from 195 to 266 million, most of the growth occurring in the metropolitan areas, where 70 percent of the population already lived. Calculating the current rate of sprawl–approximately 30 acres per 100 people–as therefore consuming 10.5 million acres, he proposed instead that building 350 new towns of 100,000 people would accommodate half this growth and cover merely 3.5 million acres. (94) New towns were meant to be qualitatively different from early postwar large-scale residential communities such as Westchester and Lakewood in Los Angeles, or the Levittowns, built near New York and Philadelphia, which were new suburban districts, where people commuted to the nearest city to work. New Towns, adapting Garden City principles, would have distinctly identifiable communities, offer a variety of housing types, have one or more mixed-use centers, and, most importantly, be partially self-sufficient by offering service, office, and industrial jobs.

14 Fred Usher, author interview, Santa Barbara, 1998, 2000; and Usher Papers. Also sketches and notes, *"1976"- Victor Gruen Associates,* July 30, 1955-Jul 23, 1956, AHCVGC box 15.

A New Urban Pattern

In 1955, Gruen had the chance to develop for a popular audience the second strand of his city-building theory–that cities were by nature finite entities and growth must be supported by new centers. He was asked to develop concepts for an NBC television documentary about how we would live in 'the world of the future' 20 years hence, in the bicentennial year 1976. The project produced sketches that ranged from overall city and regional settlement patterns to lighting and furniture for new dwelling types.[14] Gruen's sketches described a regional metropolis arranged in a planetary form, with a metropolitan core surrounded by smaller cities and towns, all well spaced from each other by green belts. A feeder road connected the entire complex to a nearby super-highway. Like the close network of villages in many European regions, Gruen's plan combined density with dispersal. Individual towns and districts were also spatially distinct, each having its own central y-shaped public space, recalling Clarence Perry's neighborhood unit diagram of 1929. The "1976" project synthesized the visionary models of the future skyscraper cities with their residential satellites exhibited at the New York World's Fair of 1939, and the "new type of 'poly-nucleated city,'" described by Lewis Mumford, with whom Gruen corresponded. In his 1938 book *The Culture of Cities*, Mumford had proposed that the giant, anti-human industrial city be replaced by a multicentered regional metropolis, in which a cluster of communities, "adequately spaced and bounded, shall do duty for the badly organized mass city" (489). Gruen wasn't going to advocate abandoning the old city center, but when a city reached a certain size, it needed more than one center; it also needed strong urban subcenters.

A year later, in 1956, the editors of *Architectural Forum* devoted their "What City Pattern?" issue to the intractable problems of the American city and asked Gruen to propose not a solution but a working method that could bring order to the simultaneous forces of "concentration, dispersion and scatteration" at work in metropolitan areas. In her introduction, "First job, control new-city sprawl," Catherine Bauer acknowledged urbanization as a process and the region as the field of action: "Now we must recognize that this renewal is only part of an over-all regional pattern of

"1976," (1955). Left, unpublished sketches in the first working through of the cellular metropolis idea. Here a view of a town with the metropolitan center in distance. Right, Y-form pedestrian center for a metropolitan town, published in the U.S. News and World Report.

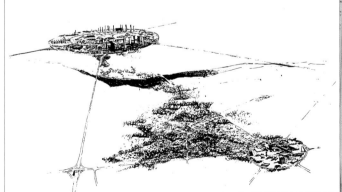
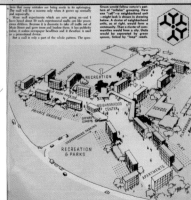

What is the relationship between the individual and the city?
Gruen's scale of progressive communal order: the modular system of the cluster,
or cellular, metropolis.

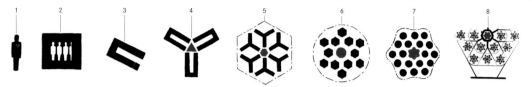

1 One module equals one human.

2 Three or more modules equal one family.

3 A number of families equal one group, a social unit.

4 A number of groups form a neighborhood, which chrystallizes around a neighborhood center offering social, cultural and economic facilities, elementary schools, churches, meeting rooms and facilities for everyday shopping.

5 A number of neighborhoods ring a constellation of clusters of a different nature: working nucleus for offices, labs, light industry; trading nucleus for retail and services, cultural nucleus, educational nucleus, recreational nucleus—together forming a community center.

6 The community centers with their satellites of neighborhoods surround a town center which offeres work, trade, entertainment, cultural and social facilities of still greater size, depth and variety.

7 This center and its galaxy of communities is formed of 50,000 to 200,000 "modules"—human beings. It constitutes a town. Some such towns would be self-sufficient. Others would be part of a large metropolitan area. The metropolitan towns would be ranged in the magnetic field of a highly potent activity center—a main creator of urban energy, the metropolitan center.

8 This center fulfills the functions we identify with the large central city core. It consists of a complex group of clusters (intimately connected by pedestrian overpasses, moving sidewalks, small electric shuttle buses and similar devices for easy flow and interchange) serving public administration, regional, statewide and national business, tourism, and those cultural and recreational activities that can be supported only by large numbers of people. Each unit in this entire cluster system—whether primarily residential or industrial or commercial—is based on the measuring stick of the walking distance acceptable for its specific conditions and purposes. This is what is meant by the human being as module. Each unit is held to a definite shape by its own centripedal force. The cluster groupings and constellations of groupings are defined and separated by neutral open areas which serve many purposes. Some are used for recreational parks, some for sports, some for agriculture, gardens, orchards, fields. These neutral areas also give us the opportunity of arranging rationally such communications as railroad tracks, automobile freeways, trucking express roads and, up above, airline air rights. By a combined radial and circular system they will connect clusters, in some cases encircle clusters, in other cases partly penetrate into clusters, but in no case will they cut through or enter into the protected zone of human activity.

Gruen, "How to handle this chaos...," 131, 132

urbanization taking in spaces far beyond, and between, old cities. Cities used to be an incident in the countryside; now countryside is becoming an incident in the City" ("First job...," 103).

In "How to Handle This Chaos of Congestion, This Anarchy of Scatteration," Gruen showed diagrams that gave more concrete form to the progressive build-up of the city model he had developed for "1976." They began with the module of a single individual, followed by a family, neighborhood, community, town, city, and finally a multicentered regional metropolis organized around a single metropolitan core. Between each element, neutral green areas of varying width could be devoted to transportation infrastructure, recreation, or even agriculture, thus ensuring access to open space. In this new pattern, the factor determining the arrangement of buildings would no longer be the road, which served the automobile, but instead the cluster, which created space for people. In contrast to Gottman's and Doxiades' visions of the city, Gruen set out to develop a city model that was bounded, with a hierarchy of centers, a community based on the attraction of public space and public life. This articulated development had spatially distinct communities that would retain a local identity within a metropolitan structure.

15 Gruen, "Environmental Architecture," 97.

The fourth strand of Gruen's theory of city-building was to define the role of the architect as the "generalist" team coordinator, in a way that would maintain his leadership in an ever more complex building and planning process. This had been, as we've seen, a theme of growing intensity in Gruen's work, ever since his development of merchandising principles for Milliron's. The transformation of the American cityscape and landscape now positively threatened the entire discipline of city and regional planning.

By the early '60s, with many downtown redevelopment projects underway, Gruen was moving more decisively from architectural concerns and focusing on the city and its planning. In a 1962 *Fortune* article by Walter Guzzardi, Jr., entitled, "The Environmental Architect," Gruen offered a provocative distinction between architecture and planning and further qualified the role he saw for himself as the leader of a multidisciplinary team in the design of the whole environment:

We do not belong to the Form Givers. We have no desire to create new fashions in architecture. There is little value in the building of buildings alone. The only thing that really matters is taking the whole area and creating an environment, comfortable and convenient for the people who live there, work there, or shop there. It is environmental architecture that really calls for imagination today. Architectural style is secondary (77).

Gruen believed that the "search for style" would only lead to frustration and was a waste of creative energy. "In a complex society," he said, "the individual building lost its significance because it depended on the environmental conditions surrounding it."[15] There was no point in focusing on the building if it was surrounded, whether in a city center or along a suburban highway, by a disordered landscape. Of course an architect could focus on producing a singular architectural object, but the task of creating the wider environment also fell to architecture—if not architects, who else?

In the last phase of work in the U.S., Gruen would have the chance to apply his city-building theory in projects for new towns and new cities, some, like his plan for the World's Fair, that were not built, and others, such as Valencia, that were, and are still in development today.

From Cluster Planning to New Cities

World's Fair 1966, Washington D.C.

In 1959, Gruen took the opportunity to translate his "1976" diagrams and his published theories into a real project when a new World's Fair was be planned for 1964. A number of cities, including New York, Los Angeles, and Washington, D.C., competed for the site, so President Eisenhower set up a three-man commission to examine the proposals and present their recommendations.

Washington's Department of Trade invited Gruen to develop a project that would be supported financially by Roger Stevens.[16] The premise of Gruen's project, planned for a 6,000-acre open site 10 miles east of downtown Washington, near Largo, Maryland, was that the institution of the World's Fair had become exhausted. Not only had it become a propaganda demonstration for industry and tourism, but also, after the enormous investment in administration and the six-month exhibition period, the host city was left with nothing. Gruen proposed that a Washington Fair be an opportunity to experiment with new urban form, a new network between centers and communites, and new alternatives for urban living. After the fair closed, buildings and fair-grounds could become the core of a new town.[17] Gruen would have been familiar with the areas of European cities that had originally been parts of fairs, especially in Germany, where parts of cites had been developed as International Building Exhibitions. The "*Weissenhofsiedlung*" (1927) in Stuttgart, for instance, had been a demonstration of modern architecture, and in Berlin, the "*Interbau*" (1957) was conceived as a model urban residential district using the towers, slabs, and small apartment blocks that would become typical of postwar building.

Designed for 50 million visitors over six months and with a staff of thousands, the fairgrounds could ultimately be transformed into a new city of 100,000. In Gruen's diagrammatic plan, the fair site was a series of concentric zones, whose form could be adjusted to topographic and programmatic conditions. At the center, the exhibition pavilions and other fair attractions took a more compact form than in the "1976" project by being built on two levels. Ground level would be used for traffic, services, and storage, while the upper level, consisting of a cluster of large island platforms connected by bridges, would be the location for Fair buildings, exhibition areas, and public spaces. In the center of this archipelago of platforms lay a park with a lake that could stage water shows and marine exhibits. In the transition from Fair to city, the fairgrounds themselves would become the new downtown, with the Fair's administration and reception buildings becoming the new city hall and convention center. Some of the new residents would live in high-density buildings in the central area, but most would live in low-density units or individual homes, erected as needed in the outer ring, along with schools, parks, shopping centers, and other facilities. The Fair's theaters, amusement parks, concert halls, and hospital would all remain for the benefit of the new city.

16 Stevens was a real-estate promoter and theatrical producer, with whom Gruen had become acquainted through his involvement with the theater in New York. Stevens also financed VGA's East Island (Roosevelt Island) project of 1960-61.
17 *Traeumer*, 258-60. In his autobiography, Gruen described the World's Fair (Washington, D.C.), East Island (Roosevelt Island, New York), and Valencia (California) as his "Unfinished Symphonies." However kitsch the reference to "Unfinished Symphonies" may be, like many architects, Gruen's goal was to build a city.

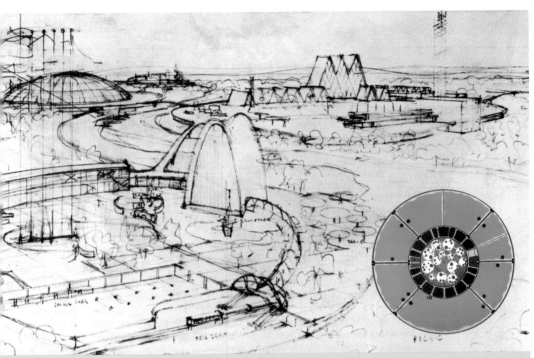

World's Fair Project, Largo, MD (1959). Sketch of fair buildings looking towards central lagoon; (inset), plan diagram of fair.

Sketch of fair buildings converted into the central area of a satellite city; (inset), plan diagram of a new city for 100.000 people. The outer quadrants in the fair, used for parking, temporary accommodation, and services, would be the site for low-density residential communities and light industrial areas in the new city.

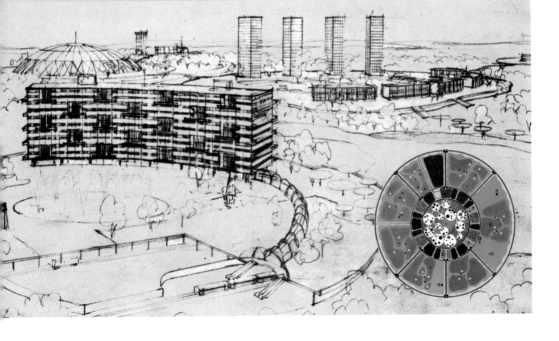

At the end of October 1959, the potential sponsor cities, together with their design teams, made their presentations to Eisenhower's panel. At first, the panel favored the logic of Gruen's "reusable" project, but later, after hard political and economic lobbying behind the scenes, the decision went to New York.[18] In reaction to the decision, Frederick Gutheim, an architectural observer of the Washington scene, reported in *Progressive Architecture*,

Gruen's grasp of the practical details of city planning, and his resolution of the transportation, housing, and other needs of both fair and the ultimate satellite city, were compelling factors in his presentation. He also impressively urged the merits of the plan as "an opportunity to demonstrate new approaches and new ideas in the field of city planning," and argued that the new town approach would show how to deal with urban sprawl and slums. The operation was a success but the patient died! ("Washington's planning problems..." 86)

The subject was not yet closed, though, for early in 1960 the cultural magazine *Horizon* published an eight-page article by the architectural critic of *The New York Times*, Ada Louise Huxtable, praising Gruen's concept and appealing to the administrators of the New York Fair to follow its basic idea: "New Yorkers, who are becoming increasingly victimized by their urban problems, anticipate plans for their 1964 World's Fair with trepidation. If this is to be the best of all possible Fairs . . . . the ideas of the Gruen plan might well be applied" ("Out of a Fair...,"87). The New York Fair Administration, however, ignored this plea. After the six months of the Fair, the usual debt and unused buildings were left behind.

---

18 "How New York Won the World's Fair," *Business Week*, 70. Gruen complained that although the utilities and infrastructure from 1939 remained in place, because of encroachments, by the end of the 1950's Flushing Meadows had become even smaller than the 1939 site. In 1939, there had been parking space for 20,000 cars, and for 1964 no more space would be available. For the New York, point of view, see: Stern et al, *New York 1960*, 1027, and notes, 1320. See also: Canaday, "The World's Fair: Architects and Critics See a Monster Developing for 1964-65."

In 1962, while in Europe, Gruen learned of the sudden death, from a brain haemorrhage, of his third wife, Lazette. After her funeral in New York, he took a leave of absence from his office and immersed himself in writing *The Heart of Our Cities—The Urban Crisis: Diagnosis and Cure*, published in 1964. The title of the book, echoing the CIAM 8 theme of a dozen years earlier, synthesized Gruen's arguments for returning to the city its role as the center for culture, commerce, and even enjoyment; the latter idea must have seemed optimistic at the time. Although he warned that the unplanned recentralization taking place in the suburbs was a threat to downtown, he argued that planning should support the strategic interdependence between the historic urban core, surrounding urban areas, and regional subcenters.

While repeating his claim that the center city was the rightful urban center, "the heart and brain" of its region, Gruen devoted a whole chapter, as well as the cover illustration, to the "Cellular Metropolis," which was a planning model for both creating new cities and restructuring growth in existing metropolitan regions. In the chapter "The Emerging New Pattern," he elaborated this model, giving it a stylized form with a scale and population for each element. Gruen used the example of the ubiquitous cellular structure in nature, and particularly the biological cell, with its nucleus, cytoplasm, and boundary wall, as a model for urban planning. Individual cells could be arranged in clusters of different sizes, some serving a single function and others serving many. Gruen's cell-like settlements were given a progressive scale of communal order comprising neighborhoods, communities, towns, and cities; ultimately the federation of elements would build up to a regional city of 3.3 million, inhabiting a metropolitan area of 694 square miles or 444,485 acres, at the time roughly the size of Cleveland but with one and a half times the population, and far more green space. The settlement units were interconnected by networks of traffic infrastructure and separated by greenbelts. Thanks to short travel distances—between neighborhood, community, town, satellite city, and metropolitan core—the Cellular Metropolis would establish close connections while giving each element its own spatial identity and sphere of governmental influence. As he had explained eight years earlier in "How to Handle This Chaos of Congestion, This Anarchy of Scatteration," the city was to be built up from the scale of a single human individual walking.

The Cellular Metropolis of Tomorrow was illustrated by a circular geometric diagram meant to be comprehensible to a lay reader. It was not a design for a city, and, as Gruen explained, the symmetry and repetition of elements would in reality be irregular, due to existing conditions. The cellular units would not only be of different sizes and shapes, but the spaces between would reflect the local landscape. If the diagram were to be applied as a model for the restructuring of an existing metropolitan area, then the pattern would be affected by buildings, large-scale elements such as highways, economic factors, and political boundaries.

The graphic representation of Gruen's settlement, built up from neighborhood to regional metropolis, resulted in a networked planetary diagram. It was a development model that could relate suburban enclaves to local urban centers, and, in turn, link these to a regional metropolitan core. It was obviously an improvement over current suburban planning, but was it a city? The pattern of the Cellular Metropolis belongs to the tradition of city planning influenced by the Garden City movement and by various subsequent arguments for decentralizing the city in the name of urban and social reform. Although Gruen was well aware of the current state of planning and architecture through the '50s and '60s, he was no historian. He claimed to have discovered Howard's Garden City model only when he started to work on large-scale community-planning projects (*The Heart of Our Cities*, 272). However, given his base in New York, and his familiarity with the ideas of Lewis Mumford, he would have been aware of the planning precedents of Radburn and the Greenbelt Towns.

The Cellular Metropolis of Tomorrow from The Heart of Our Cities (1964). Gruen's highly geometricized ideogram stands for three general planning principles: the transition between private and public transport, the pattern of built and unbuilt space, and the rhythm of high and low density.

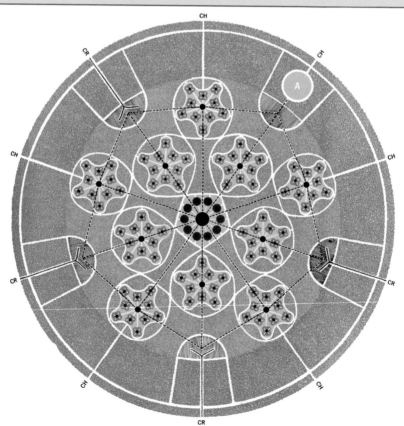

The Cellular Metropolis, four movement and space diagrams: 1) public transport–always passing through the community centers; 2) private transport–always moving around communities; 3) park and ride transfer stations (inner area), and freight transshipment centers (outer area); and 4) relationship between built-up urban elements and green space (forests, meadows, and recreational open space).

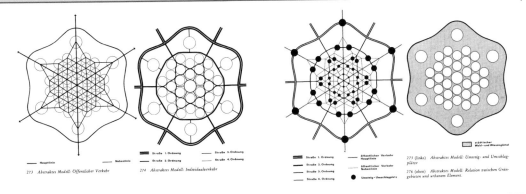

273 Abstraktes Modell: Öffentlicher Verkehr   274 Abstraktes Modell: Individualverkehr   273 (links) Abstraktes Modell: Umsteig- und Umschlagplätze   276 (oben) Abstraktes Modell: Relation zwischen Grüngebieten und urbanem Element.

Planetary systems as a metaphor for urban growth: a repeating motif throughout the 20th century. four (of many) precedents: 1) Ebenezer Howard, Garden City (1908); 2) sketch of a city, Raymond Unwin (1922); 3) Gaston Bardet's Cellular Structure of the City (1940); and 4) Robert Cristaller's Central Place Theory (1930).

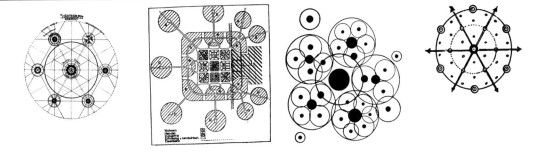

Eliel Saarinen's Dispersed City Plan of Talinn (1913) from "The City," (1944).

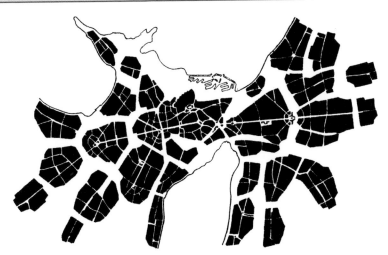

The Cellular Metropolis indeed employed various city-planning clichés such as cells, diseased and healthy tissue, and especially the concept of city growth and development as "organic," adapted from Eliel Saarinen's ideas about "organic decentralization." Gruen's diagram takes its place among many other planetary city-region development diagrams that have recurred regularly throughout the century, including, besides Howard's, Erich Gloeden's Polynuclear Metropolis (1923), Walter Christaller's Central Place diagrams (1933), and Gaston Bardet's Cellular build-up of a city (1940), to name a few. Gruen admitted that the planetary structure was merely a diagram; he was perfectly willing later on to reconfigure it to show how a real region—for instance, Vienna—could be restructured.

In "The Ordering Principles of Cities," a review of Gruen's *Heart of Our Cities*, Nathan Silver claimed that the Cellular Metropolis was like "pre-relativity physics after Einstein," describing it as a perfect "tree," Christopher Alexander's term for the hierarchical diagrams beloved of planners. Silver compared Gruen's city model unfavorably with Alexander's new structural paradigm, the "semi-lattice." This was an informal network pattern formed by a structure of overlapping flexible grids with built-in redundancy.

To examine Gruen's Cellular Metropolis critically, we must retrieve it from abstraction and consider the planning measures necessary for its implementation in an existing metropolitan area: 1) a recentralization policy to support local sub-centers; 2) concentric beltways to both distribute and intercept radial traffic flows; 3) new types of public transportation 4) subcenters at transportation junctions, supported by parking garages with park-and-ride transfers to public transport; 5) revitalization of the city core, through commercial and residential development. This city planning to-do list was hardly radical, yet its implementation would require consensus, collaboration, and leadership at every political, economic, and professional level. Unfortunately, the simplicity of Gruen's deliberately stylized two-dimensional diagram cannot represent the complexity implied by his plea for the three-dimensional interweaving of different functions in compact centers, and multiple transfer points between public and private transport. Yet there have always been hierarchies of scale and hierarchies of centers. Gruen's progressive scale of communal order, with each settlement partly self-sufficient, is similar to the sustainable model of the "City of the short ways," now a goal for European planners. The public-private transportation network and the system of greenbelts is inherently flexible and echoes to various degrees proposals by individuals as diverse as Eliel Saarinen, O.M. Ungers, and Andreas Duany and Elizabeth Plater-Zyberk.[19]

Will California Be one Sprawling City by 1970?

The urbanization of Southern California was a complex process that involved the expansion not only of Los Angeles but also of other provincial towns. Anticipating postwar growth, Los Angeles planners had imagined a region of garden cities, with industry and commerce added to regional agricultural centers, yet this idea was not robust enough for the sheer number of people moving to the region, nor was it accompanied by planning that would regulate subdivision practices.[20] At the same time that Jean Gottman was applying his "Megalopolis" thesis to the conurbation between Washington and Boston, the real-estate industry in Southern California was growing alarmed that if automobile use and suburban development continued at its current pace, then by the 1970s, 200 miles of coastline would be one sprawling city, from Santa Barbara to the Mexican border.[21] Although Southern California's great attraction was its climate, topography, and landscape, common subdivision development practice—clear cutting, reduction of the site through mechanical grading, and repetitive layouts—obliterated just these qualities. The acceptance of the automobile as the primary mode of transport meant that Southern California's downtowns were becoming ever more inconvenient. In contrast, however, to the problem of creating a large-scale development in the congested east-coast cities, where urban areas were inevitably under multiple-ownership, California had a particular advantage. Large parcels of land, some of it near urban areas, lay under single ownership, a legacy of the land division into ranches by the early Spanish settlers. Beginning in the 1950s, ranchlands were beginning to change hands, and wealthy individuals—but especially large corporations—were interested in developing planned communities.

19 For example, the organically dispersed city diagrams of Eliel Saarinen, *The City*, 10, 16. In his 1978 article Cities within the City, O.M. Ungers proposed allowing disused areas of West Berlin to become part of a green network. The remaining city fragments would become part of a structure of an archipelago. In their book, *The New Civic Art* (2003), Duany, Plater-Zyberk, and Alminana showed a masterplan for the new city of Bandar Nusajaya, Malaysia (1997), whose neighborhoods and urban districts were organized on a cellular principle with green belts running between. Examples of planetary urban structure were gathered in Schoof, "Idealstaedte und Stadtmodelle, 1965.

20 Hise, "The Airplane and the Garden City," 166-7. Hise describes the tradition of dispersed community planning in the Los Angeles metropolitan region. "In 'Congestion de Luxe-Do We Want It?' (1926), Clarence Dykstra argued that, contrary to the 'centralization complex' manifest in the, 'the city of the future ought to be a harmoniously developed community of local centers.'" By the end of World War II, the Los Angeles Regional Planning Commission envisioned a coordinated metropolitan region composed of discrete satellite communities.
21 Mulcahy, "Careful Planning Saves Beauty of Coastal Areas." See also, Edwards, "The Way A City Grows - In California Scatteration is Preferred," 11-13.

The Master Plan Grows out of the Land. ← Laguna Niguel, Orange County

As VGA gained prominence in Southern California, the firm was asked to design several new community projects for the rapidly developing Orange County coastal area. First, in 1960, VGA prepared, a 10-year development plan for a new settlement called Laguna Niguel for Cabot, Cabot & Forbes (an engineering and real-estate firm from Boston). The plan covered 11 square miles on the old Moulton and Schumaker ranches located just south of Laguna Beach and extending eastward from the coast through rolling hills and valleys to the San Diego Freeway. Gruen planned mixed residential accommodation on 7,000 acres for 40,000 people, who would be served by new local shopping centers, schools, and office and industrial areas. The residential accommodation integrated low-rise and high-rise apartment buildings together with single-family homes clustered around the local shopping areas. The Laguna Niguel Plan was one of the first and the largest new communities to be approved by the over-all Orange County Plan. The project clarified the importance of integrating residential, commercial, and industrial development with the local character of the landscape; Gruen described his strategy as "the masterplan grows out of the land."[22] The aim at Laguna Niguel was to concentrate development in community clusters, thus allowing a great part of the land to retain its character, and the project was cited as an example of efficient land use in the Congressional Record report on Urban Sprawl and Open Space.[23]

Laguna Niguel, Orange County, CA (1959-64). Masterplan diagram and view of Beach and Country Club area where Laguna Niguel meets the Pacific Ocean. Phase one villages to be built on the slopes behind.

VICTOR GRUEN ASSOCIATES ARCHITECTURE·ENGINEERING·PLANNING

22 "Look at this big tract of ranch land and see a new town in the making," *House & Home*, 149.
23 Williams, Senator Harrison (New Jersey), Congressional Record. Williams brought debates from the February 6, 1961 Conference of Mayors to the discussion of the draft bill concerning open space. The discussion also included the merits of cluster planning as used by Gruen in his Laguna Niguel project, and particularly in the project for the Whitney Estate in Long Island mentioned above. See *Architectural Forum*, Jan. 1961; and, *The Heart of Our Cities*, 141.

El Dorado Hills, Sacramento → "...the idea is to have a community that still has the California way of living..."

Soon afterwards, during the development of the Fresno plan, Gruen and Edgardo Contini had the chance to plan what they called "a satellite city," to be named El Dorado Hills, near Sacramento. The 9,000-acre area featured valleys, ridges, plateaus, and woods, and it lay in the path of growth northwest from Sacramento, whose population was expected to double in 20 years. In deciding to place a new town there, developer Alan H. Lindsey sought to meet a trend in California, in which people were more interested in their outdoor environment and had more leisure to enjoy it. The Gruen planning strategy for El Dorado Hills was developed from six basic concepts: 1) keep a large amount of open land free, especially steep slopes and wooded areas; 2) build simultaneously on a number of different areas of the site; 3) offer a variety of living accommodations, with a strong emphasis on apartments; 4) emphasize the recreational use of the site; 5) provide for all types of commercial and service uses, to assure a well-balanced, semi-independent community; and, 6) create a rural as well as an urban character for the entire project.

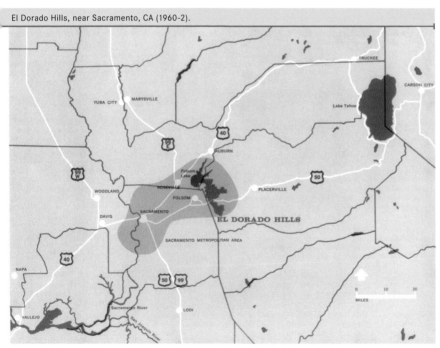

El Dorado Hills, near Sacramento, CA (1960-2).

Planned eventually to reach a population of 75,000, El Dorado Hills was structured as a network of 12 villages, linked to a boulevard. Each village, which included both houses and multi-family buildings, in a wide price range, would have its own identity, based on different kinds of recreation—tennis, boating, hunting and fishing, golf, and horseback riding. Gruen believed that the synthesis of leisure activities with the character of the local topography, together with the different functions in the village centers (shopping, community, and school), would create identity and self-sufficiency and demonstrate an alternative to sprawl: "We are guarding against any appearance of urban sprawl—the idea is to have a community that still has the California way of living—to take full advantage of the landscape and climate that are the area's heritage." [24]

During the planning phase, El Dorado Hills was featured in *House and Home* as a "new model for tomorrow's satellite cities" ("El Dorado Hills…" 107). But Sacramento didn't grow as fast as anticipated, the demand for housing dried up, and the developers were forced to offer whatever single-family house types the market would bear on a reduced version of the original plan.

Sketch of first phase village; visible is the loop road taking off from the parkway and serving individual neighborhoods.

24 "Massive Subdivision Plans Unveiled Here," Sacramento Union; and, "El Dorado Hills: new model for tomorrows satellite cities," House & Home, 107-15.

At Laguna Niguel and El Dorado Hills, Gruen learned the importance of combining the quality of the landscape with specific sport and leisure programs to create a thematic context for the neighborhoods. In his next project, he sought to experiment with the town-center arrangement to reduce local automobile trips. Rather than multiple low-density centers distributed across the site, the town center would be built in a linear form that could expand with the further development of the town itself. In 1964, VGA were asked to create a masterplan for 20 years of growth, financed entirely by private capital, for a self-sufficient community of 75,000 on 12,000 acres to be called Litchfield Park, near Phoenix, Arizona.

Since the early 1960s, Phoenix had been one of the fastest-growing major cities in the U.S., transforming its economic base from agriculture to manufacturing; now the Goodyear Tire and Rubber Co., which owned 38,000 acres west of the city, sought to make the classic western shift from farming to real estate. The site already had a small existing settlement, which included not only the lushly planted country-club and cottage colony originally designed for company executives, but also the popular Wigwam resort and a new 36-hole golf complex designed by Robert Trent Jones. This ensemble of loosely arranged buildings set in groves of palms and oranges was to set the pattern for later development.

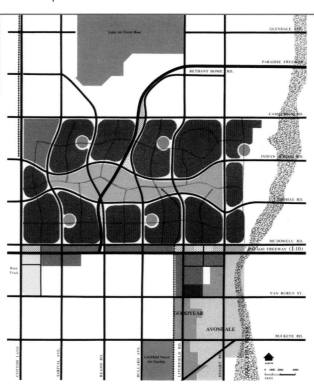

Masterplan for the New Town of Litchfield Park, Phoenix (1964-6). In the middle is the linear core area with regional commercial functions in the center; the circles are the community centers. To the right is the Agua Fria riverbed, and below the planned I-10 Interstate highway.

Arrangement of communities relative to the linear town center;

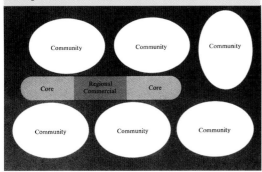

Each of the communities consists of two villages bounded by an arterial road (4), served by a commercial center (2) and high school (3).

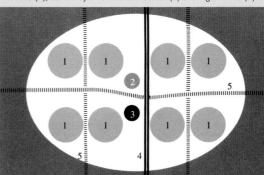

One village (7,500–10,000 people) is made up of four neighborhoods (1), each with an elementary school (4); in the center are the commercial, social, and cultural functions.(2, 5 and 6)

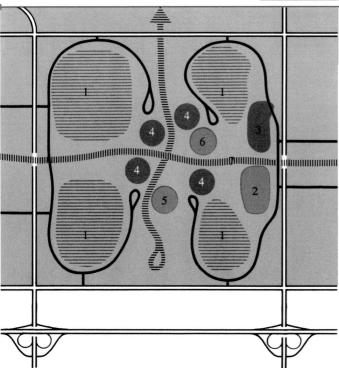

25 Cartsonis, E., "Ten-minute Town: Litchfield Park, Arizona designed around bike and golf paths," *Landscape Architecture*, 40-2. See Victor Gruen & Associates,"Litchfield Area Plan, Maricopa Co., AZ." Land Planners; Larry Smith, Real Estate Economics; Lawrence Halprin, Landscape Systems, 1965. LoCVGP; also, Litchfield Park Properties, Litchfield Park – A New City Takes Form.
26 Fred Usher, author interview, Santa Barbara, 1998; and telephone conversation with Mike Cartsonis on August 30, 2000. Also Interview between Anne Gray and Edgardo Contini, March 19, 1988: 10-11.
27 Gruen, "New Towns and Urban Centers in the U.S.,"

Already in the early '60s the Southwest was becoming a retirement area as well as attracting new families, and half the residents of the proposed new town were likely to be elderly people and children, so the aim at Litchfield Park was to create a settlement pattern in which residents could circulate safely and comfortably without depending on cars. The plan was described at the time as facilitating a "leisure of movement"; following the example set at Radburn, a major design element was a system of 12- to 15-foot-wide landscaped paths for bicycles and electric carts linking residential areas to all public facilities, without crossing vehicular streets.[25] The pathway system, around which all community facilities were based, was also meant to make the second or third family car unnecessary and provide an alternative to superfluous automobile trips. The particular demographics meant that schools would be very important; in the emerging lifestyle of young families, the school was in fact "the beginning and the end of planning," forming the basis of social and cultural life.[26] Thus the hierarchy of each settlement—neighborhood, village, community, and central core—was to be scaled in proportion to its school (elementary school, junior high, high school, or college). Gruen wrestled continuously with the question of whether a center for a large-scale, low-density development could be urban. In his earlier new-town projects, a single area was designated as the future center; at Litchfield Park, however, as the town developed, the core would not only expand horizontally as additional communities were added along its sides, but also grow vertically; for example, parking would ultimately be multi-level, accompanied by clusters of high-rise apartments and offices.

The first phase, involving some 2,100 acres, began in 1967 around the existing settlement. But the completion of the transcontinental Interstate Highway (I-10), planned for 1972, was delayed, which slowed the demand for homes, and later Goodyear sold its interest in Litchfield Park. The site was later developed with conventional sub-divisions.

Although Laguna Niguel, El Dorado Hills, and Litchfield Park (along with other Gruen masterplans) were touted in the press as new towns or even new cities, Gruen later considered them to be hybrid projects that were simply larger and better planned bedroom communities near established cities.[27] One of the problems with developing a new town in a free-market economy was that if the market slowed, developers would cut their losses and build only houses. Also, the stop-and-go progress of these large planning projects frustrated Gruen, especially as Robert Simon's Reston, William Pereira's Irvine, and James Rouse's Columbia were, until the economic slowdown of the early 1970s, proceeding as planned.

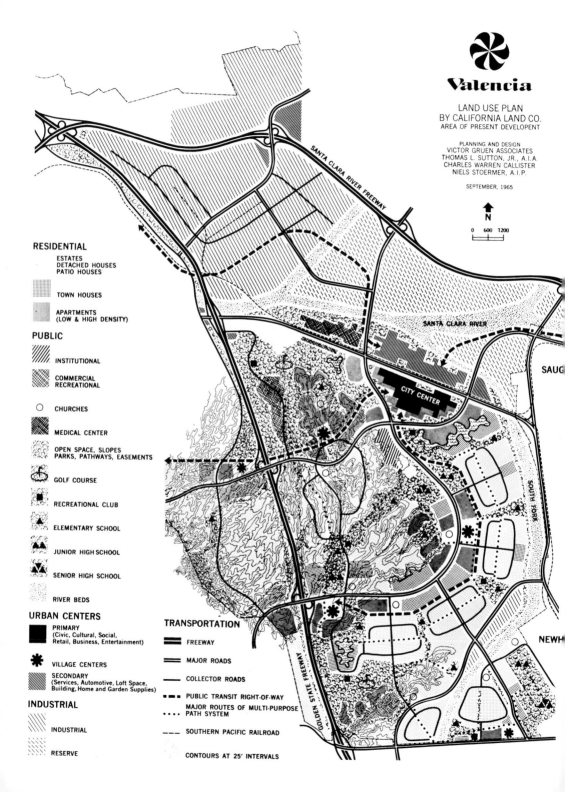

Valencia

LAND USE PLAN
BY CALIFORNIA LAND CO.
AREA OF PRESENT DEVELOPMENT

PLANNING AND DESIGN
VICTOR GRUEN ASSOCIATES
THOMAS L. SUTTON, JR., A.I.A.
CHARLES WARREN CALLISTER
NIELS STOERMER, A.I.P.

SEPTEMBER, 1965

N

0   600   1200

RESIDENTIAL

ESTATES
DETACHED HOUSES
PATIO HOUSES

TOWN HOUSES

APARTMENTS
(LOW & HIGH DENSITY)

PUBLIC

INSTITUTIONAL

COMMERCIAL
RECREATIONAL

CHURCHES

MEDICAL CENTER

OPEN SPACE, SLOPES
PARKS, PATHWAYS, EASEMENTS

GOLF COURSE

RECREATIONAL CLUB

ELEMENTARY SCHOOL

JUNIOR HIGH SCHOOL

SENIOR HIGH SCHOOL

RIVER BEDS

URBAN CENTERS

PRIMARY
(Civic, Cultural, Social,
Retail, Business, Entertainment)

VILLAGE CENTERS

SECONDARY
(Services, Automotive, Loft Space,
Building, Home and Garden Supplies)

INDUSTRIAL

INDUSTRIAL

RESERVE

TRANSPORTATION

FREEWAY

MAJOR ROADS

COLLECTOR ROADS

PUBLIC TRANSIT RIGHT-OF-WAY

MAJOR ROUTES OF MULTI-PURPOSE
PATH SYSTEM

SOUTHERN PACIFIC RAILROAD

CONTOURS AT 25' INTERVALS

SANTA CLARA RIVER FREEWAY

SANTA CLARA RIVER

CITY CENTER

SAUG

NEWH

SOUTH FORK

GOLDEN STATE FREEWAY

In 1964, the project on which Gruen set his hopes as best expressing his urban-planning philosophy was the design of a "new city" for 250,000 inhabitants 30 miles north of Los Angeles. If the plan were carried out, "Valencia" would come closest to his vision of a self-sufficient city and, with its planned dense urban center, would form the newest cell of what was forecast to become the "Southern California metropolis."[28] The starting point for the developers was well put by Norval La Vene, "We don't intend merely to compete with other residential developments already on the market," he said, "we plan to actually create desires for new homes just as the automobile industry has been doing successfully with their new-model cars."[29]

The development site, the 44,000-acre Newhall Ranch, lay at the junction of two major freeways. Originally a royal Spanish land grant, the site extended from the spine of the Santa Susanna mountains on the south to the base of two high ranges to the north and east, which separated the fertile Santa Clara river valley from the Mojave desert. It had been used for ranching until the early 60s, when, with the help of Thomas L. Lowe, executive vice president of the Pacific Mutual Life Insurance Co., plans were made to transform it into a settled landscape. Of utmost importance were what Gruen called "the deep pockets" of the developers, Newhall Land. As Valencia would be developed over 25 to 30 years, Newhall Land planned to undertake a substantial initial investment in infrastructure and services, which they believed would enable the city to weather subsequent economic downturns.

Gruen started off somewhat wildly with a design that was reminiscent of his Roosevelt Island project for New York. The first Valencia was to be a two-mile-long urban superblock, bordered with a series of parking garages, where people would leave their cars and walk or use electric carts to reach their destinations in the city. James Dickenson, president of Newhall Land, described the first project euphemistically as a "challenging marketing problem. We did not want Gruen to be the designer of unbuilt cities."[30] Gruen's final design was linear but less dense, with a series of villages oriented closely to the existing topography and the main infrastructural armature, McBean Highway, that led from the Interstate to the city-center site. Conceived for the future, McBean Highway was planned with a right-of-way along the central reservation, which was reserved for a computer-controlled public transit system.

Gruen wanted to give Valencia, named after the Spanish city for reasons of mood and promotion, characteristics that would distinguish it from his previous attempts at new towns; above all, it should provide employment as well as homes. The masterplan set aside 600 acres to be developed as an industrial center that would provide jobs for many of its inhabitants, giving the community some self-sufficiency called for in the classic definition of a new town.

28 "Valencia - Land Use Plan," (Project Brochure) California Land, nd., 13, LoCVGP.
29 Norval LaVene, Vice President, California Land. Qtd. O' Kane, "New Town Rising Near Los Angeles."
30 Newhall, "Valencia's Designer Dies,"

At Valencia Gruen followed his tenets in the Cellular Metropolis: four neighborhoods of 400 to 700 families in single homes would comprise a village, anchored by a local center, which would have apartments for a further 300 to 500 families. Though separated by parks and lakes, the villages would be linked by an extensive network of 20- to 40-foot-wide landscaped pathways for pedestrians, bicycles, and electric carts, with over- or underpasses at street intersections; thus, everyone would be able to choose between private or public transport, or simply walk. "In Valencia, you need only one car!" [31] Twenty such villages arranged along McBean Highway would be served by the densely planned city center, which, like the smaller village centers, would have its own residential population of 2,000 to 3,000 families in apartments.

At Laguna Niguel and El Dorado Hills, VGA had undertaken the general planning but could influence neither the design of individual houses, which had been given over to residential architects or merchant builders, nor the urban design form of the village centers. At Valencia, however, in contrast to the different single and attached residences offered by the market, Gruen designed land-efficient patio houses, linked to pedestrian walkways, which he called "paseos." The patio houses, adapted from the courtyard houses of Mexico and Mediterranean areas, would stand on half-size lots, shielded by eight-foot-high walls at front and rear. The lot area would thus be reduced by the elimination of front and side yards, which Gruen believed were under-utilized spaces that added much less to family living than private courtyards.

Valencia's first phase, to be completed by 1972, would be built on a 4,000-acre parcel of the Newhall Ranch and would include five villages with 6,000 people each, together with a complete range of facilities—housing, recreation, schools, churches—as well as the first phase of the industrial area and the high-rise city center. Ground was broken for the first homes in October 1965, by which time Valencia already had an 18-hole public golf course designed by Robert Trent Jones. People stayed up all night to bid for the first village houses. [32] The following year, construction started on a county administration building, and Walt Disney offered to build a campus for a new university of the arts.

31, 32 Dan Branigan, author interview, Los Angeles, 1998.

View of paseo running between the zero-lot-line patio houses;

One of Valencia's underpasses - the classic device from Radburn and Greenbelt lives on

Plan of one of Valencia's villages. Along the left boundary, formed by McBean highway, are the village center, garden and tower apartments, and junior high school. The three communities to the right are separated by elementary schools.

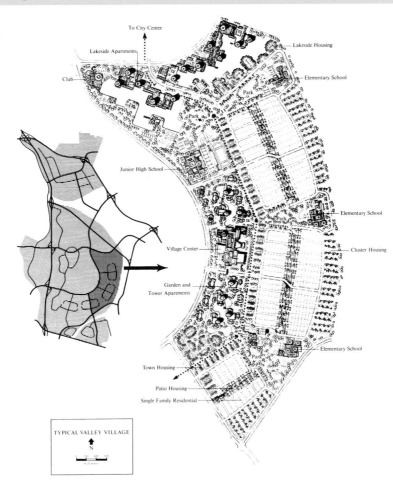

To City Center

Lakeside Apartments

Lakeside Housing

Club

Elementary School

Park

Park

Junior High School

Elementary School

Village Center

Cluster Housing

Garden and
Tower Apartments

Club

Elementary School

Town Housing

Patio Housing

Single Family Residential

TYPICAL VALLEY VILLAGE

N

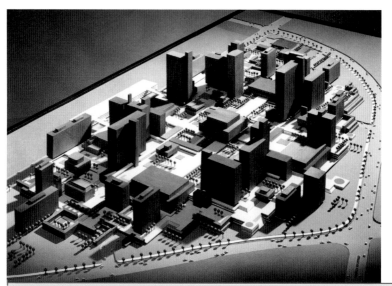

Model photo of proposed dense city center

Aerial photograph showing Valencia's slowly developing low-density center.

Don't Rush the Market

Ten years after the Fort Worth Plan, Victor Gruen saw the city center of Valencia as his first chance to demonstrate his urban-core ideas in a new-town context. Covering 4,000 acres and with a projected population of 10,000, the center would offer the primary shopping, civic, and business activities for both the new town and the region. The rise and fall of the land would allow it to be built over a "podium," which would contain parking and through which the road and rail infrastructure would cross the site. The center, designed with cross axes of retail, offices, and cultural functions, was surrounded by residential terraces that formed a kind of topography, stepping up two stories above the podium to give views into the center and outwards to landscape, and stepping down, where the topography demanded, to conceal the rim of the city-center platform parking decks.

As the design proceeded, differences appeared between Gruen's vision for Valencia and that of his clients. Believing that an urban core formed both magnet and identity for the surrounding region, Gruen wanted to follow European new towns and jump-start Valencia by building the high-rise offices and county facilities in the city center in the first phase. His clients, however, wanted to start with the neighborhood to attract homebuyers. Their differences were even more marked with respect to the center: VGA and Newhall Land argued about size and density, mixing rather than separating functions, the maintenance of the rights-of-way along McBean Highway for future public transport, and the involvement of other architects.

Gruen lost the battle. Valencia would never have the dense center he envisioned. Despite his clients' deep pockets and commitment to carrying the project through, the project had to lie dormant during downturns in the housing market and changes in development politics. Gruen had hoped that Valencia would be a climax to his American career; he was disappointed when economic pressures, lack of state or institutional support, and a slowdown in population growth forced alterations on his original concept.

Yet Valencia, long after Gruen's retirement and death, continued its slow development. Despite fluctuations of the real-estate market and the abandonment of his ideas about density and central-area planning, the new town of Valencia carried out many of Gruen's innovative planning and development concepts, some of which have since become established practice in master-planned communities throughout the U.S. Of the several dozen new towns planned or started in the 1960s, Valencia is one of only a few that have fulfilled their original vision of becoming virtually self-contained communities, and it is still being built by its original developer.

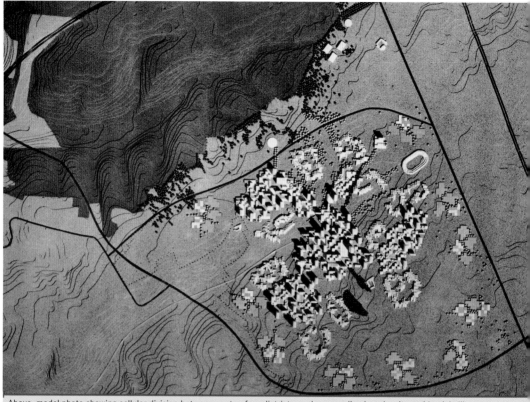

Above, model photo showing cellular division between center, four districts, and surrounding low-density residential villages.

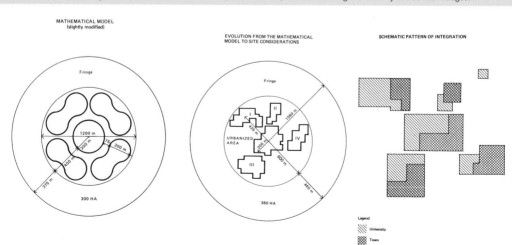

MATHEMATICAL MODEL
(slightly modified)

EVOLUTION FROM THE MATHEMATICAL
MODEL TO SITE CONSIDERATIONS

SCHEMATIC PATTERN OF INTEGRATION

Fringe

1200 m

300 HA

Fringe

URBANIZED
AREA

350 HA

Legend

University

Town

Strategic Plan for the Development of a New University Town, Louvain-le-Neuve, Ottingies, Belgium (1968-71).

33 Author interview, Fritz Waclawek, Architect, and Erik Bramhas, City Planner, Vienna, 23 May, 2002. Also conversations with Prof. David Vandenburgh, UCL, Louvain-la-Neuve, 2001, and Fabienne Lewis-Sowa, Karlsruhe, 2004.

But Europeans Want Suburban Space . . . .

After the opening of Fresno in 1964, Gruen—with an eye on his retirement—had begun to give increasing attention to work in Europe. In addition to the main offices of VGA in Los Angeles and, since 1952, in New York, he opened Victor Gruen International in Vienna, where he began to spend more time. During this transitional period, he made preliminary studies for a new university town in the Walonic (French and Catholic) area of Belgium. After demonstrations and continued unrest between the Flemish- and French-speaking students at the University of Leuven, the Belgian government decided to create a new francophone university town, Louvain-la-Neuve, near Ottignies, about 25 kilometers south of Brussels. Rather than create two separate suburban entities, Gruen proposed joining university and town in a dense cellular cluster, thus creating an urban atmosphere but with a close proximity to nature. Following the principles of the Cellular Metropolis, the first plan, initially developed in Los Angeles in 1967, consisted of an urban core—very much like the center of Valencia—surrounded by four densely built-up communities. It combined university departments and residences, altogether totaling 70,000 people on 865 acres. Besides its new highway access, the center would be connected to the nearby town of Ottignies by a new rail line. Green areas would separate the four communities from the urban core. The rolling countryside enabled both the main and local centers to be built onto podia containing parking and services.

In *Centers for the Urban Environment*, Gruen claimed that in 1968, VGI were informed that, "due to national sensitivities," further development of the project would be undertaken by Belgian architects. Gruen later wrote that the dispute was between rational planning and a local desire for "romantic planning" (228). He had, however, wilfully planned not only a dense urban form for the center, but also smaller-scale urban ensembles for the surrounding villages. This ignored the wishes of town leaders and faculty members, who wanted to live in single-family houses with gardens. Gruen had also planned a shopping district in the central area to be a magnet for further growth and ensure the mix between academic and non-academic populations. This was deleted from the project, as the academic council believed that commercial uses didn't belong near a university and would be better located outside.[33] Most likely, however, the Belgians baulked at the image of an "American" late-international-style project, which they considered "outdated." Of course, they wanted to do it themselves.

The final project, planned for a population of 50,000, covered a much larger area of 2,100 acres and consisted of a center surrounded by six communities built not quite so densely, each with its own center and surrounded by three suburban-style neighborhoods. Except for the town center, which would still be served by the shuttle train, the podium planning principle was dropped, and the outer neighborhood clusters were allowed to be developed with single-family houses with gardens. In 1970, the academic council accepted the plan and turned it over to Belgian architects for development. Despite the conflicting visions, French sociologist François Choay subsequently wrote, "The best example of what a town should be, the town which most closely corresponds to what people nowadays want, is in Belgium, in Louvain-la-Neuve."[34] The architecture was post-modern Belgian, and the center had become a "humanist megastructure."

The problems Gruen had encountered at Valencia were repeated in Belgium. Louvain-la-Neuve would be executed by Belgian architects in a "natural" or postmodern style, and Gruen's hierarchical cluster planning—from suburban neighborhood to a dense urban core—was only partly realized. Gruen had argued that in northwestern Europe, there simply was not enough land to build in the dispersed pattern that was taking place in the U.S.; however, despite the initial enthusiasm for a project that reflected the urban density and public spaces of the old university town of Leuven, the allure of lower density had prevailed. Once the regional shopping center that Gruen had proposed was deleted from the town center plan, the motor for urban density had been removed.

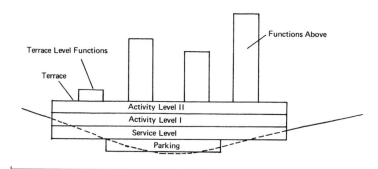

Schematic section through the podium structure of the city center;

Gruen's late modernist sketches: View of town center with terraced housing and Pedestrian bridges.

34 *Louvain-la-Neuve - Freedom of the City*, UCL-External Relations, 1997. The initiative for the second, "Belgian" project, was led by Professor Michel Woitrin, and Professor Raymond Lemaire. The planner was Architect Jean-Pierre Blondel, a professor at La Cambre, Brussels, who set up a student team. Construction began in 1971, and completion of the transfer of students from Leuven was completed in 1979. The population in 1997 was 16,000, and growing at an average of 3 percent a year.

View of the town in the mid 1990s.

In "First Job, Control City Sprawl" (1956), Catherine Bauer had written, "People who look to urban renewal to solve our city problems for the next 20 or 25 years have been fast asleep." She contended that, rather than the "fix-up fallacy in our city planning," attention should be focused on "new cities" of up to one million that should be planned away from existing cities. Years later, while the planning for Litchfield Park and Valencia proceeded–and when the problems of creating such new towns were becoming painfully apparent–Gruen returned to the idea of promoting fully self-sufficient new cities. In the summer of 1966, VGA submitted a report called "New Cities, U.S.A." to the Department of Housing and Urban Development (HUD).

"New Cities, U.S.A." was the result of meetings with federal and state officials including the Secretary of the Interior, Stuart Udall; Senator Joseph D. Tydings of Maryland; and Dr. Charles Haar, Assistant Secretary for Metropolitan Development in HUD. In the report, VGA argued for the planning and building of up to 20 new cities of 1.5 million people each, far from existing urban centers. These new cities–unlike new towns, which were clustered next to and were to a degree dependent on the adjacent city–would be programmed from the beginning as full-fledged urban structures. Yet even if this enormous program were undertaken, it would only absorb one third of the projected population growth over the next 20 years.

With their belief in centrally organized urban structures, Gruen and Contini worried that if contiguous growth continued indefinitely–as in Jean Gottman's Megalopolis–the benefits of a city would diminish; its residents, unable to comprehend its immensity, would withdraw from metropolitan events and limit their civic participation to their own communities or families. Would the U.S. at the turn of the century have two-thirds of its population concentrated in a dozen megalopoli–clusters of urbanization of between 15 and 20 million people each? This was already becoming the case. In "Anonymity and Identity," Peter Hall identified 3 "megalopoli" that had formed in the U.S. by the end of the 1970s: Boston-Washington with a population of 39 million, Chicago-Pittsburgh with 20 million, and San Francisco-San Diego with 25 million. "New Cities U.S.A." argued that earlier in the U.S., there had been many planned new cities,

---

35 Bogard, GEC. Qtd. Friedlander, "Birth of the 'New City,'" 80-1. Friedlander went on to list 12 principal 'new cities' in the U.S.: Clear Lake City, Houston, TX; Columbia, MD; El Dorado Hills, CA; Irvine, CA; Janss/Conejo (Ventura Co.), CA; Laguna Niguel, CA; Lake Havasu, CA; Litchfield Park,AZ; Mission Viejo, CA; New Orleans East,LA; Reston,VA; and Valencia, CA. As can be seen, 7 were located in California and 4 were by VGA. VGA were also involved in the preliminary planning at Mission Viejo, and were building the shopping center at Conejo.

36 "Big Plans" (Forum) *Architectural Forum*, June 1966, 32, 87. The *Forum* reported that the Committee for National Land Development Policy, which included Richard Neutra and a number of large land developers, proposed building 25 "molecular cities," each with a population of one million, far away from older metropolitan areas.

such as Philadelphia, Savannah, Kansas City, Salt Lake City, and Washington, D.C. Since then there had been no such initiatives. If the creation of new cities from a government initiative seemed to contradict the more recent laissez-faire attitude toward building and planning, Gruen and Contini pointed to experimentation in social security and agriculture as evidence of the government's changing role and its assumption of expanded responsibility. Given the current debacle of American center cities, a program for new cities would stimulate urban research. In existing cities, experimentation with political, economic, or social structures seemed impossible, but planning new cities would be an opportunity to develop new forms or techniques—much as Gruen's World's Fair project had proposed to do. One of the most promising fields of technological innovation might be transportation and the chance to reconcile the benefits of private mobility with new forms of mass transit. A second area for research was the field of building itself. Gruen and Contini criticized the building industry for failing to advance at the same rate as the manufacturing, automobile, and even farming industries. Buckminster Fuller's arguments about the permanence and obsolescence of structures could be brought to concepts of the renewal and creation of cities. Perhaps it was only the "urban structure that should be seen as a durable and stable frame, within which its component elements—somewhat as the cells of a living organism—periodically regenerate themselves by orderly cycle." Questions of urban structure, building, and communications systems and concepts such as "planned obsolescence" precipitated the interests of architects and industry not only in Japan, where the Metabolist group were creating experimental projects for new urban structures, but also in the U.S. In 1967, for example, at a planners conference, George T. Bogard of the General Electric Company (GEC) said that his firm was considering the creation of new prototype communities: "GEC feels that the new cities will permit industry to introduce exciting new products, building materials, techniques, and new practices." Building practice in the U.S., he said, was generally impeded by archaic building codes and zoning ordinances.[35] At the time VGA submitted "New Cities, U.S.A.," various other propositions were being put forward in a similar direction. Richard Neutra, together with a group of developers, proposed new "molecular" cities of more than one million each in an article published in the June 1966 *Architectural Forum*.[36] In the mid-1960s, however, the population growth of the U.S. began to slow, and the pressure for rebuilding old and building new cities dissipated.

Valencia was the last of Gruen's American new-town projects. Although he tried repeatedly to sell the idea of building town centers with a certain density to support urban diversity, this was an argument that in California he would always lose. In mid- to late-1960s America, real-estate development could sustain high-quality residential communities for a selected market, but despite the best intentions of architects and planners, it could not, or would not, invest in dense forms of urban development with their implied diversity.

The idea of new towns in America was riddled with problems of political will, social equity, their unplanned effect on inner cities, and even questions of architecture. Edgardo Contini, who had been partner-in-charge of many of VGA's new-town projects, believed that the idea of new towns, as they had been planned in England, for example—as a government-supported program embodied in the New Town Act of 1946—should have been taken up in the U.S. directly after the war, when there was a tremendous impetus to build. Of course, to speak of a national settlement policy in the 1950s, Contini said, would probably have been considered socialist. By the late 1960s, and despite the news of the vast investment that the French government was planning to devote to a system of new towns around Paris, Contini believed the chance had been missed.[37] It was no use comparing conditions in Europe and the U.S.; James Rouse had also made the pilgrimage to Europe and declared that the high-density development grouped around a rapid-transit station at Vållingby, one of the new towns outside Stockholm, was "a notion strange to an America of cars and wide open spaces, and they had been built under real-estate laws and government arrangements that bore little resemblance to the situation in the United States."[38] In the American context, privately financed new towns built at the periphery of big cities would merely become bedroom communities. Other critics would be more severe, such as Robert C. Weaver, Secretary of HUD, commenting in *Business Week*: "The vast majority (of new towns) appear destined to become country club communities for upper-income families . . . . They really are very nice towns if you are docile and have no plans of your own and do not mind spending (*your life*) among others with no plans of their own" ("Where city planners...," 103).

37 Interview Anne Gray and Edgardo Contini, March 19, 1988: 12.
38 Olsen, *Better Places, Better Lives*, 131-2. The developer James Rouse, had started as a mortgage banker, and viewed Vållingby from the point of view of current financing and development practice in the U.S. However "foreign" Vållingby may have seemed, as a planning type it was based on many of the same principles as Rouse's own new town of Columbia, and today would be considered a model of Transit Oriented Development (TOD).

39 Letter from Sybil Moholy-Nagy to Victor Gruen, June 16, 1970, LoCVGP.
40 Peter Smithson. Qtd. Gruen, *Approaches to Urban Revitalization...*, 192.
41 Gruen, "New Towns and Urban Centers in the U.S.," Paris, 1969: reprint. LoCVGP. Gruen sarcastically charged that new towns in the U.S. were profit-making exercises for the middle-class, while in Europe, they were designed for the lower income classes.

One of Gruen's harshest critics was his friend Sibyl Moholy-Nagy. The fallacy of new towns, she believed, was that they were based exclusively on residential development. Further, they drew attention, energy, and investment from the desparate needs of the cities. Their promotors, she wrote, were purveyors of "dreadful clichés such as 'superior environments,' 'complete range of urban functions' (Victor Gruen), and most hypocritically of all, 'serving the people,'" probably a reference to James Rouse's claims for Columbia.[39]

In 1962, at a lecture at the Architectural Association, London, where Gruen spoke enthusiastically about the New Town of Vällingby, Peter Smithson added a further critique, complaining that architects had utterly failed to find an architecture commensurate with this new planning instrument:

There is (however) something wrong with the way that the buildings are organized . . . . All these projects do not reflect a culture but rather, in a confused way, an international airline kind of language . . . . there is something screwed up about New Towns and urban redevelopment projects in terms of the actual architecture. Mr. Gruen may very well claim that it is not a question of architecture, (but) it is a question of what architecture is now, if it has indeed changed to become 'environment,' then a sense of space and a feeling for structure–architecture–still has to be found.[40]

In *Fortune* magazine of the same year, Gruen claimed that the context made the building; creating the context meant the reshaping of an area, including the activities, to create a comfortable, convenient, and lively living and working environment (Guzzardi, 77). Yet many architects would argue that they could not control more than their building, and thus the architecture had to be strong enough to mediate, if not make, the context. Gruen was only half-right; there must indeed be "architecture."

Although, at the time, Gruen's new-town projects attracted attention as new forms of community building that were great improvements on sprawl and much more predictable as investments, Gruen later considered them to have turned out as merely glorified subdivisions. The private market in the U.S. could hardly match the commitment of a national government program. In a speech in Paris in 1969, Gruen finally agreed with Moholy-Nagy and charged that "in the U.S., so-called new towns had even become more dangerous than sub-divisions–they speeded up and intensified the exodus of middle classes from cities."[41]

Gruen's criticism of his own projects is, within its own terms, valid. Yet it often obscures other possible readings of the projects. The developers of Valencia, for instance, saw what they were making and how they were marketing it quite differently than how Gruen saw it. His masterplan was indeed accepted and partially executed, but under a different development philosophy. For Gruen, the "new city" of Valencia ended up as nothing but a series of progressively planned, up-market sub-divisions, but for its developers and inhabitants, Valencia was not a self-sufficient urban new town but a regional center in a "middle landscape." In his analysis of Valencia's first 30 years from a development point of view, "Valencia, California: From New Town to Regional Center," Patrick Wirtz defined "middle landscape" as a dialectic containing aspects of city and country, urban and suburban, and the planned and unplanned. In the middle landscape of the six counties constituting the Southern California metropolis, Valencia was one of a number of semi-autonomous centers in the decentralized urban region. The continuously developed urban landscape, articulated by a network of high- or low-density centers, simply represented the dominant pattern governing metropolitan form. Gruen's masterplan had been the strategic instrument that coordinated the different land uses into a complementary arrangement that satisfied residents' needs, the developers' expectation from the market, and a prominent marketing instrument to present Valencia to the public. Wirtz claimed that except for the density of the town center, Valencia today looks very much like the city outlined in the plan of 1965.[42]

The structure of Gruen's plan may indeed have been robust enough to survive the alterations and omissions imposed upon it by the developers, but the same cannot be said of the more progressive detailed design elements. After the first residential area was built, including the zero-lot-line patio houses, the developers subsequently discontinued many aspects of the masterplan that would distinguish the layouts and house types, subtly interweave the residential villages, enable social and civic interaction, and create more collective movement patterns. Ebenezer Howard imagined that the Garden City would synthesize the best of town and country, but the developers of Valencia were satisfied to synthesize the best aspects of subdivision and country.

42 Wirtz, "Valencia, California: From New Town to Regional Center," 2. The term "middle landscape" first appears in Mumford, The Culture of Cities (1938). In his book *Making A Middle Landscape* (1991), Peter Rowe defined it as a rural-urban synthesis that attempts to mediate traditional pastoral perspective and modern technical temperament, yielding a philosophy of "modern pastoralism," (215). **43** Violitch, "Mr. Mumford and the job ahead," 31, 60; and, Violitch, "The Esthetics of City and Region," Qtd. Kevin Starr, "The Case Study House Program and the Impending Future," in Smith (Ed.), *Blueprints for Modern Living*: 137-138.

The Environmental City

Victor Gruen's final contribution to architecture and planning was his concept of an environmentally sustainable city. In 1968 he created the Victor Gruen Foundation for Environmental Planning, Los Angeles, and he brought this new interest with him to Vienna, where in 1972 he founded the *Zentrum fuer Umweltplanung* (The Center for Environmental Planning). Both were among the first organizations of their type in the world of architecture and planning. In the period between his involvement with Ladybird Johnson's "beautification" committee and the Oil Crisis of 1973, Gruen advanced his conceptual thinking from that of an "environmental architect"–a creator of public space in the urban landscape–to that of an environmental advocate, concerned with the interrelationship between the living and building processes and the newest discoveries involving ecology, energy, and pollution. His philosophy of urbanism culminated with his vision of the city as an environmental oasis–the result of the coming together of planning, his own humanistic philosophy, and the new ecological sciences. The last chapter of Gruen's life is the most surprising: the "mallmaker"–the so-called eviscerator of the old cities–is one of the earliest to plead for the sustainable city, the current goal of international planning.

From "Environmental Architecture" to Human Ecological Planning

Speculations on the balance between technological and humanistic goals for the city were for Gruen not new. In 1945, while he and Elsie Krummeck were busy with their shops and stores in California, John Entenza's *Arts & Architecture* magazine–the preeminent journal on the West Coast, which had just launched the Case Study House program–provided an occasional forum for these discussions. In "Mr. Mumford and the Job Ahead," Francis Violitch, referring to Lewis Mumford's writing on urban and regional development, presciently wrote, "Certainly, Mumford's insights into the balancing of biological, cultural, and technological needs–into the humanizing of the machine– would be desperately needed in the postwar era of urban planning and redirection."[43]

The link from Mumford and Violitch's critique to contemporary urban planning, and indeed the link between Gruen's own thinking and the CIAM debates on the city, was probably CIAM 8's 1952 book *The Heart of the City*. In an associated article, "The Humanization of Urban Life" (the subtitle of *The Heart of the City*), Sigried Gideon called for "a return to the human scale and the assertion of the rights of the individual over the tyranny of mechanized tools" (123). Two years later, Gruen referred to both Gideon and Jose Luis Sert in his *Harvard Business Review* article "Dynamic Planning for Retail Areas." The break with Le Corbusier's functional planning in the mid-1950s and the emerging Team 10 focus on a new "hierarchy of human associations," developed by Alison and Peter Smithson, was the beginning of a more humanistic and environmental modernist planning. Gruen's attempt to find a new progressive communal order with his "1976" (1955) project, based on his "discovery" of Howard's Garden City planning, parallels the Smithsons' attempt to imagine new forms of community by developing contemporary equivalents for houses, streets, districts, and cities.

By the mid-1960s, growing concern about the consequences of smog produced by traffic and industry, the politics of energy production, and the excesses of consumption informed questions about settlement pattern and community design. As these discussions were migrating from scientific and academic study to the popular press, Gruen was realizing that he and other planners were helpless to prevent continuing sprawl. Turning in a new direction, he began to bolster his arguments for environmental planning by adapting ideas from the ecological sciences and integrating them into his own vision of the humanist city. Gruen echoed Violitch, claiming that "the subject of planning is Man." In a letter to Peter Blake, he described himself as no longer a practitioner of architecture and planning but an idealistic believer in the importance of a new environmental planning.[44]

In 1968, at the age of 65, Gruen retired from VGA. In the spring, he set up the Victor Gruen Foundation for Environmental Planning to be a base for education and research on environmental planning issues, from local to national levels. In the Los Angeles area the Foundation would be a low-key reference point for this relatively new subject, and from the fall of 1969, a program of scholarships and research grants was developed. Seminars and special conferences were led by such figures as Stewart Udall, Secretary of the Department of the Interior in both Kennedy and Johnson administrations, who had energetically supported President and Ladybird Johnson in environmental issues. In Los Angeles, the foundation stimulated the State of California to form its own office of environmental education.[45]

44 Letter, Victor Gruen to Peter Blake, 1973, LoCVGP.
45 Rosemary Rabin, author interview, Los Angeles, 1998. Among the contributors and collaborators to the Foundation were: Russel Train, who became Chairman of the Council on Environmental Quality under Nixon; and California Governor Jerry Brown.
46 Scheuch, "Europas Großstadt - Licht und Irrlicht," *Arbeiter-Zeitung*. See also: Gruen, "Licht und Schatten der Europaische Großstadt"; and, Richard Neutra, "Europa und die Urbanitaet." All LoCVGP. Neutra's paper focused on the dwelling, not as a "machine for living," but rather as a living cell embedded in the landscape.

47 Kainrath, W., "Fußgaengerzonen in Wien" (editorial). In "Victor Gruen plans a pedestrian zone for Vienna," Kainrath wrote: "He does this with the grand gesture of the knowing patriarch. He complains of the great all-threatening catastrophe (environmental pollution), isolates the enemy (the automobile), presents himself as the savior (the all-knowing planning-doctor, who, "leads the trends as a hunting dog leads the pack," and, indeed knows, where the rosy future is to be found), and prescribes the inevitable resulting solution. So much for the style of democratic demogo-gery." [author's translation]

From Los Angeles to Vienna

Since the mid-1950s, Gruen had been visiting Europe regularly and talking about the work of VGA. In 1963, he had participated in the *Wiener Gespraeche* (Vienna Forum), a conference on the problems and prospects for European urban culture, whose speakers included the architects Richard Neutra, Roland Rainer, and Jakob Bakema, and the philosopher Theodor Adorno. Both Gruen and Neutra, speaking on urbanization in the U.S., described what European cities might anticipate. Gruen had just completed Midtown Plaza and was involved at Fresno. In the Viennese press, he spoke much more harshly of his American context than would have been prudent for the leader and salesman of VGA in the U.S. For Gruen, the gutting of downtown urban cores to accommodate the automobile—his favorite image was a map of downtown Los Angeles showing two thirds of the space given over to streets and surface parking—was symbolic of the gutting of urban culture. American cities had sacrificed public life for individual private comfort. He argued that the historic centers of old European cities could never sustain the pressure of modern automobile traffic and that the fine grain of their urban cores would have to be protected from it.[46]

Upon retiring, Gruen returned to his home city, where he had set up Victor Gruen International (VGI) as a consulting office. He continued his prolific public speaking, urging audiences not to repeat American planning mistakes, particularly, the uncritical acceptance of the regional shopping center, "unplanned" urban highways, and sprawl. In Vienna, Gruen, found himself engaged in many of the same battles that he had fought in previous decades in the U.S.: to stop the use of historic public spaces of the city as car parks, to convince politicians and planners not to allow American-style shopping centers to be located at the city's boundary, and to locate urban highways so that they wouldn't destroy urban fabric and urban communities.

VGI created plans for inner city shopping centers, mixed-use urban developments (always anchored by retail), and new towns. In France, he contributed to the planning of La Defence in Paris and advised on the French new-town program, particularly the new town center of Evry; in Switzerland, he produced the preliminary design and planning for two large-scale mixed-use urban shopping centers in Lausanne (unexecuted) and Zurich (built in a different form by local architects). But the projects that were most important to him were the masterplan for the new university town of Louvain-la-Neuve and a planning study for the central core area of Vienna (1969-71). In Vienna, Gruen hoped that his final project might be to return the center of Vienna to the pedestrian. He discovered, however, that the architecture and planning establishment was hardly going to cede ground to an American modernist, who had left their city 30 years before.[47]

The corollary to Gruen's environmental foundation in Los Angeles, the *Zentrum fuer Umweltplanung* (ZUP) in Vienna had as its goal to bring together scientists of all disciplines—together with planners, architects, artists, and humanists—to convince politicians and government planning departments to take responsibility for the consequences of development on the physical and social environment. In Austria, it was the first gathering place for discussion of ecological development, mass consumption, increasing automobile and truck traffic, and current energy policy.[48]

Gruen's foundations exposed him to the latest discoveries in the ecological sciences and their consequences for the politics, economics, and ethics of development. His concept of environmental planning shifted its focus from the quality of the built and natural surroundings to the new ecological concept of total living system. "Environment" came to denote no longer just the context—buildings, spaces, landscape—but the aggregate of all external conditions (aesthetic, biological, cultural, social, economic, historical) that effect the human life. Stewart Udall defined the shift in the understanding of the environment thus: "Environment, a term that evolved through the 1960s, began with conservation, but conservation began to be related to bigger problems and a broader spectrum of scientific disciplines."[49] In Vienna the corresponding transition involved a similar shift of interest from support and protection of the natural environment (*Umweltschutz*) to environmental planning (*Umweltplanung*), a discipline that would combine spatial and functional planning with issues of ecological sustainability and social equity.

Not all architects were interested in the negative consequences of development, consumption culture, and an energy policy based on fossil fuels or nuclear power plants. Perhaps only younger individuals drawn to questions of energy in design and planning, or those who were at the end of their careers, felt they had the luxury of that choice. Victor Gruen's foundations were significant start-ups. Later their work became subsumed into the growing environmental movement.

48 Prof. Dr. Bernd Loetsch, author interview, Vienna 2001 and 25 May, 2002. The ZUP had about 30 collaborators, all who worked on a voluntary basis, who were leading scientists of many disciplines, as well as some planners, artists, and economists. Also Loetsch, 2003, Symposium on the 100th Birthday of Victor Gruen, Vienna, July 17, 2003. Gudrun Hausegger wrote about Gruen's Foundations in "Gudrun Hausegger Tank," in the forthcoming symposium proceedings.

49 Concorci, "An Interview with Stewart Udall-former Secretary for the Interior," (Reprint), Zentrum fuer Umweltplanung archive, Vienna. In 2001, this archive was an unofficial and unsorted selection of material. I thank Frantz Skala.

50 Gruen, The Charter of Vienna, VGFEP, Los Angeles, 1972, 2,3. Gruen wrote that Le Corbusier's *Charte d'Athenes*, reacting to certain conditions of its time, sought to lower urban densities, and separate human activities away from industrial. "Particularly this last tenet has been practiced to such a degree in today's cities, that it has promoted the erosion of urbanity and the fragmentation of the urban organism into ghetto-like enclaves. Today, with the world's population having become inter-dependent, we can no longer accept this restriction to the white race, or the great emphasis on Europe," 4.

51 Gruen, The Charter of Vienna, 17-18. Gruen made this argument years before in "Introverted Architecture," 207-08.

Among the texts issued by Gruen's foundations was "The Charter of Vienna," a document that summarized 30 years of thinking about how we should live–what both the citizen and the community might expect from the urban environment.[50] Believing that questions of environmental control had assumed global importance and would soon overshadow all other problems of planning, Gruen once again charged his ideal, the architect-planner, with a responsibility to society and not just architecture. In "Cityscape-Landscape," Gruen had demanded that architects engage the large-scale transformations underway in the American landscape, not from their ivory towers, but "on the level on which it counts, on the battleground of reality."[51] In the Charter of Vienna, he wrote,

If any professional withdraws from contemporary life, then it can be presumed that other professionals will fill the void. This, unfortunately, is what happens in the task of shaping the man-made environment. This great challenge is taken up in a temporizing manner by the transportation and engineering specialists, by the developers and the promoters, by specialized consultants, each wearing blinders with regard to other specialized fields. The results of this quantitatively impressive but undirected activity are ruinous. To an ever greater extent, the architect is called upon in the role of "specialist," exclusively for exterior and interior decoration. (The resulting) sterility, ugliness and inhumanity are often criticized by sensitive architects but accepted by the populace as something one can alter as little as one can control the weather. Yet in the sense of the original meaning of the term "architekton," no other profession should be better equipped to shoulder the responsibility for shaping the man-made environment. (The essence of Architecture, 17)

To introduce environmental sustainability as a basis for planning was difficult in 1972, when the threat to the environment was neither widely accepted nor understood. After 20 years as an urban planner, Gruen believed that a change in human perception was necessary and could happen only through the closest collaboration between experts of all disciplines, their ideas communicated to the widest community. It must be a popular cause.

His last vision was the concept of *Die lebenswerte Stadt*, articulated in a book of the same name. Best translated as the livable or desirable city, this urban concept offers personal and social security, physical and psychological health, and good working conditions and possibilities. It proposes a city that respects the rights of its citizens; a city in which it is easy to get around; above all, a city loved by its citizens, offering them the possibility of self-fulfillment, individual development, and *joie de vivre*. Environmental sustainability underpins this humanist vision (95). The basis for achieving "the desirable city" was a series of guidelines published in various forms–in effect, a constitution for cities and regional planning–which mirrored the recommendations of the New York Regional Plan Association (1968) and anticipated the goals of the supporters of The City of Short Ways *(die Stadt der kurzen Wege)* in Europe, and the Charter of the New Urbanism and "Smart Growth" in the U.S. The *Guidelines* called for the sustainable use of urban land, the mixing of uses in a fine-grained pattern, a cellular structure as the model not only for urban districts but also for regional settlement, and the establishment of representative urban public spaces as the spaces of identity for local and metropolitan centers. The discipline of planning was to be absorbed into environmental planning, with the goal of reinventing the city as an ecologically sound, socially just, and vital urban environment.[52]

Balancing Regional Development

Gruen never accepted the idea of the regional city as continuous development; the goal of the Cellular Metropolis was to set limits to the large city to keep legible the character of both city and region. Far from being constellations of cities, the developing conurbations, he wrote, merely consisted of overlapping sprawl: "The need today is not to expand, but to contract urban development."[53] If development were to be regional, then it must also be urban–not sprawl but a regional structure of central spaces, or urban "living rooms."

Whether as a newly planned city or as a strategy for the recentralization of an existing metropolitan area, the vehicle for Gruen's ideas about city form and structure was the Cellular Metropolis. It was, he believed, an answer to imbalanced regional development, an alternative to sprawl, and a development form that offered spatial distinction and identity. Beyond the problem of legibility, one of the emerging criticisms of sprawl was its destruction of the natural surroundings. In the early 1960s, the English planner Colin Buchanen, who had prepared the landmark study *Traffic in Towns* for the British government, had come to similar conclusions about what Gruen called "enforced mobility." He assumed that the future pattern of cities would be a patchwork of "environmental areas"–that is, compact central areas where all but necessary traffic was excluded. This pattern of environmental areas or "urban rooms," separated and connected by their distributor roads, would yield a cellular pattern for a town.[54] As the U.S. drifted toward the urban riots and the Vietnam meltdown of the late 1960s, Gruen became convinced that life in a medium-sized, medium-density metropolis–he had meanwhile reduced the maximum population from 3.3 to 2 million people–freed of the usual chaos of traffic and with easy access to open space was, for most of humanity, desirable. He even believed, against all trends, that the potential quality of living would reduce consumerism, lessen the burden on the environment, and relieve the squandering of land. By the time he published *Centers for the Urban Environment* in 1973, he had recast the Cellular Metropolis as a framework for sustainable planning

52 Gruen, "Guidelines for Urban Development – 15 Principles," 10-11. LoCVGP
53 *Traeumer*, 281
54 Buchanan, *Traffic in Towns*, 42. Traffic in Towns was sponsored by the Ministry of Transport. The Working Group was headed by the architect and planner Colin Buchanen. Buchanen acknowledged H.A. Tripp in his report of 1942, *Town Planning and Road Traffic* for the idea of cellular planning and the creation of urban (pedestrian) rooms.

55 Hill, "Sustainability, Victor Gruen and the Cellular Metropolis, "312-26. Where does Gruen's organic city model lie in relation to other city planning paradigms? Hill placed the general argument for the Cellular Metropolis in the intellectual tradition of Ebenezer Howard, Lewis Mumford, Jane Jacobs and Christopher Alexander. Gruen's vision was human and metropolitan, not "anti-city" as Ebenezer Howard or Frank Lloyd Wright nor the functional city of Le Corbusier. Formally, it lies in the progression of organic city planning that started in the 20th century with Eliel Saarinen.

of new or existing settlements. Gruen no longer described a city model, but rather the process of urbanization itself. He believed that regional (global!) urbanization could be marshalled by means of an "abstract urbanization model," and an "abstract transportation model" that would cluster settlement around metropolitan cores. The goal was to "safeguard the biological and ecological balance between the man-made, man-influenced, and natural environment" (203). Despite the inherent value of Gruen's theories for a new environmental planning, he didn't have the right tools; architects and planners of the 50s and 60s knew little of environmental science and nothing of natural processes. Gruen's arguments lacked a crucial component that could only come from landscape planners and ecologists.

But if Gruen's Cellular Metropolis model was just another architect's utopian city design, it was a settlement model that sought to balance the relationship between urban development and nature, between high and low density, and between neighborhoods, urban centers and open space. It sought a workable compromise between American desire for private mobility and the obvious need for public transport. Reviewing the Cellular Metropolis from the perspective of the early 1990s, the planning historian David R. Hill pointed out that the formal synthesis of compact urban clusters, representative public spaces, and dispersed residential communities, connected by an overlapping mix of public and private transport, was practicable and went part-way to meeting the desire for low-density community planning.[55] Gruen's model is relevant today because his hierarchy of communities would support identity and legibility in the increasingly "unreadable" multi-centered regional city. It may not be necessary or desirable, either in North America or Europe, to build an entirely new city, but the idea of linking both old and new communities and urban cores in their region by means of a graduated network of both private and public transport reflects current goals of planning.

Wright's Broadacre, Hilbersheimer's Dispersed Settlement, Gruen's Cellular Metropolis, Gottman's Megalopolis, Doxiades' Dynopolis, and Webber's Urban Realm are all part of the long tradition of architects' and planners' speculations on a changing urban environment, speculations that proliferate in periods of violent transformation; the late '60s saw an explosion of such critical and utopian visions. From 1944 to 1961, the Acts of Congress had set in motion an extraordinary paradigm shift in the role and form of the American city, and as we know, the suburbs continue to expand. How much of the future urban landscape should be "city" in the traditional sense? Should this new urban landscape, as Wright had threatened, merely form itself?

It took only 30 years for the American landscape that Victor Gruen found in 1938 to take the rough form it has now. As his successes and failures encompass or prefigure every important commercial retail, development, and planning trend since WWII, his work is a crucial vehicle for understanding how this transformation of the American cityscape and landscape happened—as an essential first step in asking the question: what kind of city do we want?

Since his death in 1980, many of the questions Gruen faced remain unresolved, and others are increasingly urgent: the further development of the suburbs versus revitalization of the downtowns; the desire of most Americans for a dispersed settlement scaled to the automobile versus the urbanist's argument for a dense pedestrian environment; the aims and capabilities of private development versus the planning responsibilities of public authorities; and the emerging American city region—a cityscape-landscape organized by a network of centers—versus the model of traditional cities and towns, with its radial-concentric hierarchy. The suburbs continue to be built out and are filled with shopping centers, many of them failing. To have a free-standing single-family house, one must live still farther from the old city center, perhaps near an "edge city," and suffer increasingly difficult and unsustainable traffic. For those remaining in inner-city neighborhoods or first-ring suburbs, society is unable to create the opportunities for social, economic, and racial equity. After practically three quarters of a century of highway building in and around cities, there has been almost no improvement in urban traffic: American cities still struggle with the private automobile. Finally, as an ever greater percentage of humanity gathers itself in cities, questions of environment, sustainability, and humanistic values are no longer part of an alternative culture, but assume a global urgency. These are all conditions that were spawned in the decades after World War II, and relatively few architects were there to witness or manage the birth of this landscape, concerning themselves instead with "High Architecture."[1] If the history of the American cityscape and landscape should teach architects and planner anything, it should be that this time around they recognize and engage every aspect of the built environment, especially the new, undefined, and popular zone around and between cities. In facing the persistent questions, then, of how to balance mobility with the desire for a private home, how to create a sustainable city, and what to make of the ever-evolving commercial landscape and the urban forms it generates, the work of Victor Gruen should provide a base line for discussion.

1 As a self-appointed representative of "high architecture," Phillip Johnson compared himself with Gruen: "I like to take a space and create a beautiful building and that is as far as I go. Gruen goes beyond. In playing on people and suggesting what they ought to do, he is a master. And he gets good things like the sculpture done . . . his is a civic art, a civic sense. I'm not sure any of us artistic architects could do what Victor does. He's able to sit down and put things together. . . .I wouldn't get together with him to talk design. Victor feels that when you talk design you are ignoring the whole sweep . . . His architecture is clean—hardly architecture, no flights of fancy. But when you get through with the complex, you've got something beyond the design . . ." Qtd. in Guzzardi, 138.
2 Gillette, Evolution of the Planned Shopping Center, 457.
3 Breckenfield, "The Jim Rouse Show Goes National," 49.
4 Olsen noted, in describing the reaction to the opening of Faneuil Hall at the Boston Festival Marketplace, that "Disney" had become a dirty word amongst intellectuals. 270.
5 Olsen, 241.

Commerce as the Generator of New Urban Space, New Urban Images

In North America, the impact of retail shopping on the development of the suburbs, the renewal of the downtowns, and the spatial and programmatic order of the new metropolitan regions can be first traced in the built work of Victor Gruen. Yet his evolution from retail designer to philosopher of urbanism was not an isolated career trajectory. His fusion of retail with the idea of social and cultural center is the first link in a chain of projects leading from the postwar suburban regional shopping center to the "branded" urban districts today.

After Gruen, this evolution is seen most clearly in the work of developer James Rouse and architect and planner Jon Jerde. Each became known by his shopping centers, but then went on to design urban districts and new towns. And each described himself as a community builder, set for himself (whether he met them or not) the highest social goals, and believed in the possibility of a new humanistic city. Their work, though underappreciated, situates them (and the program they served: retail shopping) not at the edge of architectural culture but at its center.

James Rouse's particular innovation was to link retail, historic structures, and tourism, a strategy that led to his trademark "Festival Marketplaces."[2] Boston's Quincey Market (1976) and Baltimore's Harborplace (1984) were exemplary public-private projects of their time and required close cooperation between innovative city mayors, the developer, and his architects. The link between Rouse and Jerde is that they both believed, as Rouse put it, that "one became 'urban' by 'experiencing' the city."[3] Citywalk, in Los Angeles' Universal City, was Jerde's breakthrough project and amounted to a new development type, the Urban Entertainment Center. Even more explicitly than Rouse's Festival Marketplaces, Citywalk posed questions for urbanists: what is urban and what is city? Overturning private/public and real/artificial, Citywalk–ironically–is both private and artificial, while being popular and urban.

Developing commercial retail, entertainment, and "experience" projects is one way that cities and regions compete for business, investment, and jobs. To serve this need, planning, urban design, and architecture are being forced to engage issues such as image and "brand"; their work must not only communicate, but tell a story. Whatever the considerable differences among the work of Gruen, Rouse, and Jerde, a point of reference common to all three is Walt Disney, long a taboo name in modern architecture and planning.[4] What interested Gruen in Disneyland was how public spaces might be serviced from below or behind: that is, how technology could serve public space. What astonished Rouse on his visit to Disneyland was seeing how people were engaged with the sequences of themed "public" spaces.[5] Disney and his theme parks were hardly an issue for Jerde, whose Citywalk project finally fused shopping, entertainment, and public space. Jerde uses the word "story" often, much as Disney did, and his carefully scripted spaces, as Norman Klein wrote, "absorb the real and the false into a new synthesis" ("The Electronic Baroque," 114).

While global entertainment and media corporations are developing "branded" urban spaces and even "branded" urban districts, more and more people have come to expect urban space that not only is safe and convenient but also narrative and fun.[6] Yet these new large-scale commercial ensembles raise many of the same problems and questions that were leveled against suburban and urban shopping centers. Can the design of the marketplace lead to urban and social renewal? Under what conditions do corporations want to play a more positive social, cultural, and environmental role? Will new urban districts developed by Disney or Sony and new theme parks created by Volkswagen or Adidas generate further building and development, and thus establish a more heterogenous urban core? Or will they replicate the exclusion of socially disadvantaged groups that characterized other private themed environments? Architects and cultural critics have rebuked the extent to which these consumption sites rely on mass tourism and impulse purchases, their "artificiality," and their heterotopic quality—for they are worlds unto themselves that exclude contrasting elements of urban life, especially those that could be perceived as threatening.[7] It may be easy to criticize the misfit between new retail environments and old, especially historic, urban fabric, but there have, frankly, been few alternative planning and investment strategies to draw investment for the new urban core areas. To offer new forms of housing, transit, public places, and even urban districts, architects and planners will have to learn from these commercial environments. In contrast to the critical reception of these urban retail projects and the perceived "suburbanization" of the city, these experiments in citymaking give a new quality to the life of the metropolis and confirm the central place that commerce, the marketplace, and public space play in social and cultural life of the city.

6 "The American downtown as playground...," in Jones, „Downtown of Tomorrow?" A1; and, Elizabeth Stabler and Nancy Huggins of the International Downtown Association, quoted in, Roush, „Kalamazoo Mall Turns 30," A1.
For "branded urban spaces . . . branded urban districts," I have referred to Hoeger, " Emerging Corporate Urbanism in Europe - Developing Responsive Strategies within Brandhubs in the Experience Society," (Unpublished research proposal). ETH, 2004: iii, 1. Hoeger defines "Brandhubs," as comprehensive mixed-use environments developed by global corporations, sometimes in close cooperation with city governments and local communities, 1.
7 The transition from post-war prosperity to a culture of consumption and its effect on cities and suburbs has drawn criticism from a wide array of commentators. See, for example, from the

mid-1960s, "The Future Of The American Out-Of-Town Shopping Center," Ekistics, 100 (referred to in Part 2); Gruen's self-criticism in the late 1970s (see Part 2); and two examples from the 1990s: Michael Sorkin, (Ed.). *Variations on a Theme Park*, see "Introduction," by Michael Sorkin, (xiv); "The World in a Shopping Mall" by Margaret Crawford, for example, (30); "Cities for Sale," by Christine Boyer, (200).
8 Webber, "Non-place Urban Realm," 89. The argument was developed further in the articles in note 11 below.
9 "The View From the Road: A Highway Designed For the Drama of Driving." *Architectural Forum*, 75-8. The article was a preview of Appleyard, Lynch, and Myer, *The View from the Road*, Cambridge, 1964.
10 Jackson, "On the Road, Behind the Wheel, or On Foot."

What Kind of City Does the Car Want?

"The motor has killed the great city. The motor must save the great city." (Le Corbusier, *City of Tomorrow*, 277) By the sprawling 1990s–the S.U.V. decade–the automobile had become the main instrument of typological change in the 20th century for houses, cities, and landscape. Especially in the South and West, Americans have created a new kind of city: dispersed rather than dense, with multiple centers rather than a single historic downtown, and made of freestanding buildings rather than city blocks. The undeclared goal is a city that reflects how a mobile consumer society wants to live rather than a modernization of traditional urban living patterns. Although this experiment had begun to meet both practical and environmental limits even in the 1970s, still it continues to evolve. Are attempts to control the space of the automobile and impose a traditional vision of urban culture compatible with the reality of today's automobile-oriented urbanization? What are the arguments and advantages for the new automobile-oriented city? Can the car in fact be an instrument of a new urbanity?

The benefits of mobility and access are described by three great North American theorists, whose work makes it possible to construct an image of a new kind of dispersed regional city. Melvin Webber argued in his 1964 article "Non-Place Urban Realm" that, for the spread-out Western city, with its myriad starting and destination points, the private automobile was an instrument of personal freedom and, more important, gave access to employment, health care, recreation, and social interaction.[8] Kevin Lynch's 1964 book *The View From the Road* proposed that the design of urban highways could render the complex urban landscape legible and present urban space as an unfolding narrative.[9] The landscape historian J. B. Jackson described two counter-intuitive trends that are helping create a vernacular type of city: loosely structured, fluid, and expansive. First, trucks and vans, which are essential work tools for many Americans, are reintroducing small-scale services and skills into the private realm. Second, the passenger car is relocating many of the experiences and pleasures (once identified with private life) back in the public realm. Jackson wrote, the variation and versatility of automobiles promises a miraculous revival of street life; young people in their cars forming ad-hoc groups in strips or partially empty parking lots create unstructured public spaces for spontaneous, temporary group interaction.[10]

Despite Jackson's enthusiasm for the vernacular, Lynch's proposition that the design of movement could make the city comprehensible, and Webber's embrace of a new form of city and mobile lifestyle, the proliferation of cars and trucks, dispersed development, and the need for ever more roadspace is well known to be a self-sustaining cycle that both engenders and is nourished by sprawl. Cities, even in the South and West, may be continuing to spread out, but they are also becoming more dense, and that means more problems with traffic. Even Webber acknowledged that in contrast to telecommunication advances, the capacities of the auto-highway system have been falling while costs have been rising.[11]

More than 50 years after the Housing Acts made bank loans available for first-time home buyers and therefore helped produce the suburban landscape, a critical turning point in the debate on the form of the city and the problem of sprawl came in 1995 from the Bank of America, which concluded, "This acceleration of sprawl has surfaced enormous social, environmental, and economic costs, which until now have been hidden, ignored or quietly borne by society. . . . We can no longer afford the luxury of sprawl."[12] The "enforced mobility" that Gruen lamented had become an everyday condition.

Yet however logical the separation of traffic or the success of individual pedestrian zones, Americans will not accept total banishment of cars and trucks from their downtowns. The urban landscape of the future will have to be more nuanced than both Gruen's strictly divided pedestrian and vehicular spaces and the exclusively automobile-accessible spaces ever more frequent today. Urban planning needs not a single mechanism for balancing the needs of pedestrians and vehicles but a series of measures, from inter-modal transport interchanges at the edges of urban centers, to smaller-scale interventions in residential areas. Gruen's concept of use classification for streets can also play an important role: highway, boulevard, street, and exurban roads have to be reinvented and re-equipped. Today we need to try to understand traffic as a function in itself, with degrees of complexity, scale, and speed. In 1989, Vittorio Gregotti echoed Gruen's call to architects in "Cityscape-Landscape" by pleading that it was time for architects to "return the road to the settlement event."[13]

11 Webber, "The Joys of Spread City," in Simmonds and Hack, (Eds.), *Global City Regions*, 279. See also "The Joys of Automobility," in Wachs and Crawford (Eds.), *The Car and the City*.
12 "Beyond Sprawl: New Patterns of Growth to Fit the New California," Bank of America and others, San Francisco, 1995. Qtd. Dolores Hayden, *Building Suburbia*, 157.
13 Gregotti, "About Roads," 118.
14 Gruen described this development in his own terms in *Centers for the Urban Environment*, 3-7, 203. In 1987, sustainable planning was officially defined as: "meeting present needs without compromising the ability of future generations to meet their own

needs." Our Common Future," (The Brundtland Report), Oxford University Press, Oxford, UK, 1987. (World Commission on Environment and Development). Peter Calthorpe and Sim van der Ryn described sustainability in their book *Sustainable Communities - A New Design Synthesis for Cities, Suburbs, and Towns*, 1986.
15 McHarg, Qtd. in Rome, The Bulldozer in the Countryside, 187. See also: McHarg, Design with Nature.
16 The Portland Growth Boundary has been consistently supported by voters since its inception in 1976. See Yaro and Hiss, A Region at Risk, 209; and Calthorpe, *The Next American Metropolis*, 32.

Towards the Sustainable City

Gruen's call for a "human ecological planning" was eventually taken up independently by others.[14] Incorporating aspects of ecological planning, reconsidering traditional urban design strategies, and proposing a new design-oriented regional planning, the sustainable-planning movement seeks to replace the *laissez faire* model of sprawl. The main question for architecture and planning is, how shall cities maintain, as they continue to expand into their region, a high-quality urban environment, spatially, socially, and ecologically? Three inherently flexible systems—the transition between public and private transport, the pattern of built and unbuilt space, and the rhythm of high and low density—should be the basis for negotiation between the demands of the commercial and technologically driven world and the need for a social and environmental sustainability.

Ecological Determinism

In 1969, while the work of Gruen's Foundation for Environmental Planning was getting underway, the Philadelphia-based landscape planner and ecologist Ian McHarg published *Design with Nature*, a book that combined a sharp and sometimes ironic critique of contemporary development practices with a planning method that focused on the actual capacity of land to sustain development. McHarg believed that developers, planners, and citizens needed a new set of values. They needed to reconsider the relationship between human communities and the nonhuman world and, above all, to confront the myopic logic of economic determinism, which held that the function of land was to provide profits. Instead of economic determinism, what was needed was "ecological determinism."[15] His work made clear that the process of urbanization and the ecological cycles of the regional landscape must be considered together in any new regional planning or large-scale design.

Re-establishing Regional, Urban, and Neighborhood Space

McHarg's vision required a new planning, and a new regional design and planning movement emerged out of the postmodern architectural and urban critique of the 1970s and '80s. Beginning in the mid-1970s, Portland, Oregon, and later Seattle, Washington, began to consider how to manage growth not only in their immediate metropolitan areas, but across their respective region. The first result of this change in thinking was the Urban Growth Boundary for the city of Portland, published in 1976.[16] This regional planning tool was complemented several years later by a model for a new kind of neighborhood. Seaside, Florida (1983), a planned vacation community, offered both a neotraditional layout and an urban design and architectural code that claimed to offer a more social and urban town life. At the same time, two new strategic and spatial concepts emerged as building blocks for a progressive urbanization of the suburbs. "Pedestrian Pockets" were to be dense mixed-use suburban developments, which were less reliant on frequent use of the car. Linking these pedestrian islands to the central city through regional transit lines, or creating park-and-ride stations for buses, resulted in the concept of "Transit Oriented Development." By incorporating public transit in a new development philosophy, the chances will increase that this consistently neglected area of design and technology may be renewed.[17]

Growth boundaries, neotraditional neighborhood design, and transit-oriented development: these new tools and planning paradigms enable a rethinking of both urban and suburban community development models. Yet what is the overarching concept that can be the basis for social, economic, and spatial consensus? For Peter Calthorpe and others, design is the decisive component of a new regional planning, not merely in terms of the practice of designing, but also as a creative and critical way of thinking. It is the common denominator that links large to small scale–from the scale of the region (1:50,000) to the scale of the community and public space (1:200). Robert Fishman defined this all-inclusive design as starting with a regional concept; continuing with the design of the process of communication, management, and participation; and ending with the design of the infrastructure for movement and open spaces. Design is the action that brings intelligence from the overall vision to the everyday detail–what you see and touch.[18]

Basing their work on a critique of sprawl, over reliance on the automobile, and consumption culture as represented by the shopping center, the New Urbanists and the advocates of a new regional planning believe that their well-developed design and development process, together with their pattern books of physical design elements, will restore a recognizable and sustainable town and urban culture. Over time, the sprawling landscape of strip and subdivision will wither, be renovated, or be replaced. Revitalizing the centers of the numerous historic cities, towns, and villages in the contemporary regional city, adding to their form, and integrating new transit options is a job well suited to supporters of New Urbanism. Yet what of the expanding cityscapes described by Melvin Webber and J. B. Jackson?

17 Kelbaugh, (Ed.), The Pedestrian Pocket Book – A New Suburban Design Strategy, 1989. For "Transit Oriented Development," see: Calthorpe, The Next American Metropolis, 1993, 56-75.
18 Calthorpe and Fulton, *The Regional City*, xv, xvi. This recasting of traditional urban design principles was formalized in 1993 by the establishment of the Congress for New Urbanism. Calthorpe and Fulton's book includes the text of the Charter of New Urbanism. Many of the general development guidelines that Gruen had formulated in his Charter have reappeared in the CNU as a set of principles, backed up by precise codes.

19 Johnson, Robert, "Why `New Urbanism' Isn't for Everyone." Johnson, citing research from the American Association of Homebuilders, claimed that less than 20 percent of consumers want to live i an urban setting. Building industry estimates put the share of "New Urbanist" homes at 10 percent of all new homes sold annually.
20 A description of the components of the European "Zwischensta dt"–the cityscape and landscape around, between, and in cities–is described in Oliver Bormann, Michael Koch, Astrid Schmeing, Martin Schroeder, and Alex Wall. Zwischen Stadt Entwerfen, Zwischenstadt Andernorts. Wuppertal: Verlag Mueller+ Busmann, 2005

Designing Cityscape Landscape Today

Designing Cityscape Landscape Today

After 50 years of successive waves of dispersed growth–of investment and disinvestment–this apparently *laissez-faire* process of development can no longer be adequately described as "suburbanization," nor is it any longer merely "sprawl." The overlapping of suburbs from adjacent towns and cities is an urbanization process that cannot be simply corrected by the planning and urban-design tools developed for the early 20th century city. Driven by the search for spatial and economic advantage, the thousands of intersecting investment decisions have resulted in a form of self-organizing urban landscape that waxes and wanes according to market demands; it cannot be effectively engaged by fixed spatial and functional design codes. In this new cityscape and landscape, as highway, road, and rail infrastructure are added, previously peripheral areas become central, and a regional network comes into being that changes the status of older centers. Supporters of New Urbanism and smart growth–on both sides of the Atlantic–are determined to "correct" this form of development and the desires and practices that support it. But although the number of New Urbanist and smart-growth projects are increasing, more people today live, work, shop, and play outside of or between established centers, and they have chosen to do so.[19]

Other architects and planners, however, are willing to meet the current reality of regional urbanization on its own terms and thus provide space, amenity, and identity for diverse and fragmented communities.[20] In the traditional city, designers may work with street, block, plaza, and district, but outside of densely built-up urban areas, these elements are not the only relevant design and planning components. Outside cities, between cities, and even in central urban areas, development may better be described not in terms of built components, but of spatial and programmatic operations. These include the treatment of edges between different functional areas, the deployment of short-term functions within large buildings, the coordination of (sometimes large-scale) temporary events across a region, and the programatic enrichment of transportation infrastructure. The character and potential of this new urban, yet dispersed, cityscape and landscape depend on the synergy produced by apparently unrelated functions, the temporary existence of new public spaces by the appropriation of disused or underused areas, and the infiltration of traditional functions by new consumption practices. Yet it is a landscape difficult to read and understand, certainly from a single vantage point. Set into a traditional land-use plan, the arrangement of these buildings and functions also makes little sense. Kevin Lynch understood that as one moves through the contemporary city, its disparate parts make themselves known and form a comprehensible narrative–urban space is mediated by movement, and time.

The new cityscape/landscape, with its shopping centers, industrial areas, theme parks, and airports–new institutions which are, by virtue of their program and the large numbers of people who use them, unmistakably urban–is part of what city? It is a developing urban form that cannot be corrected to become a traditional urban pattern, but must mature into a new pattern, different, yet complementary to the old. Architecture alone cannot engage this process. Gruen's expression "cityscape-landscape" implies the coming together of urban and landscape planning and design–a synthesis he could not achieve. At the time of writing, regional urbanization is developing as dynamically in Europe as it is in the U.S., forcing architects and planners to develop new forms of practice and innovative design and planning strategies, many of which may be described as "landscape urbanism."[21] Much as Gruen and others fashioned new building types for the nascent suburbs–the regional shopping center, research parks, and the suburban corporate head office–the new regional urban landscape around and between cities will lead to new kinds of buildings and landscapes that accept the heterogeneity and temporality of sprawl; this is already happening. As the Belgian urbanist Marcel Smets said, the conflicts and potential of urbanization at the edge of and between cities will lead to "the renovation of planning and the rescue of architecture."[22] Planning will have to liberate itself from the straitjacket of successive regulatory "refinements" and seek new flexible forms of negotiation. There are not two cities: traditional centers on one hand, and, on the other hand, recent development around and between cities. There is a single phenomenon of urbanization, which includes and changes older centers, while creating and experimenting with new ones.

In this context, Gruen's vision of the architect-planner as an interdisciplinary team leader should be updated: while remaining a generalist, he must take on a more entrepreneurial role. More and more, his task will not be to conceive and strategize space and built form, but to conceive and strategize forms of design, management, communication, and negotiation. Only by engaging the new urban landscape on its own terms, is it possible to produce the forms and spaces that will make it legible, usable, and urban yielding - an architectecture that is "urban," and a new planning that is made legible by design.

21 See my "Programming the Urban Surface," in James Corner (Ed.), Recovering Landscape, 1999.

22 Smets, Marcel. Unpublished workshop discussion at the Centre de Cultura, Barcelona, 1989.

LA DEFENSE ZONE A
ETUDE DE LA PARTIE OUEST . 6910

SITUATION LOCALE

1 / 6000   NOV 69   3

equipe d'etude
VICTOR GRUEN urbanisme et architecture s.a.
ch saachlen. karnberg suisse
FREEMAN FOX WILBUR SMITH & associés
conseillers pour la circulation
19   dartmouth st. london sw1. angleterre
LARRY SMITH & co.
conseillers economiques
7 rue desmartin. paris s. france

Picture Credits

Cover, title page Courtesy Gruen Associates. Photo: Joseph Molitor Photography, New York. (Cherry Hill: Cherry Court)
Backcover *Fortune*, Jan. 1962. Photo: Baskerville (Victor Gruen Associates. Clockwise from lower right: Victor Gruen, Karl Van Leuven, Ben Southland, Rudi Baumfeld, Edgardo Contini, Herman Gutman)
0-1 Library of Congress, Prints and Photographs. Gruen presenting *Shopping Centers of Tomorrow* to Margaret Arlen of CBS (1953)
2-3 (table of contents) Courtesy Gruen Associates. Photo: Warren Reynolds, Infinity, Inc. (Southdale, Side Promenade)

Part 1 Commerce is the Engine of Urbanity.
16-17 (spread) Courtesy Gruen Associates. (Altman & Kuhne: oblique view of display wall towards rear of store)
25 (left) Duany, Plater-Zyberk, and Alminana, *The New Civic Art*. New York: Rizzoli, 2003: 207.
(Camillo Sitte, Rue de la Regence, Brussels, 1890s)
25 (right) Le Corbusier 1910-60. Editions Girsberger Zuerich, 1960: 291. (Le Corbusier: Une ville contemporaine, 1922) © Vegap
26 (left) Library of Congress, Prints and Photographs. Victor Gruen Papers. (Interior: Bristol perfume shop)
26 (right) *l'Architecture d'Aujourd'hui*. Apr. 1938: 19 (Bristol perfume shop)
27 American Heritage Center, Victor Gruen Collection. (Stoff Singer, Vienna, 1936)
28 Library of Congress, Prints and Photographs. Victor Gruen Papers (The new Singer fabric shop on the Rotenturmstrasse, Vienna, 1936)
29 (left) *Architectural Review*, April 1938: 171. (Deutsch Herrenmoden, Vienna 1936)
29 (right) *l'Architecture d'Aujourdhui* April 1938: 18. (Richard Löwenfeld Women's Fashion Boutique)
31 (above) Courtesy Gruen Associates. Photo Ezra Stoller. (Lederer de Paris, New York, 1939, Lobby)
31 (below) American Heritage Center, Victor Gruen Collection (Perspective drawing. Ciro's and Lederer de Paris)
33 Courtesy Gruen Associates (Altman & Kuhne: Interior view towards rear of store)
35 *Architectural Forum*. Sept. 1941: 192. Photo Robert M. Damora. (Barton's bonbonniere, New York)
36 *Architectural Forum*, Sept. 1941: 196. Photo: Baskerville. (Grayson, Seattle, facade, night view)
37 (left) *Architectural Forum*, Sept. 1941: 197. (Grayson, Seattle, view of sunken display area)
37 (right) *Architectural Forum*, Sept. 1941: 196. (Grayson, Seattle, plan and section)
39 *Architectural Forum*, Oct. 1944: 91. ("Victory Store," Grayson's, San Francisco, CA)
41 *Progressive Architecture*, May 1947: 73. Photo: Roger Sturtivant.

(Joseph Magnin, Sacramento, CA. 1946)
42 American Heritage Center, Victor Gruen Collection. (Millirons, Westchester. *Stores*, March 1949, cover)
43 (above) *Architectural Forum*, June 1949: 105. (Millirons future site in the planned Westchester shopping district)
43 (below left) *Architectural Forum*, June 1949: 105. (Site plan. Millirons Department Store, Westchester)
44 *Architectural Forum*, June 1949: 109. (Millirons, Westchester. Cutaway diagram)
45 (above) Courtesy Gruen Associates. Photo Julius Schulman. (Millirons, Westchester. Rear elevation)
45 (below) Courtesy Gruen Associates. Photo Julius Schulman. (Millirons, Westchester. Aerial view)
46 Courtesy Gruen Associates. Photo Julius Schulman. (Millirons, Westchester. Night view of side entrance with ramp behind)
47 (above) Courtesy Gruen Associates. Photo Julius Schulman. (Millirons, Westchester. View of circular layout with escalators)
47 (below) Gruenbaum and Krummeck, *Merchandising Controls Store Design*, 1950: 7. (Millirons, Westchester. Ground floor plan)
49 Courtesy Gruen Associates. Photo Julius Schulman. (Millirons, Westchester. Night view of ramp to roof)

Part 2 Think of it as an Experimental Workshop.
54-55 (spread) *Esquire*. June 1955: 71. Watercolor: Juliette Kida Renault. (Northland, Detroit. *Esquire*'s Avenue of Fashion)
63 Longstreth, R. "J.C. Nichols, the Country Club Plaza, and Notions of Modernity." *Harvard Architecture Review* 5, 1986: 128. (Country Club Plaza, Kansas City, MO. Preliminary design, E.B. Delk)
64 (upper left) Stein, C.S. *Towards New Towns for America*. Cambridge: MIT, 1966: 129 (Greenbelt, MD, 1935-8. General plan–reversed)
64 (upper right) *Architectural Forum*, March 1943: 39. (Town Center plan, Willow Run, Saarinen, Saarinen and Swanson)
64 (lower left) *Architectural Forum*, Sept. 1944: 85. (left-Site plan, Linda Vista Shopping Center, 1944)
64 (lower right) *Architectural Forum*, Sept. 1944: 81. Photo: Alfred Eisenstaedt. (View of the "lawn." Linda Vista Shopping Center, 1944)
66 American Heritage Center, Victor Gruen Collection. (Aerial view. Northgate, Seattle, WA, 1950. John Graham)
67 Ketchum, M. *Shops and Stores*, New York: Reinhold, 1948: 279. (Aerial perspective. North Shore Center (project)
68 *Architectural Forum*, May 1943: 101. (194X, perspective: "Drug Store and Dining Terrace,"
69 (upper left) *Architectural Forum*, May 1943: cover.
69 (upper right) *Architectural Forum*, May 1943: 102. (194X, Building Plan)
69 (lower right) *Architectural Forum*, May 1943: 101. (194X, Site Plan)

71 *Chain Store Age*, July 1948: 22. (Perspective sketch, Harvey Park, 1948 (project)
73 (above) Courtesy Gruen Associates. (Alternate department store design. Olympic Shopping Center, East Los Angeles)
73 (below left) Courtesy Gruen Associates. (Location plan. Olympic Shopping Center, East Los Angeles)
73 (below right) Courtesy Gruen Associates. (Brochure cover. Olympic Shopping Center, East Los Angeles)
74 Courtesy Gruen Associates (Detroit, Master decentralization plan)
76 (left) *Architectural Forum*, Aug. 1950, 115. (Eastland I. Perspective of circular department store)
76 (right) *Architectural Forum*, Aug. 1950: 113. (Eastland I. Perspective of shopping arcade)
76 (below) *Architectural Forum*, Aug. 1950: cover. Model photo: R. Marvin Wilson (Eastland Plaza (project)
77 *Architectural Forum*, Aug. 1950: 113. (Eastland Plaza project). Plan of store block showing arcade space and double access)
79 *Architectural Forum*, Aug. 1950: 110. (Diagram of team set up to execute the J.L. Hudson shopping centers)
81 Boeckl, M., (Ed), *Visionaere und Vertriebene*. Berlin: Ernst & Sohn, 1995: plate XXV. (Exciting Northland brochure)
82 (left) Courtesy Gruen Associates. (Northland, Model photo showing reverse graded parking fields)
82 (right) Gruen and Smith, *Shopping Towns, U.S.A.*: 124. (Northland, Site Plan showing access)
83 Gruen and Smith, *Shopping Towns, U.S.A.*: 133. (Northland, Merchandising plan)
84 (above) Courtesy Gruen Associates. (aerial view of Northland)
84 (below left) *Esquire*. June 1955: 71. Watercolor: Juliette Kida Renault. (Northland, Detroit. *Esquire*'s Avenue of Fashion)
84 (below right) Courtesy Gruen Associates. (Northland, Detroit. View of store block arcade)
86 *Architectural Forum*. June 1954: 104. Photo: Ben Schnall (Northland, Night view showing entrance to truck tunnel (below left)
87 Courtesy Gruen Associates. (Northland, North Mall with the Totem Pole shortly after opening)
88 *Monthly Bulletin, Michigan Society of Architects*. March 1954: 43. Photo: Photograph House. (Northland's power plant and water tower)
90 Courtesy Gruen Associates. Photo: York Photographic Studios. (Northland: Aerial view)
91 American Heritage Center. Victor Gruen Collection. (Montclair: Perspective of site layout, with Weslyan Avenue running under)
92 Courtesy Gruen Associates (Southdale: a) Bruce Dayton and Gruen with model of the first project; and, b) Hermann Gutman, Gruen, and Rudi Baumfeld in central court)

93 Courtesy Gruen Associates (Southdale: Site plan of first project (single department store), and surrounding community).
95 (left) Courtesy Gruen Associates (Southdale: Plan view of model of final project)
95 (right) Courtesy Gruen Associates (Southdale: Model of central court)
96 *Architectural Forum*. Dec. 1956: 114-15. (sections and site plan. 1) Southdale; 2) Mondawmin; 3) Shoppers World.
97 (above) Courtesy Gruen Associates. (Southdale: short section)
97 (below) *Architectural Forum*. Dec. 1956: 121. (Southdale: Ground floor plan)
98 (above) *Architectural Forum*. Dec. 1956: 116. Photo: Infinity Inc. Warren Reynolds. (Southdale: "The court of eternal spring.")
98 (below-left) Courtesy Gruen Associates. Photo: Anthony Lane. (Southdale: Opera Ball with the Minneapolis Symphony Orchestra)
98 (below-right) Courtesy Gruen Associates. Photo: Anthony Lane. (Southdale: Fashion show)
100 American Heritage Center. Victor Gruen Collection. Photo: Chester Frieden. (Southdale: Aerial view "Inverted architecture")
104 *The Architectural Record*, June 1962, 177. (Cherry Hill: Site Plan)
105 Courtesy Gruen Associates. Photo: Joseph Molitor Photography, New York. (Cherry Hill: Cherry Court)
106 (above) Courtesy Gruen Associates (Randhurst: Plan of public areas with Pavilion)
106 (below) Courtesy Gruen Associates. Photo: Gordon Summers. (Randhurst: Aerial view showing apartment buildings at edge of site)
107 Courtesy Gruen Associates. Photo: Gordon Summers. (Randhurst: Interior view of Pavilion)
110 Courtesy Gruen Associates. Photo Alexandre Georges. (Eastland shopping center: Woman and child)
112 Gruen and Smith, *Shopping Towns U.S.A. (1960)* (cover)

Part 3 The Car and the City
114-15 (spread) Courtesy Gruen Associates (Westchester Plaza (project) model photo and painting montaged into aerial photo of site)
118 Gruen, *The Heart of Our Cities*: 100. (Cartoon from *Paris Match*, Cartoon by Bosc.)
119 *Architectural Forum*, Sept. 1956, 104. (Graphic of car ownership and population increase)
125 Greater Fort Worth Planning Committee, *A Greater Fort Worth Tomorrow*: 18-19. (diagram: creation of a pedestrian central business district)
127 American Heritage Center. Victor Gruen Collection. (front page: Fort Worth Press)

128 (above) Greater Fort Worth Planning Committee, *A Greater Fort Worth Tomorrow*: 2-3. (Aerial view of Fort Worth in 1955.
128 (below) Courtesy Gruen Associates. (Fort Worth: Photomontage: Photo: Gordon Sommers)
130 (above) Greater Fort Worth Planning Committee, *A Greater Fort Worth Tomorrow*. 19. (Diagrams: Circulation diagrams, and scaled to Midtown Manhattan)
130 (below) *Architectural Forum*. Sept. 1956: 117. Photo: Gordon Sommers. (Diagrams: Belt highway and parking garages drawn over plan)
132 Greater Fort Worth Planning Committee, *A Greater Fort Worth Tomorrow*: 6, 10, 27. (Approach and arrival sequence sketches)
133 Courtesy Gruen Associates. (Sketch perspective-gouache- "salt & pepper"- open space)
134 Greater Fort Worth Planning Committee, *A Greater Fort Worth Tomorrow*: 31. (Chart showing administrative structure for implementation.)
135 Greater Fort Worth Planning Committee, *A Greater Fort Worth Tomorrow*: 22. (coloured plan)
136 Courtesy Gruen Associates (Photo of sketch model of garage, district plaza, and building cluster)
137 (above) Greater Fort Worth Planning Committee, *A Greater Fort Worth Tomorrow*: 8. (Fort Worth future scenario: a businessman looks out over the new city)
137 (below) Greater Fort Worth Planning Committee, *A Greater Fort Worth Tomorrow*: 11. (Fort Worth future scenario: a suburban housewife enjoying a day downtown)
138 Courtesy Gruen Associates (Fort Worth: sketch model: parking garage and building group)
139 *Today's Business*, August 1959 (cover) (Burdick Street Pedestrian Mall, Kalamazoo)
140 *Architectural Forum,* Feb. 1959: 93. (Downtown Kalamazoo reconceived as a giant regional shopping and civic center)
141 Attoe and Logann. *American Urban Architecture*. Berkeley: University of California, 1989: 83. (Downtown Kalamazoo; legend shows projects added to Burdick Street Mall)
142 (above) Courtesy Gruen Associates. (Midtown Plaza: Location plan and plan of new beltway and linking streets)
142 (below) *Architectural Forum*, June 1962, 110. (Midtown Plaza: 2 photos: Existing conditions, Project and as built)
157 American Heritage Center. Victor Gruen Collection (Midtown Plaza: Basement parking, Street level plan and First Floor plans)
144 (above) Courtesy Gruen Associates (Midtown Plaza. Model photo)
144 (below) Gruen, *Centers for the Urban Environment*: 128. (Midtown Plaza: Section)
145 American Heratage Center. Victor Gruen Collection. (Parking level, and ground floor plans)

146 (above) Courtesy Gruen Associates. (Midtown Plaza: View as built)
146 (below) *Architectural Forum*, June 1962, 108-9. (Midtown Plaza: Interior plaza view)
147 Edwards Press. Rochester, New York. (Postcard: Midtown Plaza: Clock of the Nations)
151 *Progressive Architecture*. July 1959: 155 (State of California location plan: Fresno and the great central valley)
152 American Heritage Center. Victor Gruen Collection (Fresno: Comprehensive plan with highway interchanges)
153 (above) Courtesy Gruen Associates (Fresno: model photo showing dense center)
153 (below) American Heritage Center. Victor Gruen Collection (Fresno: Central Business and pedestrian shopping District plan)
154 Gruen, *The Heart of our Cities*, 227. (Fresno, "Life on the Mall." Perspective drwg.)
155 Gruen, *The Heart of Our Cities*, 227. (Fresno: "Life on the Mall." Perspective drwg.)
156 Courtesy Gruen Associates (Fresno: Aerial view of Fulton Street Pedestrian Mall)
162 (left) American Heritage Center. Victor Gruen Collection (Gratiot Urban Renewal Project: view from apartment)
162 (right) American Heritage Center. Victor Gruen Collection (Gratiot Urban Renewal Project: (yellow) shadow plan)
164 (left) Gruen and Smith, *Shopping Towns U.S.A.*: 269. (Charles River Park: Perspective by Carlos Diniz, Photo: Gordon Sommers)
164 (right) American Heritage Center. Victor Gruen Collection (Charles River Park: Perspective view from apartment window)
170 American Heritage Center. Victor Gruen Collection (Stamford, CN: Masterplan)
172 American Heritage Center. Victor Gruen Collection (Stamford, CN: perspective of pedestrian mall)
173 American Heritage Center. Victor Gruen Collection (Cincinnati, OH: Masterplan and Perspective)
177 Gruen, *The Heart of Our Cities*: 124 (aerial view of downtown Rochester before redevelopment)

Part 4 Alternatives to Sprawl

178-9 (spread) Bordner Aerials, Bloomington, MN. 941125-43PC-20 (View looking over Southdale towards Minneapolis)
181 (above) Gruen, *Centers of the Urban Environment*: 86. (The Vicious Circle)
181 (below) Gruen, *Centers of the Urban Environment*: 87. (The suburban labyrinth)
183 Gruen, *The Heart of our Cities*: 106. ("The masked builder strikes again." Virgil I. Partch, cartoonist, Los Angeles Times, Publishers Newspaper Syndicate)
187 (left) Gottman, J., *Megalopolis*: 26. (Northeast Corridor)
187 (right) Doxiades, C., *Architecture in Transition*. New York: Oxford, 1963: 107. (Plan for the extension of Washington D. C.)

187 (below) Doxiades, C., *Architecture in Transition*. New York: Oxford, 1963: 103. (Dynopolis)

188 *Architectural Forum*, " Sept. 1956, 129. (Strip and Cluster)

191 Maki, F., *Investigations in Collective Form*: 6. (Group Form diagram)

193 Gruen, *The Heart of Our Cities*: 140. (Whitney Estate)

194 Mastering the City, Vol. II. Rotterdam: NAI, 1997: 47. (Town Center, Vållingby)

196 *Architectural Forum*, Sept. 1956: 131-2. (Progressive Communal Order diagrams)

197 (left) American Heritage Center. Victor Gruen Collection ("1976" Oblique view of a town with metropolitan center in distance)

197 (right) *U.S. News and World Report*, June 20, 1960: 87 ("1976" Oblique view of a town with metropolitan center in distance)

199 (above) *Horizon*, May 1960: 82, 84. (World's Fair Project, Sketch of Fairgrounds with inset Plan)

199 (below) *Horizon*, May 1960: 83, 85. (World's Fair Project, Sketch of New City with inset Plan)

202 Gruen, *The Heart of Our Cities*: 273. (Fold-out plan)

203 (above) Gruen, *Centers of the Urban Environment*: 207-9. (Cellular Metropolis: movement and space diagrams)

203 (middle) Schoof, H. "Idealstaedte und Stadtmodelle.": 81, 86, 184. (Howard, Unwin, Bardet, Christaller)

203 Saarinen, Eliel, *The City*: 210. (Organic dispersal plan for Greater Talinn, 1913)

206 (left) Courtesy Gruen Associates. (Project brochure: structure digram of Laguna Niguel)

206 (right) Courtesy Gruen Associates. (Project brochure: Laguna Niguel, bird's eye view of Beach Club)

207 Courtesy Gruen Associates. (Project brochure: El Dorado Hills, View of village).

209 Courtesy Gruen Associates (Litchfield Park: Concept Plan)

210 American Heritage Center, Victor Gruen Collection (Project brochure: Litchfield Park: Diagrams: One City-six communities; One Community-two villages; One Village-a cluster of neighborhoods)

212 Courtesy Gruen Associates. (Valencia, CA: masterplan)

215 (above) Courtesy Gruen Associates. Photo: Julius Schulmann. (Valencia, CA: drawing: perspective of Paseo; photo; Underpass and kiosk)

215 (below) Courtesy Gruen Associates. (Valencia, CA: plan of a village group)

216 Courtesy Gruen Associates (Valencia, CA: model photo of dense city center)

218 (above) Gruen, *Centers of the Urban Environment*: 225. (Louvain-la-Neuve: model photo of first project)

218 (below) Gruen, *Centers of the Urban Environment*: 223-4. (Louvain-la-Neuve: abstact model diagrams)

220 Gruen, *Das Ueberleben der Staedte*: 284, 302, 305. (Louvain-la-Neuve: section diagram; perspective views)

221 (above) Courtesy Gruen Associates (Louvain-la-Neuve: views of town center and pedestrian bridges)

221 (below) *Louvain-la-Neuve - Freedom of the City*: 4. (aerial/oblique photo)

Part 5 The Desirable City

234-5 (spread) *Architectural Forum*, Sept. 1956: 131-2. (Progressive Communal Order diagrams)

248-9 (spread) AHCVGC. EPAD, Victor Gruen International, Freeman Fox and Wilbur Smith, Larry Smith (La Défense, Zone A, Southwest Quadrant, 1970)

270-1 (spread) Courtesy Gruen Associates. Photo: Gordon Sommers (Maryvale Shopping Center, Phoenix, AZ, 1961)

Works Cited

Author's note, Biographical references, and Archives
The principle archives are: Victor Gruen Papers: Manuscript Division, mm 92081474, Library of Congress, Washington, D.C., Accession date 1995; the Victor Gruen Collection, American Heritage Center, University of Wyoming, Laramie, WY, 5809-84-09-10; and the Stadt- und Landesarchiv Wien.
The principle source of biographical information is "Gruen, V., "Ein Realistischer Traeumer," Ruckblicke, Einblicke, Ausblicke," LoCVGP, Container 77. This 424 page manuscript, which Gruen hoped to have published, was dictated (in german) in Vienna from 1979. Translations from "Ein realisticher Traeumer" are mine.
I take this unpublished manuscript as Gruen's final edit of previous notes. These include: Notes for New Book - Autobiograhical work about Victor Gruen, dated 26 March, 1975, in the LoCVGP, Container 20; Victor Gruen, untitled manuscript (notes for an autobiography) 1977, LoCVGP, Container 20; Victor Gruen, "General Book Plan," September 1977-April 1978, Lo-CVGP, Container 77, folder 2; and, "Biographische Notizien",the preparatory notes in german for "Ein Realistischer Traeumer," also LoCVGP, Container 20.
Some information in Ein realistischer Traeumer is corroborated or contradicted by, for example, "The Partners talk about Victor Gruen Associates, c. 1970 (Karl Van Leuven, Edgardo Contini et al.) LoCVGP, Container 78. Further corroboration and contradictions come from Interview and notes (unpublished), and texts of Edgardo Contini. Collection Anne Gray, Los Angeles.
Victor Gruen's speeches are bound in four volumes, and are to be found in the LoCVGP (boxes 80-84), AHCVGC, and at Gruen Associates.

WORKS BY GRUEN
Books:
—. Centers of the Urban Environment - Survival of the Cities. New York: Van Nostrand Reinhold Co. 1973.
—. Ein realistischer Traeumer: Ruckblicke, Einblicke, Ausblicke (unpublished manuscript for an autobiography), Wien: December 1979. LoCVGP, box 77.
—. The Heart of Our Cities - The Urban Crisis: Diagnosis and Cure. New York: Simon and Schuster 1964.
—. Ist Fortschritt ein Verbrechen? Umweltplanung statt Weltuntergang. Vienna: Europaverlag 1975.
—. Die Lebenswerte Stadt: Vision eines Umweltplaners. Muenchen: List Verlag 1975.
—. Meine Alte Schuhschachtel. Vienna: Europaverlag 1973.
—, and Larry Smith. Shopping Towns U.S.A. The Planning of Shopping Centers. NewYork: Reinhold Publishing Corp. 1960

Articles—including speeches, project reports, brochures and catalogs:
—. "A City Reborn," (film). Victor Gruen Associates, 1968. LoCVGP Film Division. There is also a videotape in the AHCVGC; also Gruen Associates, Los Angeles.

—. "A New Look At Past, Present and Future Shopping Centers." Architectural Record, Apr. 1968: 167- 171.
—. "A Proposed Solution (How to Handle this Chaos of Congestion, this Anarchy of Scatteration)." Architectural Forum, Vol. 105, No. 3, Sep. 1956: 130-35.
—. "Are Centers Necessary?" Speech E 132, Bergen, Norway, 11 February, 1967.
—. "A Shopping Center Is More Than A Collection OF Stores." Practical Builder (Chicago) Oct. 1953: 64-67.
—. "Approaches to Urban Revitalization in the United States." Architectural Association Quarterly, Dec. 1962: 178-194.
—. "Architect Gruen States the Challenge that Graphic Design Presents." Architectural Record, (Building Types Study: Commercial Buildings: Signs and Symbols). Sep. 1956: 244-247.
—. "Architect's Complete Control of Design and Furnishings Effects Large Saving for Owner." Southwest Builder and Contractor, Apr. 22, 1949: 8-9, 11, 40.
—. "Art and Architecture in a man-made environment." Rochester Chronicle, December 4, 1958: reprint LoCVGP.
—. "The better to see, reach, and touch." Furniture Forum, n.d. 1955: reprint, LoCVGP.
—. "The Case for the Flexible Ceiling." Electrical West, Sep. 1949: reprint LoCVGP, OV 60.
—. "The chain's stake in planning the center." Chain Store Age, May 1954: 34-41.
—. The Charter of Vienna, Victor Gruen Foundation for Environmental Planning (VGFEP), Los Angeles, 1972. LoCVGP.
—. "Cities in Trouble–What Can Be Done." U.S. News&World Report (interview), June 20, 1960: 86-93.
—. "The City As Designed Structure." Pratt Alumnus - Spring 1962: reprint, LoCVGP. Speech D 90: Pratt Institute, Brooklyn, NY. 12 Dec. 1961.
—. "The City in the Automobile Age." Perspecta. Spring 1956: 50-1. AHCVGC.
—. "Cityscape Landscape." Arts & Architecture, Sep. 1955: 18, 19, 36. Reprinted in Architectural Culture 1943-1968. Ed. Joan Ockman, and Ed Eigen, Rizzoli, New York, 1993: 194-195.
—. "Controlling Factors in the Establishment of Regional Shopping Centers." Regional Conference on the Effect of Current War Conditions on Real Estate Market and Valuation Problems, 1943. Speech A 01, LoCVGP, container 81.
—. "Defence on the Periphery." Speech A05, National Convention of the American Institute of Architects, Chicago, May 8, 1951. AHCVGP
—. "Downtown Appleton, Its Future?" Victor Gruen, A.I.A., Sep. 1953. Gruen Associates, Los Angeles.
—. "Dynamic Planning for Retail Areas." Harvard Business Review, Nov.-Dec. 1954: 53-62.
—. "El Dorado Hills: New model for tomorrow's satellite cities." House and Home, March, 1963: 107-115.
—. "Emerging urban pattern." Progressive Architecture, 40, 7. July 1959: 115-166.

—. "Environmental architecture." *American Institute of Architects (AIA) Journal*, 38 Dec. 1962: 96-97.

—. East Island: A Proposal for the Conversion of Welfare Island, New York to a Residential Development, 1961. Victor Gruen Associates. AHCVGC; LoCVGP.

—. "From the Shopping Center to the Planned City." *Stores,* Mar. 1966: 14-17 (see speeches - NRMA Jan. 1966 Retail Research Institute).

—. "Guidelines for Urban Development – 15 Principles." Victor Gruen Center for Environmental Planning, Vienna, Jan. 1973. LoCVGP.

—. "Highways and the American City." Speech B45, Hartford, CN, September 9, 1957: 468.

—. "How to handle this chaos of congestion, this anarchy of scatteration." *Architectural Forum* (What City Pattern?), 105 September 1956: 130-5.

—. "Introverted architecture." *Progressive Architecture* 38, 5. May 1957: 204-208.

—. "Is there a gap between architect and merchant?" letter to the editor published in *Chain Store Age*, May 1953: 66, 70. AHCVGC, Box 11.

—. "Kalamazoo, 1980, A Planning Study by Victor Gruen Associates and Larry Smith & Company, 1958." History Room, Kalamazoo Public Library.

—. "Licht und Schatten der Europaische Großstadt." in Scheuch, M., "Europas Großstadt - Licht und Irrlicht," *Arbeiter-Zeitung* (Profile), 9 Jun. 1963. LoCVGP.

—. List of Work Done in the Years: 1924-1937. LoCVGP.

—. "Litchfield Area Plan, Maricopa Co., AZ." Victor Gruen & Associates, Land Planners; Larry Smith, Real Estate Economics; Lawrence Halprin, Landscape Systems, 1965. LoCVGP.

—. "Lighting Fixtures Used for their Psychological and Decorative Value." *Lighting & Lamps*, Oct. 1952: 46.

—. "Lighting Today's Interior." *Lighting & Lamps,* Jan. 1953: 30-31.

—. "Modern Architecture." *Michigan Society of Architects*, Dec. 1956: 23.

—. *New Cities U.S.A.: A Statement of Purpose and Program,* prepared for the Department of Housing and Urban Development. Victor Gruen Associate, Summer 1966.

—. "New Towns and Urban Centers in the U.S.," Speech F144, Paris, July 1969.

—. *"1976"* (unpublished project sketches and text). *Victor Gruen Associates,* July 30, 1955-July 23, 1956. AHCVGC box 15.

—. "No more offstreet parking in congested areas." *American City,* Sep. 1959: 161-63.

—. Olympic Shopping Circle - Los Angeles Hotspot, Olympic Shopping Circle Inc., Los Angeles, CA, 1950. Gruen and Krummeck - Victor Gruen, Architect. Collection, Gruen Associates, Los Angeles.

—. "The Peoples Architect." Rice 1964. Speech D 94: Rice University, Houston, TX. 9 Jan. 1963.

—. "The Planned Shopping Centers of America." *Zodiac* 1, 1957: 159-67.

—. "The Present Pattern." *Progressive Architecture* (The Emerging Urban Pattern), July 1959: 126-129.

—. "Regional Shopping Centers and Civilian Defense – A Memorandum With Special Reference to the Eastland Shopping Center in Detroit." Victor Gruen Associates, 1953: 10-12. AHCVGC.

—. "Renewing Cities for the Automobile Age." *Traffic Engineering,* May 1957. Speech before the Potomac Chapter of the National Housing & Redevelopment Officials, Washington, D.C., 3 Jan. 1957.

—. "Retailing and the automobile." *Architectural Record*, Mar. 1960: 192-210.

—. "The sad story of shopping centers." *Town and Country Planning* 46, 7/8 July-Aug. 1978: 350-353.

—. "Shopping Centers of Tomorrow." *Arts & Architecture* 71, Jan. 1954: 12-17.

—. *Shopping Centers of Tommorrow*, Catalogue of an Architectural Exhibit circulated by the American Federation of the Arts; designed by Victor Gruen Associates, Victor Gruen, A.I.A., R. L. Baumfeld, Karl O. Van Leuven, Jr., A.I.A., Edgardo Contini; catalog by Madden/Shipman. 1953. AHCVGC Box 33.

—. "Shopping Centers, Why, Where, How?" Zentrum fuer Umweltplanung, Vienna, 1978 - (Speech for the Third Annual European Conference of the International Council of Shopping Centers, Hilton Hotel, London, 28 Feb. 1978. LoCVGP box 78.

—. "Store Designing for the 'Feminine Touch'." *West Coast Feminine Wear*, Tues. 29 April, 1947: reprint, LoCVGP.

—. "Triple target for economy." *Chain Store Age,* July 1949: 18-19,63-4.

—. "Twelve Checkpoints for Regional Planned Center." *Women's Wear Daily*, 28 December, 1953: reprint, LoCVGP.

—. "Urban Planning for the 1960s." *Commerce* (Chicago), Oct. 1960: 25-6, 44, 47, 50. Speech C 72 to the annual U.S. Conference of Mayors, Chicago, May 1960.

—. "What to look for in shopping centers." *Chain Store Age*, July 1948: reprint LoCVGP.

—. "What's Wrong With Store Design?" *Women's Wear Daily*, 18 Oct. 1949: 62.

—. "Where is modern architecture taking us? (with Eero Saarinen). *American Institute of Architects (AIA) Journal*, 28 August 1957: 239-241.

—. "Who is to Save Our Cities?" *Harvard Business Review*, May-June 1963: 107-115.

—. "Yardstick for Shopping Centers," *Chain Store Age*, Feb. 1950: 23-5, 35.

Victor Gruen Associates – Architecture/Engineering/Planning, 1958 (office brochure).

Victor Gruen Associates – Architecture/Engineering/Planning, 1968 (office brochure).

Victor Gruen Associates. "Litchfield Area Plan, Maricopa Co., AZ.", Land Planners; Larry Smith, Real Estate Economics; Lawrence Halprin, Landscape Systems, 1965. LoCVGP.

Victor Gruen Foundation for Environmental Planning (VGFEP), 1968. LoCVGP, AHCVGP.

Gruen (Gruenbaum) et al:

Gruen, Victor, and Morris Ketchum, "What to look for in Shopping Centers", *Chain Store Age* (Store Modernization Issue), Administrative Edition, Jul. 1948: 63-6.

Gruen, Victor and Elsie Krummeck, "letter: Architect Bites Client." *Architectural Forum*, Feb. 1948: p 34, 46.

Gruen, Victor and Elsie Krummeck. *"Merchandising Controls Store Design."* Los Angeles: Victor Gruen, AIA., 1949.

Gruen, Victor, Carol Meeks, Christopher Tunnard, and Edith Kerr. "On Architecture and Planning–A Yale Report." *Arts and Architecture,* Oct. 1959: 24.

Gruen, Victor, J.L. Sert (moderator), et al. "Urban design: Harvard Conference." *Progressive Architecture* Aug. 1956. Aug: 97-112.

Gruen, Victor, and Larry Smith. "Shopping centers: The new building type." *Progressive Architecture* 33, 6. June 1952: 67-94.

Gruen, Victor, Eric von Storch, and D.C. Ehrlich, "Urban Renewal,"*Architectural Metals*, Aug. 1962: 10-18, 21-26.

Gruenbaum, Victor, "Some Notes on Modern Store Design." *Architect and Engineer*, Feb. 1942: reprint.

Gruenbaum, Victor and Elsie Krummeck, "Face to Face," *Apparel Arts*, Jun. 1940: 52.

Gruenbaum, Victor, Elsie Krummeck and Michael Auer, "The Case of Displayman versus Store Designer," *Display World*, Sep. 1941: reprint, LoCVGP.

WORKS BY OTHERS

Adamson, Paul. "Looking Back on Our Future: conflicting visions and realities of the modern American coity," in Thomas Deckker (Ed.), *The Modern City Revisited*. 242.

Aex, R.P., "Rochester unveils America's first midtown bazaar." *American City,* March 1959: 173-75.

Albrecht, Donald (Ed.). *World War II and the American Dream - How Wartime Building Changed a Nation*. Cambridge, MA: MIT Press 1995.

Appleyard, Donald, Lynch, Kevin, and Meyer, J.R. *The View from the Road*, Cambridge, MA: MIT Press 1964.

Attoe, Wayne, and Donald Logann. *American Urban Architecture*. Berkeley, CA: University of California 1989.

Augenfeld, Felix. "Modern Austria, personalities and style." *Architectural Review,* Apr. 1938: 165, 171.

Austin, K. "Elsie Krummeck has dramatised with her patented metal dolls..." *New York World Telegram* 22 June 1936. Clipping. Peggy Gruen Collection.

Baker, Geoffrey and Bruno Funaro. *Shopping Centers – Design and Operation*. New York: Reinhold Publishing Corporation 1951.

Balcolm, Lois. "Best Hope for Our Big Cities," *The Reporter*, Oct. 3, 1957: reprint, LoCVGP.

Banham, Reyner. *Megastructure - Urban Futures of the Recent Past*. London: Thames and Hudson 1976.

Bauer, Catherine. "First job: control new-city sprawl." *Architectural Forum* 105, Sep. 1956: 105-12.

Beauregard, Robert. *Voices of Decline - The Postwar Fate of U.S. Cities*. New York: Routledge 2003.

Blau, Eve. *The Architecture of Red Vienna 1919-1934*. Cambridge, MA: MIT Press 1999.

Boeckl, Matthias., (Hrsg), "Visionaere und Vertriebene," Oesterreichische Spuren in der modernen amerikanischen Architektur. Berlin, Wien: Ernst & Sohn, 1995.

Bormann, Oliver, Michael Koch, Astrid Schmeing, Martin Schroeder, and Alex Wall. *News From Nowhere*. Wuppertal: Verlag Mueller+ Busmann, 2005.

Bradford, H. "Gruen's Mall Visit Mends Some Fences." *Kalamazoo Gazette* May 11, 1960, (Business).

Breckenfield, Gurney. "The Jim Rouse Show Goes National." *Fortune* July 27, 1981: 48-54.

Browning, David L. "The Legacy of a Planning Legend: The Victor Gruen Plan for a Greater Fort Worth Tomorrow." *CRIT* 12, Winter 1983 (AIA, Washington, D.C.): 5-10.

Buchanen, Colin. *Traffic and Towns*. London: HMSO, 1963.

Calthorpe, Peter. *The Next American Metropolis - Ecology, Commuinty, and the American Dream*. New York: Princeton Architectural Press, 1993.

Calthorpe, Peter, and William Fulton. *The Regional City City - Planning for the End of Sprawl*. Washington, D.C.: Island Press, 2001.

Calthorpe, Peter and Van der Ryn, Sim, *Sustainable Communities - A New Design Synthesis for Cities, Suburbs, and Towns*. San Francisco: Sierra Club Books, 1986.

Canaday, J. "The World's Fair: Architects and Critics See a Monster Developing for 1964-65." *New York Times*, undated-probably 1961. reprint, AHCVGP

Carson, Rachel. *Silent Spring*. London: Penguin, 1998 (1962).

Cartsonis, E. "Ten-minute Town: Litchfield Park, Arizona designed around bike and golf paths." *Landscape Architecture*, Oct. 1966: 40-2.

Chung, Chuihua J., Jeffrey Inaba, Rem Koolhaas, Sze T. Leong (Eds.). *Harvard Design School Guide to Shopping*, Cologne: Taschen, 2001.

Clausen, Meredith. "Northgate Regional Shopping Center–Paradigm from the Provinces." *Journal of the Society of Architectural Historians* (JSAH) 43 May 1984: 144-161.

Clay, Grady. "What makes a good square good?" in Jacobs, Jane. "Downtown Is For People." *The Exploding Metropolis*. Ed. William Whyte. Berkeley: University of California (1958) 1993: 172.

—. "Main Steet 1969." (A Citizens Planning Conference organized by the American Planning and Civic Association). *Landscape* Vol. 7, No. 1, Autumn 1957: 2.

—. "Metropolis Regained," *Horizon* Vol. 1, No. 6, July, 1959: 4-15.

Cohen, Gary. "A Mecca for Suburbanites." *U.S. News & Word Report* (Special Report "The American Century"). Dec. 27, 1999: 49-50.

Cohen, Lizabeth. "From Town Center to Shopping Center: The Reconfiguration of Community Marketplaces in Postwar America." *American Historical Review* (AHR) 101.4 Oct. 1996: 1050-1081.

Collins, George R., and Christine C. Collins. *Camillo Sitte and the Birth of Modern City Planning* (Columbia University Studies in Art History and Archaeology, No. 3). London: Phaidon Press, 1965.

Concorci, C."An Interview with Stewart Udall-former Secretary for the Interior." *EQM* May 1973. Reprint. Collection Oekostadt, Wien.

Contini, Edgardo. "The Renewal of Downtown Fresno: A Case Study." Speech presented at the Urban Design Symposium, Auckland City Development Association, Auckland, NZ, 13 May 1969. Collection of Anne Gray, Los Angeles.

—. "Notes on Fresno," 1970, LoCVGP.

—. Interview with Anne Gray, unpublished manuscript, and notes from conversations with Anne Gray, 1988. Collection Anne Gray, Los Angeles.

—. "Urban Renewal, Performance and Prospects," *Urban Land* 225, May 1963, 3-7.

Le Corbusier, *The City of To-morrow and its Planning*, Translated from the 8th French edition of *Urbanisme* by Frederick Etchells (first english english translation published by Payson and Clark Ltd., New York about 1929), repub. New York: Dover, 1987.

Crawford, Margaret. " Daily Life on the Home Front: Women, Blacks, and the Struggle for Public Housing." *World War II and the American Dream*. Ed. Donald Albrecht. Cambridge, MA: MIT Press, 1995: 90-143.

—. "The World in a Shopping Mall," Ed. Michael Sorkin, Variations on a Theme Park.

Crawford, Margaret and Wachs, Martin, Eds. The Car and the City, Ann Arbor: University of Michigan, 1992.

Crear, W. Jr. "Southdale 1951-71: Discussion on New Suburban Town Center." Unpublished Notes for a presentation. ICSC, New York, May 17, 1971. LoCVGP.

Cunningham, Allen. "The Modern City Revisited - envoi." *The Modern City Revisited*. Ed. Thomas Deckker. London: Spon, 2000: 247-50.

Dames, T.A., and W.L. Grecco. "A Survey of New Town Planning Considerations." *Traffic Quarterly*, Oct. 1968: Reprint. LoCVGP.

Deckker, Thomas (Ed.). *The Modern City Revisited*. London: Spon Press, 2000.

Ditch, S., and P. Rouse Eds. "A Larger Vision James Rouse and the American City." (excerpts from speeches). The Rouse Corporation, Columbia, MD: nd.

Divine, Robert (Ed.), *The Johnson Years, Vol. Two: Vietnam, The Environment, and Science*. Lawrence, KA: University of Kansas, 1987.

Doxiades, Constantine, *Architecture in Transition*. New York: Oxford, 1963.

Duany, Andreas, Elizabeth Plater-Zyberk, and Robert Alminana, *The New Civic Art: Elements of Town Planning*. New York: Rizzoli, 2003.

Dyer, Stephanie. "Markets in the Meadows: Department Stores and Shopping Centers in the Decentralization of Philadelphia, 1920-80." Dissertation in History, University of Pennsylvania, 2000. Ann Arbor: University of Michigan Dissertation Services.

Dykema, Ray. "Ray Dykema remembers when: the making of the mall." *Encore*, Apr. 1987: 28-32, 64-66. History Room, Kalamazoo Public Library.

Ehrenkrantz, Ezra, and Ogden Tanner. "The remarkable Dr. Doxiades." *Architectural Forum*, May 1961: 115.

Feiss, Carl. "Shopping Centers." *House and Garden*, Vol. 76, No. 6, Dec. 1939: 48-66.

Fernandez, Jose. "Modernized Store Fronts." *Paint Logic*. Oct. 1947. reprint. LoCVGP

—. *The Specialty Shop, A Guide*. New York: Architectural Book Company, 1950.

Fishman,Robert. *Bourgeois Utopias: The Rise and Fall of Suburbia*, New York: Basic Books, 1987.

—. "Past and Future Influences: The American Metropolis at Century's End." Fannie Mae Foundation, Housing Facts & Findings Newsletter, 1999: 4. Also: www.fanniemaefoundation.org/research/facts/archive.html.

Forristal, T. "Grayson's Growth." *Wall Street Journal*. 1946, (The Inquiring Investor): 12. reprint, LoCVGP.

Friedel, Robert. "Scarcity and Promise: Materials and American Domestic Life during World War II Culture," Ed. Donald Albrecht, *World War II*. Cambridge, MA: MIT Press, 1995: 42-58.

Frieden, Bernard J., and Lynne B. Sagalyn, *Downtown Inc. -How America Rebuilds Cities*. Cambridge, MA: MIT Press, 1997 (1991).

Friedlander, Gordon D. "Birth of the New City: an exciting creation." *IEEE Spectrum* (Institute of Electrical and Electronic Engineers, Inc.), April 1967: 70-86.

Funaro, Bruno, and Geoffrey Baker. "Shopping Centers." *Architectural Forum* (Building Types Study No. 152), Aug 1949: 110-129.

Gallion, Arthur and Simon Eisner, *The Urban Pattern*. New York: Van Nostrand, 1980 (Fourth Edition).

Gans, Herbert J., *The Urban Villagers*. Glen Coe: The Free Press, 1962: 285.

Garvin, Alexander, *The American City - What Works, What Doesn't*. New York: McGraw-Hill, 1996.

—. "Make No Little Plans." *Unbuilt Cincinnati*. Eds. Garvin, Alexander, David R. Scheer, and J. A. Chewning. Cincinnati: Cincinnati Forum for Architecture and Urbanism, 1998, p. 21-5.

Gideon, Sigfried. "The Humanization of Urban life." *Architectural Record*, Apr. 1952: 123.

Gillette, Howard, Jr. "The evolution of the planned shopping center in suburb and city."
Journal of the American Planning Association (JAPA) 51, 4 Apr. 1985: 449-460.

Gilmore, Irving. "Plan Stirs Curiosity, Wins Praise." *Kalamazoo Gazette*, Mar. 19, 1958, Section 2: 19-34. Clippings file, History Room, Kalamazoo Public Library.

Goodman, Robert. "Dead Mall." *Metropolis*, Nov. 1993: 43-45.

Gottman, Jean, *Megalopolis: The Urbanized Northeastern Seaboard of the United States*. Cambridge, MA: MIT Press, 1961.

Gould, Lewis L. "Ladybird Johnson and Beautification." *The Johnson Years, Vol Two: Vietnam, the Environment, and Science*. Ed. Robert A. Divine. Lawrence, KA: University Press of Kansas 1987: 150-182.

Greer, G. Is your town fit to live in?. " *The American Magazine* 146, July, 1948: 50.

Gregotti, Vittorio. "About Roads," (english digests). *Casabella* 553-554, Jan.-Feb. 1989: 118.

Grunenberg, Christopher. "Wonderland: Spectacles of Display from the Bon Marche' to Prada," Ed. Max Hollein and Christopher Grunenberg, *Shopping - A Century of Art and Consumer Culture*: 18-21.

Guelft, Olga. "Department Store of the Future: Milliron´s Could Be the Model."
Interiors CIX. 3, Oct. 1949: 112-19.

Gutheim, Frederick. "Washington Planning Problems: From L"Enfant to Gruen." *Progressive Architecture* (p/a news report), n.d. 1959: 82-6. reprint, AHCVGC.

Guzzardi, Walter, Jr. "An Architect of Environments." *Fortune*, Jan 1962: 77-80, 134-138.

Hall, Peter. "Anonymity and Identity in the Giant Metropolis., Ed. Luigi Mazza." *World Cities and the Future of the Metropoles, Vol. II, International Participants*, XVII Triennale. Milano: Electa, 1988: 44.

Hanchett, Thomas. "U.S. Tax Policy and the Shopping Center Boom of the 1950s and 1960s." *American Historical Review (AHR)* 101.4 Oct. 1996: 1082-1110.

Hardwick, M. Jeffrey. "Creating a Consumer's Century: Urbanism and Architect Victor Gruen, 1938-68." Dissertation, Yale University. Ann Arbor: University of Michigan Dissertation Services, 2000.

—. *Mallmaker, Victor Gruen, Architect of an American Dream*. Philadelphia: University of Pennsylvania Press, 2004.

Hayden, Dolores, *Building Suburbia - Green Fields and Urban Growth, 1820-2000*. New York: Pantheon, 2003.

Hays, Samuel, *Beauty, Health, and Permanence - Environmental Politics in the U.S., 1955-85*. New York: Cambridge University Press, (1987) 1993.

Herbert, R., "Rebirth of Nation's Cities Owes Debt to Victor Gruen." *Los Angeles Times*, Sep. 18, 1960: 13-14.

Herman, Dan. "High Architecture," Eds. Chuihua J Chung, et al, *Harvard Guide to Shopping*. Cologne: Taschen, 2001: 390-401.

—. "Mall - Requiem for a Type (Obituary)." Eds. Chuihua J Chung, et al, *Harvard Guide to Shopping*. Cologne: Taschen, 2001: 464-475.

—. "Three-Ring Circus; Or, The *Double* Life of the Shopping Architect." Eds. Chuihua J Chung, et al, *Harvard Guide to Shopping*. Cologne: Taschen, 2001: 737-47.

Hill, David R. "Sustainability, Victor Gruen and the Cellular Metropolis. " *Journal of the American Planning Association (JAPA)* 58.3, Summer 1992: 312-26.

Hise, Greg. "The Airplane and the Garden City: Regional Transformation during World War II," Ed. Donald Albrecht. *World War II and the American Dream*. Cambridge, MA: MIT Press, 1995: 152-59.

Hoeger, Kirstin, " Emerging Corporate Urbanism in Europe - Developing Responsive Strategies within Brandhubs in the Experience Society," (Unpublished research proposal). ETH (Swiss Federal Institute of Technology), Zuerich, 2004.

Hollein, Max, and Christopher Grunenberg (Eds.), *Shopping - A Century of Art and Consumer Culture*. Ostfildern-Ruit: Hatje Cantz, 2002.

Hornbeck, J. "Signs & Symbols in Commercial Architecture." *Architectural Record* (Building Types Study 238 Commercial Buildings Signs & Symbols), Sep. 1956: 242-275.

Huxtable, Ada Louise. "Out Of A Fair, A City." *Horizon*, May 1960: 80-87.

Jackson, J.B., "On the Road, Behind the Wheel, or On Foot." *Casabella* 586-587 "America," Jan.-Feb. 1992.

—. "Truck City," in *A Sense of PLACE, a Sense of TIME*. New Haven: Yale, 1994: 171-186.

Jackson, Kenneth. "All the World's a Mall: Reflections on the Social and Economic Consequences of the American Shopping Center." (AHR Forum) *American Historical Review*, 101.4 Oct. 1996: 1111-1121.

—. *Crabgrass Frontier: The Suburbanization of the United States*. New York: Oxford University Press, 1985.

Jacobs, Jane. "Downtown is for people," Ed. William Whyte, Jr., *The Exploding Metropolis*: 157-184.

Janik, Alan and Toulmin, Stephan, *Wittgenstein's Vienna*. New York: Simon and Schuster, 1973.

Jencks, Charles. *Modern Movements in Architecture*. Harmondsworth: Penguin, 1973: 99, 303.

Johnson, Phillip. "Why We Want Our Cities Ugly." *Lotus 5*, 1968: 9.

Johnson, Robert. "Why `New Urbanism' Isn't for Everyone." *New York Times* (Perspectives), Sun. Feb. 20, 2005.

Jones, Al. "Downtown of Tomorrow?" *Kalamazoo Gazette*, Jan. 21, 1996: A1. Clippings File, History Room, Kalamazoo Public Library.

Jones, W. Dwayne. "A Greater Fort Worth Tomorrow: Victor Gruen's Vision Revisited." unpublished 20 page manuscript, Texas Historical Commission, Austin, 1997.

Kainrath, W., "Fußgaengerzonen in Wien" (editorial), *Bau*, Jan. 1971: 51.

Kapfinger, Otto. "Victor Gruen und Rudi Baumfeld: Traumkarriere einer Partnerschaft," Ed. Matthias Boekl, "*Visionaere und Vertriebene*": 255-80.

Kaufman, Gerd. "Valencia – More Than Just Another New Town." *Urban Land*, Oct. 1992: 73-75.

Kelbaugh, Doug (Ed.). *The Pedestrian Pocket Book – A New Suburban Design Strategy*. New York: Princeton Architectural Press, 1989.

Keller, A. "Let's make our fairs permanent cities." *New York World-Telegram & Sun*, June 11, 1960 (Feature Magazine Section): Reprint. LoCVGP.

Ketchum, Morris, *Shops and Stores*. New York: Reinhold, 1948.

Kiek, R. "Europe's Fifth Avenue - Lijnbaan-Rotterdam Testifies to Success of the Downtown Shopping Center." *Urban Land*, Oct. 1954: 3-6.

Kiesler, Friedrich, *Contemporary Art Applied to the Store and its Display*. New York: Brentano's, 1930.

Kirkpatrick, D., "The Artists of the Independent Group: Backgrounds and Continuities," Ed. David Robbins, *The Independent Group, Postwar Britain and the Aesthetics of Plenty*. Cambridge, MA: MIT Press, 1990: 210.

Klein, Norman. "The Electronic Baroque: Jerde Cities." Eds. Francis Anderton and Norman Klein, *You Are Here!*: 114.

Kraus, E. "Thoughts on Friedrich Kiesler's Show Windows," Eds. Max Hollein and Christopher Grunenberg, *Shopping - A Century of Art and Consumer Culture:* 125.

Kwinter, Sanford. "Virtual City: the wiring and waning of the world." *Arch+* 128, Sep. 1995.

Labo, Mario. *Architettura del Negozio*. Milano: Ulrico Hoepli, 1937.

Lapidus, Morris, *The Architecture of Joy*. Miami: E.A. Seeman, 1979.

—. "Store Design, A Building Types Study." *Architectural Record*, Feb. 1941: 120-131.

Larkin, W.P. "Closed Mall Pays Off in Leases - Cherry Hill." *Shopping Center Age*, Jan. 1962: 51-5.

—. "Midtown Plaza . . . one answer to downtown's problems." *Shopping Center Age*, Aug. 1962: 3-15.

Lear, Linda. Afterword (Carson, R., Silent Spring. London: Penguin, (1962) 1998): 258-64.

Lear, M. W. "A Master Builder Sites a Shopping Mall." *New York Times* (Sunday Magazine), Aug. 12, 1973: 82,84. Cited in Frieden, Bernard J., and Lynne B. Sagalyn, *Downtown Inc.-How America Rebuilds Cities*. Cambridge, MA: MIT Press, (1991) 1997: 5.

Lemann, Nicholas, *The Promised Land*. New York: Alfred Knopf, 1991.

Leong, S. T. "Gruen Urbanism," Eds. Chuihua J Chung, et al, *Harvard Guide to Shopping*: 380-89.

Litchfield Park Properties. Litchfield Park – A New City Takes Form: Designs for A Richer and More Fulfilling Way of Life in the Valley of the Sun: Maricopa County, AZ, 1965. LoCVGP

Logan, D., "Briefing: Shopping Centers." *Architectural Design* Vol. XLIII no. 2, 1973, 96-103.

Longstreth, Richard. *City Center to Regional Mall- Architecture, the Automobile, and Retailing in Los Angeles, 1920-1950*. Cambridge, MA: MIT Press, 1997.

—. "J.C. Nichols, the Country Club Plaza, and Notions of Modernity." *Harvard Architecture Review* 5, 1986: 121-35.

Lowe, Jeanne R. "Whats happened in Fort Worth?" *Architectural Forum*, May 1959: 138.

Loewy, H., "Wien wurde nicht geopfert." *Arbeiter-Zeitung*, 30 Oct. 1960. LoCVGP

McCoy, Esther. "West Coast Architects III - Victor Gruen." *Arts and Architecture*, Oct. 1964: reprint.

McHarg, Ian, *Design with Nature*. New York: Natural History Press (Doubleday, 1969) 1971.

McKeever, Ross J. *Shopping Centers: Principles and Policies*. Washington: Urban Land Institute (Technical Bulletin No. 20) 1953.

McQuade, Walter. "Boston: What Can A Sick City Do?"*Fortune*, June 1964: 132-37, 163-4.

McShane, Clay. "Transforming the Use of Urban Space: A Look at the Revolution in Street Pavements." *Journal of Urban History* V, May 1979: 279-307.

Maki, Fumihiko, *Investigation into Collective Form*. St. Louis: School of Architecture, Washington University, 1964 (special publication number 2).

Melosi, Marvin. "Lyndon Johnson and Environmental Policy," Ed. Robert Divine. *The Johnson Years, Vol. Two: Vietnam, The Environment, and Science*. Lawrence, KA: University Press of Kansas, 1987: 122,139.

Mennel, T. "Victor Gruen and the Construction of Cold War Utopias." *Journal of Planning History* 3.2, May 2004: 116-50.

Mueller, Peter. *Contemporary Suburban America*, Englewood Cliffs, New Jersey, 1981.

Mulcahy, F. "Careful Planning Saves Beauty of Coastal Areas." *Los Angeles Times*, Nov. 26, 1961. reprint, LoCVGP.

Mumford, Eric, *The CIAM Discourse on Urbanism, 1928-1960*. Cambridge, MA: MIT Press, 2000.

Mumford, Lewis, *The Culture of Cities*. London: Secker and Warburg, 1938.

—. "New Faces on the Avenue." *New Yorker* (The Skyline,. Sept. 15, 1939: 62-4. LoCVGP OV 11.

Neutra, Richard. "Europa und die Urbanitaet." In Scheuch, M. "Europas Großstadt - Licht und Irrlicht." *Arbeiter-Zeitung* (Profile), 9 June 1963. reprint, LoCVGP.

Newhall, R. "Valencia's Designer Dies." *Sunday Signal* (Newhall Signal and Saugus Enterprise), Feb. 17, 1980, p.1, 5. LoCVGP.

Nichols, J.C. "Mistakes We Have Made in Developing Shopping Centers." Washington, D.C.: Urban Land Institute (ULI) (Technical Bulletin No. 4) 1945: 2-13.

Nicholson, Emmerich. *Contemporary Shops*. Forward by George Nelson. New York: Architectural Book Publishing, 1945.

Ockman, Joan (Ed.) *Architecture Culture 1943-1968*. New York: Columbia Books of Architecture-Rizzoli, 1994.

O' Kane, Lawrence. "New Town Rising Near Los Angeles." *New York Times*, Sunday July 17, 1966. reprint LoCVGP.

Olsen, Joshua. *Better Places, Better Lives - A Biography of James Rouse*. Washington, D.C.: Urban Land Institute (ULI), 2003.

Patton, Phillip. "Agents of Change: Ten people who changed the way you lived." *Forbe's American Heritage*, Dec. 1994: 88-109.

Peirce, Neil. "The Shopping Center and One Man's Shame." *Los Angeles Times*, Sunday Oct. 22, 1978: (Opinion) Part IV. Reprint AHCVGC.

Peter, John. *The Oral History of Modern Architecture*. New York: Henry Abrams, Inc., 1994.

Plotkin, A.S.. "West End Development, Another Boston New Look." *Boston Globe*, nd. 1959. reprint LoCVGP.

Rome, Adam, *The Bulldozer in the Countryside - Suburban Sprawl and the Rise of American Environmentalism*. New York: Cambridge University Press, 2001.

Rose, M., *Interstate: Express Highway Politics, 1939-1989*. Knoxville, TN: University of Tennessee, (1979) 1996.

Ross, D.H. "Display Key-Notes At Magnin's, San Mateo." *Display World*, Aug. 1950. reprint LoCVGP.

—. "Elegance and Sophistication," *Display World*, Mar. 1950. reprint LoCVGP.

Roush, Matt. "Kalamazoo Mall Turns 30." *Kalamazoo Gazette*, Aug. 13, 1989: A1. Clippings File, History Room, Kalamazoo Public Library.

Rouse, James. "Why aren't there more good shopping centers?" *Architectural Forum*, Dec. 1956: 166, 170.

Rowe, Peter. *Making a Middle Landscape*. Cambridge, MA: MIT Press, 1991.

Saarinen, Eliel, *The City*. New York: Reinhold Publishing Corp., (1943) 1958.

Scheu, Friedrich, *Humor als Waffe - Politisches Kabarett in der Ersten Republik*. Wien: Europaverlag, 1977.

Scheuch, M. "Europas Großstadt - Licht und Irrlicht." *Arbeiter-Zeitung* (Profile), 9 June 1963. reprint. LoCVGP.

Schoof, Dipl. -Ing., H. "Idealstaedte und Stadtmodelle als theoretische Planungskonzepte - Beitrag zur raeumlich funktionalen Organisation der Stadt, (unpublished dissertation), University of Karlsruhe, 1965.

Schorske, Carl E.. *Fin-De-Siecle-Vienna-Politics and Culture*. New York: Vintage, 1981 (1961).

Scott, Mel, *American City Planning Since 1890*. Berkeley: University of California, 1969.

Segoe, Ladislas. Undated letter. *Urban Land*, June 1962: 2-5.

Seligman, Daniel, "The Enduring Slums," Ed. William Whyte, Jr., *The Exploding Metropolis*: 111-132.

Sert, Jose Luis. "Centers of Community Life," Eds. Jaqueline Tyrwhitt et al, *The Heart of the City*: 6.

—. et al. "Summary of the Needs at the Core," Eds. Jaqueline Tyrwhitt et al, *The Heart of the City*: 164.

Shamp, J. "Victor Gruen, designer of Kalamazoo Mall, dies." *Kalamazoo Gazette*, Feb. 15, 1980: reprint, LoCVGP.

Silver, Nathan. "The Ordering Principle of Cities." *Progressive Architecture* (Book Reviews: Heart of Our Cities), Jan. 1966: 186, 192, 198.

Simmonds, Roger, and Gary Hack (Eds.). *Global City Regions - Their Emerging Forms*. London: Spon Press, 2000.

Slote, Clare Trieb. "How to Judge A Town By Its Planning." *Management Methods* (Interview: Clare Trieb Slote with Gruen), Aug. 1960: 39-45.

Smiley, D. (Ed.), *Sprawl and Public Space - Redressing the Mall*. Washington, D.C.: National Endowment for the Arts (NEA), 2002.

Smithson, Alison and Peter. *The Charged Void*. New York: Monacellli, 2005.

Smithson, Alison (Ed.). "Team 10 Primer." *Architectural Design*. Dec. 1962: 574.

Sorkin, Michael. "See You in Disneyland," Ed. Michael Sorkin, *Variations on a Theme Park*. New York: Noonday, 1992: 205-232.

Starr, Kevin. "The Case Study House Program and the Impending Future," Ed. Elizabeth A. T. Smith, *Blueprints for Modern Living - History of the Case Study House Program*. Cambridge, MA: MIT Press, 1989: 131-143.

Stein, Clarence, *Toward New Towns for America*. (reprint) Cambridge, MA: MIT Press, 1971.

—, and Bauer, Catherine. "Store Buildings and Neighborhood Shopping Centers." *Architectural Record* 75, Feb. 1934: 176-187;

Steinhauer, Jennifer. "New York and the nation take a walk along the Kalamazoo Mall." *New York Times* (Business), Nov. 5, 1996. Clippings File, History Room, Kalamazoo Public Library.

Stern, Robert A.M., Gregory Gilmartin, and Thomas Mellins, *New York 1930 - Architecture and Urbanism Between the Two World Wars*. New York: Rizzoli, 1987.

—. Thomas Mellins, and David Fishman, *New York 1960, Architecture and Urbanism between the Second World War and the Bicentennial*. New York: Monacelli, 1995.

Taper, Bernard. "A City Remade for People." *McCall's*. April 1966. Reprint, AHCVGC box 37. Reprinted as: Taper, Bernard. "A City Remade for People." *Reader's Digest*. Oct. 1966: 146-150.

Tyrwhitt, Jaqueline, Sert, J.L., and Rogers, Ernesto, Eds. *The Heart of the City*. New York: Pellegrini and Cudahy, 1952.

Van Leuven, Karl O. "From joe's hot dog stand to a regional shopping center." *American City*, Apr. 1953: 98-99.

Violitch, Francis. "Mr. Mumford and the job ahead." *Arts & Architecture*, Nov. 1945, p. 31, 60.

—. "The Esthetics of City and Region." *Arts & Architecture*, June, 1945.

Von Eckardt, Wolf. "Escape from the Automobile." *The New Republic* (Review of The Heart of Our Cities), Jan. 1965: 18-19.

—. "Pioneering an American Idea." *Washington Post* (Style), Saturday, Jan. 15, 1972: D1-3.

Wall, Alex, "Programming the Urban Surface," Ed. James Corner, *Recovering Landscape*. New York, Princeton Architectural Press,1999: 233-50.

Warner, Sam Bass. "Foreward," Ed. William Whyte, Jr., *The Exploding Metropolis*: x and note 25, xiv.

Weaver, Robert C. "Where City Planners Come Down to Earth." *Business Week*, Aug. 20, 1966: 103.

Webber, Melvin. "Non-place Urban Realm," *Explorations into Urban Structure*. Philadelphia: University of Pennsylvania, 1964: 79-147.

—. "The Joys of Automobility," Eds. Martin Wachs and Margaret Crawford, *The Car and the City*. Ann Arbor: University of Michigan: 1992.

—. "The Joys of Spread City," Eds. Roger Simmonds, and Gary Hack. *Global City Regions – Their Emerging Forms*. London: Spon Press, 2000: 277-81.

Welch, Kenneth. "Some Projects in the Northeast." *Journal of the American Institute of Planners* (JAIP), Fall 1948: 7.

Wharton, Diane. "Those amazing shopping centers." *Plymouth Traveler*, May 1962: 17. reprint AHCVGP.

Whyte, William Jr., Ed. *The Exploding Metropolis*. Berkely: University of California Press, (1958) 1993.

Williams, Senator Harrison (New Jersey), *Congressional Record*, Proceedings and Debates of the 87th Congress, First Session ("Urban Sprawl and Open Space."), Vol. 107, No. 24, Washington, February 9, 1961.

Wilmot, James P. "Downtown Core is Revived," *Shoping Center Age*, Aug. 1962: 12.

Wirtz, Patrick. "Valencia, California: From New Town to Regional Center," June 1999: 2. University of Southern California, Lusk Center for Real Estate.

Wright, Frank Lloyd, *The Disappearing City*. New York: W.F. Payson, 1932.

Yudis, Anthony. "Is the West End Project Due for a Long Slowdown?" Boston Globe, April 28, 1960. LoCVGP reprint.

Zevi, Bruno. "Downtown come San Marco." *Urbanistica*. 26, 20 Sep. 1956: 116-17.

Zola, Emil, *The Ladies' Paradise*, (1883). trans. Brian Nelson. Oxford: Oxford University Press 1995.

Journal Articles:

"A Breakthrough for Two-level Shopping Centers." *Architectural Forum* 105, Dec. 1956: 114-126.

"A Controlled Climate for Shopping." *Architectural Record* 120, Dec. 1956: 193-195.

"A New City Rises." *Landscape Design and Construction*, Feb. 1966.

"A new suburban department store." *Arts and Architecture* 66, June 1949: 39-41.

"Altman & Kuhne shop." *Architectural Forum*, Feb. 1940: 89-93.

"Act Out Day's Program for Customers in Series of Store Windows." *Womens Wear Daily* 22, June, 1936. Clipping, Peggy Gruen Collection.

"Architect bites client." *Architectural Forum* (Letters), Feb. 1948.

"Architect Gruen States the Challenge that Graphic Design Presents,"*Architectural Record*, Sept. 1956: 244-6.

"Architect's complete control of design and furnishings effects large savings for owner." *Southwest Builder and Contractor*, Apr. 22, 1949. reprint, LoCVGP.

"The Architect's Place in the suburban retail district." *Architectural Forum*, Aug. 1950: 111-15.

"Autoists Denounce Their Urban Critics." *New York Times*, Sept. 5, 1962, LoCVGP.

"Beyond Sprawl: New Patterns of Growth to Fit the New California." Bank of America and others, San Francisco, 1995.

"Big City Project in Rochester" *Business Week*, June 24, 1961: 102-3.

"The big ideas in the big new shopping centers." *Architectural Forum*, Mar. 1953: 122-125.

"Les Boutiques." l'*Architecture d'Aujourd'hui*, April 1938: 3-21.

"Can today's big cities survive?" *U.S. News & World Report* 63, Nov. 6, 1967: 56.

"Can Cities Save Downtown Areas?" *U.S. News & World Report*, Nov. 16, 1959: 74.

"Center for Rochester." *Architectural Forum* 116, June 1962: 108-113.

"Center with a total suburban plan." *Architectural Record* 129, May 1961: p 165-188.

"Chain Apparel Shop – Gruen and Krummeck Plan a `Victory´ Store with Non-critical Materials," *Architectural Forum*, Oct. 1944: 89-91.

"Cherry Hill Shopping Center, Delaware Township, NJ." *Architectural Record* 131, June 1962: 174-179.

"Cherry Hill." *Shopping Center Age*, Jan. 1962: 46-52.

"Cherry Hill." *Greater Philadelphia Magazine*, Apr. 1963: 29.

"Cities As Long As Highways - That's America Of The Future." *U.S. News & World Report*, Apr. 5, 1957:27-31.

"Cities in Trouble-What Can Be Done?," *U.S. News & World Report* (Interview with Victor Gruen), June 20, 1960: 84-93.

Congress and the Nation Vol. I, 1954-64. A Review of Government and Politics in the Post-War Years. Congressional Quarterly Service. Washington, D.C.: 1965.

Congress and the Nation. Vol. II, A Review of Government and Politics during the Johnson Years, Congressional Quarterly, Inc. Washington, D.C., 1969.

"Donaldson's and Dayton's Merge Shopping Center in $15,000,000 Southdale Project." *Minneapolis Sunday Tribune*, 25 Oct. 1953. LoCVGC, OV 04.

"Donaldson's Had Planned Another Suburban Center." *Minneapolis Sunday Tribune*, 7 Oct. 1956. LoCVGC, OV 04.

"Do Not Enter," (video film) Bell & Howell Close Up, A Special Projects Presentation of ABC News, broadcast on 4 October, 1962, 10:30 pm. (30 minutes), directed by Nicholas Webster, with:Herbert Askwith, Henry Barnes, Victor Gruen, Jack Strauss, et al. American Museum of Broadcasting, T82:0700

"Department store of the future: Milliron's could be the answer." *Interiors,* Oct. 1949: 112-119.

"Design Decade." *Architectural Forum,* Oct. 1940: 287.

"Design for a Better Outdoors." *Architectural Record* (Building Types Study: Shopping Centers) 131, June 1962: 163-182.

"The downtown center: Rochester, New York, opens 'Midtown Plaza'." 116.4, Apr. 1962: 108-114.

"Downtown – Fresno's Future," a joint publication by the City of Fresno, the Redevelopment Agency, and the Hundred Percenters. n.d. LoCVGC.

"Downtown Gets Uplift." *Life,* Oct. 26, 1959.

"Downtown Needs a Lesson from the Suburbs." *Business Week* (Regions), Oct. 22, 1955: 47.

"El Dorado Hills: new model for tomorrows satellite cities." *House & Home,* Mar. 1963: 107-15.

"Every business district a modern shopping center." *American City,* July 1958: 137-39.

"Expansion plan revised, Northland center to be built first." *Hudsonian* 12, 1951. LoCVGP.

"Fresno and the Mall: A Story Of Community Action." Fresno with Victor Gruen Associates, 1965.

"Fresno Mall Gives a Small City New Heart." *Engineering News Record,* Jan. 12, 1967. reprint, AHCVGC box 37.

"The Future Of The American Out-Of-Town Shopping Center." *Ekistics* 16.93, Aug. 1963: 96-105. (Harvard Graduate School of Design, 7th Urban Design Conference held on April 26, 1963)

"Getting Twenty-Four Hours of Service from Store Fronts." *Chain Store Age* (Administrative Edition), Feb. 1941. reprint, AHCVGC.

'Glas' *Österreichische Glaserzeitung* 8/9, 1937. reprints, LoCVGP, AHCVGC.

"Grass on Main Street." *Architectural Forum,* Sept. 1944: 83.

Grayson-Robinson Stores, New York, Annual Report for the year ended September 30, 1946.

"Gruen and Krummeck plan a 'Victory' Store with non-critical materials." *Architectural Forum* 81.4, Oct. 1944 (Commercial Remodeling): 88-91.

"Henry Ford's Page." *Dearborn Independent,* Dearborn, Michigan, 1922. Cited in: *The Urban Pattern.* Gallion, Arthur and Simon Eisner, New York: Van Nostrand, 1980 (Fourth Edition).

"How New York Won the World's Fair." *Business Week* (Regions), Nov. 7, 1959: 70.

"HUD Award for Design Excellence." (Fulton Mall, Fresno, CA) Department of Housing and Urban Development HUD, Washington, D.C. 1968.

"HUD Award for Design Excellence." (Park Slope North Rehabilitation, Brooklyn, NY) Department of Housing and Urban Development HUD, Washington, D.C. 1968.

"Initials in the Decorative Scheme." *Display,* Aug. 1935: 233.

James W. Rouse: A Man of Vision, (obituaries and commemorative articles) The Enterprise Foundation, Columbia, Maryland. nd.

"Joseph Magnin, Sacramento." *Progressive Architecture,* May 1947: 71-75.

"The Kalamazoo Mall." City of Kalamazoo, Kalamazoo, MI, in cooperation with Kalamazoo County Chamber of Commerce and the Downtown Kalamazoo Association, 1971. History Room, Kalamazoo Public Library.

"L.S. Donaldson Joins Dayton's In New Center." *Womens Wear Daily,* 26 Oct. 1953. LoCVGP, OV 04.

"Lederer Front Is New Departure." *Women's Wear Daily,* 16 June, 1939. LoCVGP, OV11.

Litchfield Park, (development company brochure) 1965. LoCVGP

"Look at this big tract of ranch land and see a new town in the making." *House & Home,* Aug. 1960: 147-152.

Louvain-la-Neuve - Freedom of the City, (publicity brochure) UCL-External Relations, 1997.

"Massive Subdivision Plans Unveiled Here." *Sacramento Union,* Dec. 13, 1961. Reprint. LoCVGP.

"Master Plan." *Progressive Architecture,* May 1955: 12.

"The masterplan grows out of the land." *House & Home,* Aug. 1960: 147-50.

"Mobility in the place of "Automobility." Letter from Victor Gruen printed in the (Rochester, NY) *Times-Union,* 13 July, 1960. LoCVGP

"Midtown Plaza." *Urban Land Institute (ULI) Journal,* June 1962: 3-5.

"Minneapolis Crucified by Architect." *Rapid City Journal* (South Dakota), 29 Nov. 1956. LoCVGP, OV 04.

"New Buildings for 194X." *Architectural Forum,* May 1943: 69-152.

"New Thinking on Shopping Centers." *Architectural Forum* 98.3, Mar. 1953: 122-145.

"New Stores Opened By Ingenious Use of Substitute Materials." *Chain Store Age,* Jan. 1944: 24.

"The New Yorker Interviews Architect Victor Gruen." New Yorker (Talk of the Town) Mar. 17, 1956. Reprinted in *Charette,* Aug. 1956: 25.

"North Shore Center, Beverly, MA." *Architectural Forum,* June 1947: 84.

"Northland: A new yardstick for shopping center planning." *Architectural Forum,* June 1954: 102-119.

"Northland Will Be Opened." *Michigan Society of Architects,* Mar. 1954: 33-4.

"Olympic Circle Shop Center, LA." *Progressive Architecture* (Design Survey), n.d. *1951.* clipping, LoCVGP 14.

"100 Largest Architectural Firms in the U.S." *Architectural Forum,* Apr. 1963: 11-14.

"109 Store Houston Shopping Center of 1952 to feature Pedestrian Mall." *Women's Wear Daily,* Jan. 3, 1951. AHCVGC, box 47.

"Organization for Efficient Practice 6. Victor Gruen Associates." *Architectural Record,* Oct. 1961: 133-141.

"People," *Architectural Forum,* June 1960. reprint, LoCVGP.

"The Planning of Midtown Plaza." *Architectural Record,* Oct. 1961: 131-8.

"Playful chocolate shop." *Architectural Forum* 97 Aug. 1952: 100-109.

"Ein Portalumbau von Arch. Viktor Grünbaum." *Österreiche Kunst* 15 Apr. 1936: 27. AHCVGC.

"The Pros and Cons of Architecture for Civil Defence," *Progressive Architecture*, Sept. 1951: 63-81.

"Proposed Back Bay Center Development – for Stevens Development Corporation." *Progressive Architecture* (First Design Award), Jan. 1954: 73-85.

"Randhurst Center, big pinwheel for prairie." *Architectural Forum* 117, Nov. 1962: 106-111.

"Recent Work: Gruen, Krummeck, and Auer." *Architectural Forum*, Sep. 1941: 191-200.

"Redevelopment f.o.b. Detroit." *Architectural Forum*, Mar. 1955: 116-25.

"Retailer's Problem: Reviving Sick Old Downtown." *Business Week*, January 15, 1955: 42-50.

"Retail Stores: A Critique." *Progressive Architecture*, May 1947: 71-5.

"Rochester brings them back from the suburbs." *Engineering News Record* (ENR), Feb. 16, 1962: 30-32, 34, 36, 38, 40.

"Shopping Center." *Architectural Forum* (New buildings for 194X), May 1943: 102-103.

"Shun skin-deep beauty." *Men's Wear Magazine*, Aug. 22, 1947: 65-7, LoCVGP OV 14.

"600 Ton Heat Pump System Creates Eternal Spring." *Heating, Piping and Air Conditioning* (HPAC), Jan. 1957.

"Something new in stores." *Architectural Forum* 90, June 1949: 104-112.

"Southdale: It's always spring in this rooted market square in the suburbs." *Interiors* 116, May 1957: 96-101.

"Sprawling Strip Cities - They're All Over U.S." *U.S. News & World Report*, Sept. 18, 1961: 73-5.

"Store of the Month," *Store of Greater New York*, Nov. 1939, LoCVGP, OV 11.

"Suburban Retail Districts." *Architectural Forum* 93, Aug. 1950: 106-122.

"Substitute materials." *Chain Store Age*, Jan. 1944: 24.

"Symposium in a symbolic setting." *Life* (Architecture), Sep. 9, 1957: 53-4.

"$10,000,000 Shopping Center Underway." *Houston*, Jan. 1951: 22.

"Three Successful Shopping Centers." *Architectural Forum*, Oct. 1957: 112.

"The Town of Willow Run." *Architectural Forum*, Mar. 1943: 37-53.

"Trade." *Architectural Forum*, Oct. 1940: 286-291.

"20th Century Bazaar," *Life* (Modern Living), Aug. 30, 1954. reprint, AHCVGC, box 35.

"Typical downtown transformed." *Architectural Forum*, May 1956: 146-156.

"Upgrading Downtown: Urban Design by Victor Gruen Associates." *Architectural Record*, June 1965: 175-190.

"Urban Design, Award Citation." *Progressive Architecture* (Sixth Annual Awards Program), Jan. 1959: 112.

"Urban neighborhood redevelopment." *Progressive Architecture*, Aug. 1955: 100-105.

"Urban Redevelopment, Detroit, Michigan." *Progressive Architecture* (Awards), Jan. 1956.

"Urban Traffic Forum." *Architectural Forum*, Feb. 1953: 111-119.

"Valencia, A Planned New City by Victor Gruen Associates." *Arts and Architecture*, Nov. 1966: 18-23

"Valencia – Land Use Plan." California Land (Project Brochure), n.d. LoCVGP.

"Victor Gruen: Champion of Hope for Fallen Cities." *Engineering News Record*, Nov. 30, 1967: 42-5.

"Victor Gruen Associates, Architects - City planners who started out in the interiors field have never left it." *Interiors* 119 (Design Firm Case Study 4), 12 July 1960: 52-69.

"The View From the Road: A Highway Designed For the Drama of Driving." *Architectural Forum* (Transportation and the City), Oct. 1963: 75-8.

"What's Best About Rochester." *Boston Magazine*, Sep. 1962: 43.

"What people said at Connecticut General's symposium on highways." *Architectural Forum* (Excerpts) Nov. 1957, 197-8, 200-6.

"Winter or Summer." *Architectural Forum*, Mar. 1953: 126-32.

"World's Largest Heat Pump Revisited." *Heating, Piping & Air Conditioning* (HPAC), Nov. 1961: 115-119.

Acknowledgements

The initial research for this project was supported by the Graham Foundation.

At Gruen Associates in Los Angeles, I would like to thank Col. Serge Demyanenko, Ki Suh Park, and Charles Wilson. At the Victor Gruen Collection, Library of Congress, Washington, D.C., I would like to thank Harry Heiss in the Manuscript Division, and Maricia Battle and Ford Peatross in Prints and Photographs. At the American Heritage Center, University of Wyoming, Laramie, WY, I would like to thank David Daniels and Matt Sprinkle. At the Stadt- und Landesarchiv Wien, I would like to thank Dr. Michaela Laichmann, and at the Suedwestdeutschesarchiv fuer Architektur und Ingenieurwesen, Dr. Gerhard Kabirska. Further material, especially photographs, was gathered from the collection of Peggy Gruen. I also thank Anne Gray for access to her collection of unpublished notes, articles, and an interview of Edgardo Contini.

Critical conversations and interviews were an invaluable source of information. I thank the following: John Belle, Jack Beyer, Dick Blender, Jim Bishop, Erich Bramhas, Dan Branigan, Mike Cartsonis, Beatrice Contini, Fernando Costa, Elsie Krummeck Crawford, Margaret Crawford, Chris Cummins, Bruce Dayton, Bill Dahl, Carlos Diniz, Stephanie Dyer, Lavonne Easely, John Farko, Georg Frankl, Alexander Garvin, Frank Gehry, Charles and Karen Gomez, Anne Gray, Mark Gunderson, Michael Gruen, Peggy Gruen, Gary Hack, Gudrun Hausegger, Frank Hotchkiss, Otto Kapfinger, Norman and Betty Katkov, Gere Kavanaugh, Richard Longstreth, Chris Van Leuven Mikami, Ki Suh Park, Cesar Pelli, Rosemary Rabin, Joyce Repya, David Rosen, Marion Sampler, Henry T. Segerstrom, Bob Simpson, Anne Taylor, Fred Usher, Fritz Waclawek, and Greg Walsh.

Margaret Crawford was my host in Los Angeles and shared her wealth of knowledge and contacts. Likewise Gere Kavanaugh and Gudrun Hausegger generously shared their contacts.

Margaret Crawford and Gary Hack read preliminary drafts of the shopping center and urban planning chapters. Bjoern Erik Behrens read the manuscript, created graphic material and the timeline. Jane Alison, read early drafts, edited the manuscript, and provided critical and strategic advice; there would be no book without her support. Andrea Kahn read the final manuscript and provided critical advice.

Publisher
Actar (www.actar.es)

Author
Alex Wall

Graphic designer
Reinhard Steger

Editorial coordinator
Albert Ferré

Editorial assistant
Anna Tetas

Digital poduction
Oriol Rigat

Printing
Ingoprint SA

Distribution
Actar-D
Roca i Batlle 2
08023 Barcelona
office@actar-d.com
Tel +34 93 4174 993
Fax +34 93 4186 707

DL 43442
ISBN 84-95951-87-8

Printed and bound in the European Union
Barcelona 2005